Videoblogging
FOR
DUMMIES®

Videoblogging For Dummies®

Quick Storyboard Template

Slip this under your notebook page for a quick-and-easy template for your storyboards!

65765273

Diagram for Lighting an Interview

Here's a lighting arrangement for an interview that should put you and your subject in the most flattering light.

Backlight

Interview subject

Fill light   Camera   Key light

Video Recording Supplies to Take with You

When you're preparing to record video outside your home, remember to take along the following items:

- Padded camera bag
- Video camera with lens cap and UV filter
- 2 extra blank tapes
- Mini-tripod or monopod
- Extra battery and charger
- Digital still camera for backup
- FireWire and USB cables or card reader
- External microphone or audio recorder

- Clapstick if you're using an external audio recorder
- Model-release forms
- Brightly colored stickers for non-released participants
- Pen and notebook for director notes and planning
- Storyboard template or this Cheat Sheet
- Inexpensive clamp lights

Videoblogging For Dummies®

Asking for a Release

Use the following as an example of what to say when you're asking someone for permission to film:

"Hi, I'm _____. I'm taping a video for my non-commercial Internet blog, and I'd like permission to include you/your child/your location in the movie. I have a short flyer explaining what this is about, and where you can view the movie later. Would you be willing to sign this release form or state on-camera that you are granting permission to be filmed?"

If you get a no-don't-film-me response from the person (or people) you asked, use the following as an example of an appropriate response:

"I respect your desire for privacy and thank you for taking the time to talk with me. So I don't accidentally get you in the shot, would you be willing to wear this brightly colored sticker? That way, when I'm editing I can make sure to edit out any scenes with you in them, and the bright color will help me remember to point the camera away from you during today's event."

If the person prefers not to wear a sticker, don't push it; jot down something distinctive about the person's appearance to look for in the edit later on.

Definition of a Videoblog

Sometimes you'll need to explain what a videoblog is. Here's a short description that many people seem to understand easily:

A *blog* is basically an online journal, a Web site where people post entries that appear in chronological order. Because a blog is a Web site, a blog entry can include a hyperlink to another Web page, a link to an audio file, or even a link to a video file. So a *videoblog* is a blog that contains video files.

In addition to watching the videoblog on a Web site, people can also subscribe to videoblogs using another program, like iTunes, which can automatically check for new videos and download them.

Wiley, the Wiley Publishing logo, For Dummies, the Dummies Man logo, the For Dummies Bestselling Book Series logo and all related trade dress are trademarks or registered trademarks of John Wiley & Sons, Inc. and/or its affiliates. All other trademarks are property of their respective owners.

For Dummies: Bestselling Book Series for Beginners

Videoblogging FOR DUMMIES®

by Stephanie Cottrell Bryant

WILEY

Wiley Publishing, Inc.

Videoblogging For Dummies®

Published by
Wiley Publishing, Inc.
111 River Street
Hoboken, NJ 07030-5774
www.wiley.com

Copyright © 2006 by Wiley Publishing, Inc., Indianapolis, Indiana

Published by Wiley Publishing, Inc., Indianapolis, Indiana

Published simultaneously in Canada

WILEY

About the Author

Stephanie Bryant is a technical writer from Santa Cruz, California. She's been writing professionally for ten years, and has written two books on Web design and graphics. Her first video posted to the Internet was a 30-second clip of finding her first book on HTML in a Parisian bookstore.

In May of 2005, Stephanie started a personal videoblog, after having been a text blogger for three years. She now co-presents seminars on videoblogging and the law, covering technological aspects to help those in the legal professions to make informed arguments about the intellectual property and other legal aspects of this emerging technology.

When she's not writing, Stephanie writes! A four-year winner in National Novel Writing Month, she's written five novels, keeps several blogs and videoblogs, and still maintains a healthy handwritten correspondence with a few friends and family members. She is married and has one cat and several betta fish.

Dedication

This book is dedicated to Stuart Cottrell, who unknowingly introduced my sister and me to science fiction and fantasy and opened our imaginations to questions beyond "what if this happened?" and into "what if this *could* happen?" The future is made with such questions. Thank you, Dad.

Author's Acknowledgments

Most people look at a book and think the name on the cover is the only person creating it. Well, that's rarely the case, and this book is no exception. It would simply not have come to pass without the wonderful help, support, and encouragement of many, many people. Naturally, any mistakes or errors in this book are my fault, not theirs — the buck stops somewhere on my very messy desk.

In particular, I'd like to help the friends and cheerleaders in my life, who have really given me a lot of moral support and understanding friendship along this path. Naturally, the first of these is my husband, John, who sacrifices more for my books than anyone. Thanks also to my mother Bonnie Beck, and friends Molly Landers, John Daniels, Brian Kolm, Patrick Reilly, John Simmons, and Ben Rice. A special shout-out to Ben Carey and Henrik Delchag, whose book *This Book Will Change Your Life* was the humorous inspiration for my earliest videoblogs.

Thanks also to the hardworking souls who labored on this project: Margot Maley Hutchison, my agent; the folks at Wiley, including Steve Hayes, acquisitions editor, Jean Rogers, project editor, Leah Cameron, editorial manager, Barry Childs-Helton, copy editor, and the graphics and layout techs; and Sean Gilligan, technical editor.

I've had a lot of support and cheerleading from the videoblogging community, and there's no way I can thank each of the 2,000 or so people who vlog regularly and inspire, communicate, and debate with me about videoblogging. So I'll have to settle for the short list; if you search for any of these folks, you'll find great vlogs and tools: Bill Streeter, Enric Teller, John Leeke, Paul Knight, Amanda Congden, Andrew Michael Baron, Marcus Sandy, JD Lasica, Eric Rice, Ryanne Hodson, Jay Dedman, Michael Verdi, Schlomo Rabinowitz, Heath Parks, Steve Garfield, Zadi Diaz, Josh Leo, Justin Day, Kaveh Kardan, Sheldon Pineo, Matt Savarino, Peter Doyle, Chad Aaron, Israel Hyman, Daniel Lyss, Jerry and Orrin Zucker, Kent Nichols, Douglas Sarine, David Peck, Greg Smith, August Trometer, Warren Murray, and Leanne White.

Publisher's Acknowledgments

We're proud of this book; please send us your comments through our online registration form located at www.dummies.com/register/.

Some of the people who helped bring this book to market include the following:

Acquisitions, Editorial, and Media Development

Associate Project Editor: Jean Rogers

Senior Acquisitions Editor: Steve Hayes

Copy Editor: Barry Childs-Helton

Technical Editor: Sean Gilligan

Editorial Manager: Leah Cameron

Media Development Specialists: Angela Denny, Kate Jenkins, Steven Kudirka, Kit Malone

Media Development Coordinator: Laura Atkinson

Media Project Supervisor: Laura Moss

Media Development Manager: Laura VanWinkle

Media Development Associate Producer: Richard Graves

Editorial Assistant: Amanda Foxworth

Sr. Editorial Assistant: Cherie Case

Cartoons: Rich Tennant (www.the5thwave.com)

Composition Services

Project Coordinator: Tera Knapp

Layout and Graphics: Claudia Bell, Stephanie D. Jumper, Alicia B. South

Proofreaders: John Greenough, Leeann Harney, Christine Pingleton, Dwight Ramsey, Techbooks

Indexer: Techbooks

Publishing and Editorial for Technology Dummies

　　Richard Swadley, Vice President and Executive Group Publisher

　　Andy Cummings, Vice President and Publisher

　　Mary Bednarek, Executive Acquisitions Director

　　Mary C. Corder, Editorial Director

Publishing for Consumer Dummies

　　Diane Graves Steele, Vice President and Publisher

　　Joyce Pepple, Acquisitions Director

Composition Services

　　Gerry Fahey, Vice President of Production Services

　　Debbie Stailey, Director of Composition Services

Contents at a Glance

Table of Contents

Introduction

· ·

*E*ver want to get away from the spoon-fed content on your television? Do you wonder what life is like inside other people's houses (or, for that matter, heads)? Did you ever want to share some amusing observation about your life with the world? Behold the videoblog: the emotional voyeur's (and exhibitionist's) way of sharing with the world the most up-close and personal views of a human life. It's a step beyond what you may have heard about blogs. In a text blog, you can capture and present such a moment in words, but it has all the immediacy of a newspaper article. Add pictures, and it's visually interesting, but still kind of ho-hum.

But drop a video into that blog, and suddenly you have people riveted! Whether your interest is just a personal video diary, an instructional video, a promotion, or to tell the political story you feel hasn't been told, videoblogs are a powerful and immediate medium for telling your story.

About This Book

This book isn't meant to be read from front to back. It's more like a reference. Each chapter is divided into sections, each of which has self-contained information about a specific task in videoblogging.

You don't have to remember anything in this book. Nothing is worth memorizing. The information here is what you need to know to get by and nothing more. And wherever I mention a new term — or am possessed by the need to get geeky with the technical descriptions — I've been sure to let you know so you can decide whether to read them or ignore them. (I am thoughtful, aren't I? You're welcome.)

Conventions Used in This Book

I know that doing something the same way over and over again can be boring (the way Mr. Rogers always wore the same kind of sweater), but sometimes consistency can be a good thing. For one thing, it makes stuff easier to understand. In this book, those consistent elements are *conventions*. In fact, one of those is the *italic* typeface I use to identify and define new terms.

Whenever you have to type something, I put the stuff you need to type in **bold** type so it is easy to see.

When URLs (Web addresses) appear within a paragraph, they look like this: www.dummies.com. If I need to show you code (for example, a snippet of HTML to embed a video in your blog), I use a code font like this:

```
<a href="http://www.example.com/Video.mp4"
   rel="enclosure">
<br />Click here for the movie! (MPEG-4 format)</a>
```

This book covers both Macintosh and Windows computers, but the emphasis is on Macs running Mac OS X. When I mention Windows, I focus on Windows XP, because it's the first Windows platform to natively support editing movies, with Windows Movie Maker.

What You Don't Have to Read

You don't need to read the sidebars if you don't want to — they're extra details, notes, and information to help you figure things out, or cool little tidbits to make your vlogging experience more fun.

Likewise, any paragraph next to a Technical Stuff icon beside it is similarly optional reading, because those paragraphs are where I get a little more geeky than normal.

Foolish Assumptions

I have to make some assumptions about you, the reader. First, I have to assume that you already have a computer and a video camera. Now, granted, I do actually give a bit of advice on buying a computer or a camera if you don't already have one — but my basic assumption is that you do, in fact, already have these basic pieces of equipment.

I also assume that you have a connection to the Internet. I also assume that your Internet connection is not a slow dial-up connection. The fact is, videoblogging is very difficult if you're not on a high-speed connection. That means satellite, DSL, cable modem, a T1, or (at the very least) an ISDN line.

Finally, I assume that you more or less know how to download and install a software program, and that if I tell you to go to a Web site and follow the directions there, you're good to go. Why would I point you to a Web site instead of telling you how to do this myself? Because some things change quickly and will be obsolete after this book goes to print. I'd hate to meticulously explain something, and then have you try it out and find out it didn't work!

The Internet changes quickly. By the time this book gets into your hands, a Web site I recommend might have changed. Please make good use of your favorite search engine if you can't find a Web page that I mention in this book.

How This Book Is Organized

I divided this book into parts, which I organized by topic. The parts point out the most important aspects of videoblogging. If you're looking for information on a specific videoblogging topic, check the index or skim the headings in the table of contents and flip to the indicated page.

By design, this book enables you to get as much (or as little) information as you need at any particular moment. Need to know something fast to set up an RSS feed? Read the section of Chapter 13 that applies. *Videoblogging For Dummies* is intended as a reference that you can reach for again and again whenever some new question about videoblogging comes up.

Part I: Zen and the Art of Videoblogs

This part gives an overview of videoblogging. It's part introduction, and part quick-and-dirty get-you-started fun. Here's where you find information on watching videoblogs, getting your computer set up for videoblogging, and creating your first, basic videoblog post.

Part II: Step Away from the Camera

Okay, this part doesn't really get away from the camera, but it does focus on the parts of videoblogging where you don't necessarily want the camera present. For example, getting feedback on your videoblog, branding a look and feel, overcoming stage fright, and planning a videoblog entry — as well as scripting it — are all in this part.

Part III: Lights, Camera, Vlog!

This part talks about more advanced filmmaking techniques, including composition, lighting, sound, and file formats and compression. If you're an experienced videographer, you'll find the file formats section interesting, but if you're new to storytelling through a lens, then you'll want to read Chapter 9 on composing shots and using the camerawork to tell your story.

Part IV: Going Public

In this part, you get the preflight briefing about putting your videoblog on the Internet, publicizing it, managing the permissions, and keeping an eye on your traffic and bandwidth expenses.

Part V: The Part of Tens

I've remained true to *For Dummies* style by including a Part of Tens. The chapters in this part can help you quickly find ten or so vlogs to watch, personal vlogging ideas, and business videoblogging ideas. The Part of Tens is a resource you can turn to again and again.

Icons Used in This Book

To make your experience with the book easier, I use various icons in the margins of the book to indicate particular points of interest.

Whenever I give you a hint or a tip that makes an aspect of videoblogging easier to do, I mark it with this little Tip thingamabob — it's my way of sharing what I've figured out the hard way, so you don't have to.

This icon is a friendly reminder or a marker for something that you want to make sure that you keep in mind.

Ouch! This icon is the equivalent of an exclamation point. Warnings give you important directions to keep you from experiencing any nightmares. (Well, at least where videoblogging is concerned. Offering premonitions about your personal life costs extra.)

Sometimes I feel obligated to give you some technical information, although it doesn't really affect how you videoblog. I mark that stuff with this geeky fellow so you know it's just background information.

Where to Go from Here

Now you're ready to use this book. Look over the table of contents and find something that catches your attention, or a topic that you think can help you solve a problem — and go for it!

If you end up needing a little help, or you want to tell me about your new videoblog, or you'd like to see some of the example videos from this book, check out www.mortaine.com/vlogdummies. You'll find examples, updated links to resources mentioned in this book, links to reader vlogs, and a way to send me a link to your own vlog!

Part I
Zen and the Art of Videoblogs

The 5th Wave   By Rich Tennant

"You're starting a videoblog? You should record something interesting to watch. The fish bowl! The fish bowl!"

In this part . . .

Videoblogging is part personal diary, part filmmaking. Part art, part science. It's a tool for broadening your horizons, or just fooling around on the Internet.

In this part, you get the standard briefing on video-blogging — what it is, what typically defines a videoblog, where to find videoblogs, and where to get the software to watch them. You also get an overview of the basic video-blogger's toolbox, and a very quick start toward creating and posting your first videoblog.

Chapter 1

This Is Your Brain on Vlogs

*V*ideo seems like the hottest new thing in the online world. It seems like everyone's posting links to videos from YouTube, or adding little clips of themselves to their MySpace accounts. You can even download full TV shows to your video iPod to watch them any time you like.

Videoblogs are one great way to share videos with friends, family, and complete strangers on the Internet. As you start videoblogging, kick back with a cold beverage and enjoy yourself.

Checking Out the Vlogging World

You may or may not be aware of it, but there's a revolution going on right now, and it involves your television. And your computer, for that matter! Videoblogging is changing the way people think about visual media, how they interact with it, and what they choose to say with it.

What a videoblog is

A *videoblog* is a collection of video files posted to the Internet using a method that makes it easy to update content quickly — combining the usability of a blog with video files. There are many different definitions of videoblogs, and fussing over the distinction between a videoblog and just video on the Internet, but here are the core qualities that most videoblogs *should* have:

✔ **Video that can be downloaded and played outside of your Web browser.** This means the video is a downloadable file, instead of a streamed video or an embedded-only format. A lot of Flash-based Web sites, which may have cool interactive animation, aren't really videoblogs because you can't download the animation and play it without being connected to the Internet, although Flash videos, which are different from Flash interactive animations, usually can be saved and played. Similarly, streaming video, although useful for longer videos, doesn't really fit into the concept behind videoblogging, because it downloads while you watch it. If your video can't be saved to someone's hard drive, then your viewers can't put it onto an iPod or download it overnight while they're asleep.

✔ **A regularly updated blog format.** Most videoblogs use a standard blog format, such as the one shown in Figure 1-1. It's not strictly necessary to have a videoblog format — certainly, you can update a Web page and your RSS feed file manually every time you want to post a vlog entry — but that's time-consuming. If you really dislike the blog layout and appearance, you can customize it, if you know some HTML and have a good eye for design. But if you offer the third quality, an RSS feed, chances are many of your viewers won't see your beautiful design anyway.

✔ **An RSS feed with enclosures.** With an RSS-enabled videoblog, people can subscribe to your feed and download your videos whenever it's convenient for them. Figure 1-2 shows how the RSS feed looks for the same blog posts shown in Figure 1-1. RSS readers will often check feeds on an automatic schedule, so when you post new entries, you can be confident that your subscribers will receive them. An RSS feed is what makes videoblogs work for most people, and what makes videoblogs work in iTunes.

RSS, Atom, and Media RSS are all similar (and, thankfully, compatible) XML-based technologies that allow users to subscribe to your videoblog feed. When you include *enclosures* in the feed, you send along a file, like an image, audio, video file, along with the blog's text. The subscriber can then view the blog entry in a separate reader.

Now, I won't say that every videoblog has all of these qualities, nor will I suggest that every videoblog *must* have them. But most videoblogs do, and new videoblogs can meet a lot of resistance if they don't have them.

The reason behind having these qualities is simple: Videoblog watchers want to download the video without having to sit and wait. They want to watch it at their leisure. With the new generation of mobile video-viewing devices, many vlog-watchers want to download videoblogs onto iPods and PlayStation Portables and watch them when they're away from the computer.

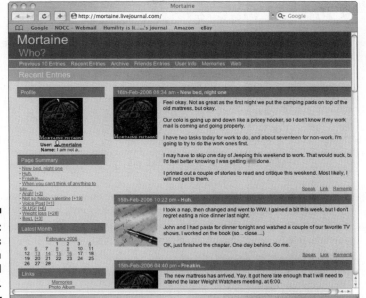

Figure 1-1:
Videoblogs often use a standard blog format.

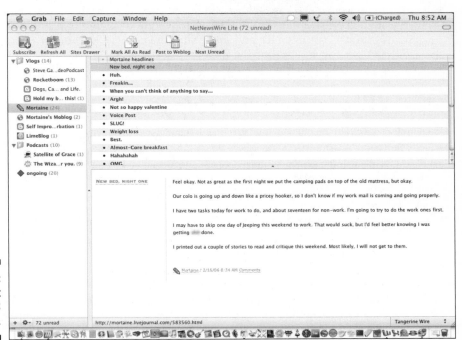

Figure 1-2:
A blog post in an RSS reader.

Who makes videoblogs

Videobloggers are a mixed group — and there are thousands of them, with more starting up every day. Most early-adopter videobloggers are enthusiastic, but not necessarily driven by a business model for creating content. Videobloggers are artists, filmmakers, technology geeks, and citizen journalists who go out and report news that major news networks may have overlooked or underreported (say, technology trade shows or unusual political activism). But many videobloggers are ordinary people who would normally share their family videos by mailing out a VHS tape every six months, but who now have this amazing format they can use to send video to family members who don't live nearby. The reasons vary — as does content.

In addition to the personal, non-commercial, and journalist videobloggers, more commercial entities are getting into videoblogging. Videoblogs now run ads for BMW cars and for beer, from lawyers providing educational outreach for potential clients, and also pure entertainment shows. Major studios are even getting into the action, with vlogs like the *Superman Returns* videoblog (www2.warnerbros.com/supermanreturns/videoblog).

No one regulates the content in videoblogs except the videobloggers themselves. Videoblogs aren't given a rating like TV shows and movies, and quite a few videoblogs contain explicit language and content. Some vlogs are even used as teasers and ads for adult Web sites that require a paid subscription. If you're searching for videoblogs to watch, be aware that not everyone's vlog is rated G (or even R), and make sure the content is appropriate for the people you watch the vlog with.

Why watch videoblogs

I asked a bunch of vloggers why they watch videoblogs, or why they think other people do. Now, granted, these are people who actively produce videoblogs, so they have a vested interest — but they are also the largest group of watchers out there right now. The reasons they stated ranged quite a bit, but here are a few:

- ✔ I have a personal connection with the videoblogger.
- ✔ I can watch videoblogs whenever and wherever I want, and I have control over what I see.
- ✔ Videoblogs are short enough to keep my attention.
- ✔ I don't have to watch what the TV networks think I should like and there are no ads.

✔ It's social — I host vlog-watching parties every week.

✔ I enjoy the diversity of people and environments represented in vlogs.

✔ I like watching creative people doing things.

Of these, the two most prevalent reasons to watch videoblogs were social networking and getting away from the network television model. When a vlogger shows you his or her personal space, home, family, and life, you get to know him or her in a way that's unusual in Internet culture. Sure, there's still the possibility that the whole thing is made up, that the vlogger is acting or not being entirely truthful in his or her videos. But you can't watch a vlogger weeping over her crashed hard drive and not connect with her in a very human way. When you as a viewer comment on someone's videoblog entry, you bring that social network into a two-way communication, and form a closer connection to the videoblogger. And when you watch videoblogs, you get away from the network television model because *you* get to specify the lineup of video content that you enjoy watching through your RSS subscriptions. If you don't like a show, you just drop the subscription.

Where to find out more about videoblogs

After you finish reading this book, you'll be well on your way to becoming a great videoblogger. But there are tons of resources on the Internet that you can tap into to discover more about videoblogging — whether you're looking for how to subscribe to and watch other people's videoblogs, or how to make your own videoblogs.

Finding videoblogs to watch

You can find videoblogs by searching in the common videoblog directories, by talking to other videobloggers, and by looking for uncommon ways to describe videoblogs.

The popular videoblog directories are

✔ **Vlogdir** (`www.vlogdir.com`): The first vlog directory search engine.

✔ **Mefeedia** (`www.mefeedia.com`): A videoblog directory and RSS aggregator; you can subscribe to and watch your favorite vlogs inside the Web site.

✔ **Vlogmap** (`www.vlogmap.org`): A geographically based directory.

✔ **FireANT** (`www.fireant.tv`): This directory plugs into the popular videoblog RSS viewer.

✔ **iTunes Music Store:** Here you can search in Podcasts for Video Podcasts, and subscribe to the ones marked Free. It's only accessible through the iTunes interface.

✔ **Yahoo! Video (`http://video.search.yahoo.com`):** You can search Yahoo! for videoblogs and their feeds to your My Yahoo! Web site.

✔ **Google Video (`http://video.google.com`):** Google's entry into the world of video directories is disappointing and doesn't offer real videoblogging options, but you can still find some interesting video-on-Internet through them.

✔ **Internet TV networks:** Veoh.com, Current.tv, and DTV (`http://participatoryculture.org`) are all Internet television models, some of which use videoblogs for content. Each one has its own search engine of channels, and many have separate downloadable programs you need in order to watch their video content.

You can also find vlogs through good old word of mouth. Videobloggers are highly self-referential, so they talk about other peoples' videoblogs in their own vlogs, and cross-link to them often. The more you vlog, the more other vloggers will notice you and your videoblogs. They'll come by, leave comments, and then you can go check out their vlogs and find interesting stuff to watch that way, too.

Finding more information about videoblogging

You've already taken the first step in learning how to videoblog by reading this book. The following list provides some additional, online resources for videoblogging:

✔ **Videoblogging.info (`www.videoblogging.info`):** A catch-all videoblogging information site.

✔ **Wikipedia (`http://en.wikipedia.org/wiki/Videoblogging`):** The Wikipedia entry for videoblogging is sometimes severely slanted by people with a financial agenda, but is mostly good information.

✔ **FreeVlog (`www.freevlog.org/tutorial`):** A tutorial on creating a videoblog for free (camera not included).

✔ **FeeVlog (`www.feevlog.com`):** A tutorial on creating a videoblog using for-pay services.

✔ **Node 101 (`www.node101.org`):** Node 101 videoblog learning centers are opening in many metropolitan areas to help teach people in a classroom how to vlog.

Videoblogging terminology

Videoblogging is a new technological phenomenon, so it doesn't have its own terminology firmly established yet. *Videoblogs, vlogs, vblogs, vodcasts,* and *video podcasting* are all terms that describe the same thing: video, delivered over the Internet, in some automated fashion. Usually those methods use an RSS feed to deliver their content.

Because the public imagination ties podcasting so intimately to Apple's iPod (even though, as *Podcasting For Dummies* by Tee Morris and Evo Terra points out, you don't need an iPod to do it), Apple coined the term *Video Podcasting* for when a podcast uses video instead of audio. However, the word "podcast" is somewhat brand-centric, in that it refers to the iPod in its name. Many videobloggers, aware of the importance of vocabulary on mindshare, choose instead to use the more generic term *videoblogging.* Similarly, the generic term for a podcast is *audioblog.* Long before iTunes offered video playback, videoblogging was available and growing strong. When Apple announced the addition of videoblogs subscriptions in iTunes, there were already over a thousand videobloggers, making movies and publishing them to their blogs.

Another potentially confusing term is for *mobile blogging* or *moblogging.* Traditionally, moblogging has referred to posting blog entries via a cell phone, often including photographs in the moblog post. To distinguish between a moblog that's limited to text and pictures and one that includes video, some people now say *mobivlogging.* I've also seen *movlogging,* but I think few people can actually say that out loud without stumbling. Personally, I think that's getting into too fine a level of detail, so I just call all of it *moblogging.*

The word *vlog* is a more colloquial way of saying *videoblog,* but it can also refer to an individual post in a videoblog. Although a few people pronounce it "vee-log," more people say "vlog," with the "vl" sounding a lot like the vl in Vladmir or Vlad the Impaler. It's uncommon (though not unheard of) for someone to say "vee-blog," and spell it "vblog." In this book, I use *videoblog* to refer to the blog space, *vlog* for the posts and movies, and *videobloggers* or *vloggers* for the people making the movies. If you feel more comfortable thinking of them as video podcasts, you're certainly welcome to do so. Just be aware that, if you search on the Internet for *video podcast,* you get only half the story.

Joining the videoblogging community

Another resource that is essential to the serious videoblogger is the Videoblogging group on Yahoo! Groups. With over 2000 subscribers, the e-mail and Web-based group has a lot of traffic and discussion of all topics related to videoblogging. This is where you make the personal connections that so many find worthwhile about videoblogging.

Unlike many other technology-oriented e-mail groups, you won't usually anger anyone by asking newbie questions. (Though if you don't bother to read the resources you're directed to, or follow the advice given, the participants will express some frustration.) Discussion ranges from technical issues to hosting sites to media trends, and the group currently gets over 2000 messages a month. Despite the high volume of posts, off-topic chatter is pretty low, though the videobloggers do consider a lot of topics to be "on topic" for videoblogging.

You subscribe to the group at `http://groups.yahoo.com/group/videoblogging`. There's a link in the upper right-hand corner of the page that says Join This Group! If you don't have a Yahoo! account, you will need to create one to join the group, and you can set your e-mail preferences to receive each message posted to the group's forum in your e-mail inbox, get a daily digest, or only read the group on the Web site.

Finding Reasons to Vlog

There are many reasons to make and post a videoblog, from purely personal to highly-charged political reasons. There are as many reasons to videoblog as there are videobloggers — perhaps more.

Personal reasons to vlog

On the personal end, videobloggers create and post vlogs because on one level or another, they enjoy it. Here are just a few of the personal reasons why videobloggers do what they do:

- Keeping in touch with distant friends and relatives
- Ego-stroking (Some people just really like to see themselves on screen!)
- Archiving family history and interviews
- Ranting about issues in their lives
- Learning more about digital video technology
- Increasing the online presence of a minority group
- Making people laugh (for comedy vloggers)
- Making new friends online

Whatever your reasons for videoblogging, make sure you get some personal enjoyment out of doing it. There's no point in taking up a time-consuming hobby if you don't really love doing it.

Professional reasons to vlog

People create professional videoblogs for the two main reasons:

- ✔ **To make money:** There are, in fact, professional videobloggers, people for whom videoblogging is their primary means of employment.

- ✔ **To promote their businesses:** In some cases, professional videobloggers use videoblogs to promote themselves, their products, or their services. In other cases, they're using videoblogs as a means of delivering their products. Or they may use videoblogs to provide an educational background for their potential clients.

Some videobloggers turn pro by offering services to other videobloggers, like video editing or production, Web hosting, or blog online services. Others may earn their keep by teaching people to videoblog.

If you want to put together a videoblog that ties into your professional life in some way, go ahead. There aren't nearly enough of them out there, and as long as you're up-front and honest about your financial and professional interests, you'll find your audience in time. However, if your vlog is just a bunch of ads that provide no value to your viewers, you'll never get off the ground. If your vlog gives some kind of value, be it important information or some humor, then you'll quickly get subscribers coming to watch your videos.

Even an ad-only vlog can offer value to the viewer. Exciting and gorgeous visuals ("eye candy") or cleverly-written ads can draw people back to your vlog even when it's just advertisements. Think about all the ads in the Super Bowl — lots of eye candy and witty writing. Some people watch the Super Bowl just for the advertisements because the ads are so expensive and so competitive, they tend to be the cream of the crop. Viewers see the ads as being valuable in and of themselves.

If you decide to go pro with a professional or commercial videoblog, you'll also have to be more careful about how you use other peoples' works in your videoblog. In this book, I talk about re-using video and music from other vloggers who have offered their work with a Creative Commons license, but you need to understand that the biggest group of Creative Commons-licensed material is available only for non-commercial purposes. If you want to use it commercially, you'll have to contact the creator and negotiate terms for its use.

Citizen journalism and political reasons to vlog

Journalism, political activism, politics, and videoblogs all go hand in hand. Just as bloggers have become a major media force in researching, reporting, and exposing political events and scandals, so too are videoblogs poised to report the news that major news outlets have ignored.

Citizen journalism refers to a movement of independent — usually individual — news reporters delivering their reports to the Internet. It also refers to the many people who, in the midst of a disaster or tragedy, think to capture the moment in photographs, video, and film. The citizen journalists present during the 2004 tsunami made history when they posted video clips to the Internet for the world to see what damage a tsunami could inflict. Similarly, photos from rescuers in areas afflicted by Hurricane Katrina helped shape public awareness of the real situation in New Orleans and the Gulf area.

As you might have guessed, citizen journalists are often also political activists in one way or another, and covering activist events and viewpoints is frequently the purpose of a citizen journalist's videoblog. The fine line between activism and journalism blurs here, but videobloggers blur the line between objectivity and personal opinions with ease. The really hard-core vloggers may come off a bit like the extreme talk-radio hosts, but because you can get body-language cues when watching someone on video, there's a greater sense of the personal in a vlog.

Politicians have jumped on the videoblogging bandwagon, realizing how powerful a medium video is, and how much more powerful their messages are when broadcast over the Internet.

Art as the reason to vlog

Of the videoblogs out there, I would classify at least half as being purely artistic in nature. Personal, diary-like vlogs, while expressive, are not necessarily artistic — they don't always aim for and achieve an artistic statement beyond a video of someone talking about their feelings and vulnerabilities. That's not to say that such videos don't have artistic value, but rather that their value is different from what many folks consider aesthetic.

Perhaps the biggest difference between an art vlog and other vlogs is that most videoblogs have at their core some kind of story to tell, a narrative that's being expressed, and the narration takes precedent over most other parts of the videoblog's composition. In an art vlog, there is a single idea or emotion being expressed, and that takes precedence over the narration or storytelling in the vlog.

If you want to create an artistic videoblog, chances are you don't need me to tell you how to do the artistic part. Artists know best how to express themselves and their art. Artists also know that the best way to learn a new tool is to use it until it becomes comfortable, whether that tool is a pencil or a video camera. But I can give you a few handy pointers on trying out the tools, and how to deliver your artwork to the worldwide Internet audience.

As you watch any artistic videoblogs, pay special attention to how the vloggers use light, sound, screen effects like the focus, and color in their vlogs to emphasize particular elements. Most artistic vloggers have a specific idea they want to express; look for it. In addition, because videoblogs connect the creator with his or her audience, go to the vlogger's blog and comment on any posts that you found really interesting or compelling, or which you really feel you understood.

When you begin videoblogging, consider a single artistic idea you want to express. Perhaps it's an emotion evoked by something visual in your life, or a particular color or shape that you'd like to explore. Go out with your camcorder and explore it as fully as you can, edit it, and perhaps set it to music. When you look at the results, look at it with your artist's eye, not your videographer's eye, and not your storyteller's eye.

Knowing What You Need: The Basic Tools and Budget

A common question about videoblogging is "but don't I have to buy a bunch of camera equipment?" While it's true that you will need a toolbox of equipment to videoblog, many vloggers do fine with a smaller set of tools than most people would expect. Additionally, vloggers are a resourceful bunch — if they can't use a video camera, they'll use a still camera. If they don't have one of those, a screencast might be the way to go. Or they'll remix videos from other sources into new vlogs to post.

Gathering your tools

Chapter 3 goes into depth about the equipment you need to create a videoblog. Here I give you the basic list of things you'll need, sooner or later, to get going as a vlogger:

✔ **A fairly recent computer.** A PC that can run Windows XP or a Macintosh that can run Mac OS X is just about the *minimum* you'll want for videoblogging. You can make do with something less, but it'll be a struggle.

✔ **An Internet connection.** Your Internet connection should be some kind of high-speed connection, be it broadband, cable Internet, satellite, or DSL. You must have an Internet connection, and if you want to watch videoblogs and upload your posts quickly, it should be fast.

✔ **A camera.** It can be a webcam, digital camera (with or without a video option), digital camcorder, or even analog camcorder with a FireWire cable. The best option is a digital camcorder, but all you really need is some way to get a video or image into your computer.

✔ **Video-viewing software.** This one is easy — the major video viewers, QuickTime and Windows Media Player, are both available as free downloads.

✔ **Video-editing software.** Windows XP comes with Windows Movie Maker, and iMovie comes pre-installed with new Apple computers, or can be purchased as part of iLife. You can also buy more advanced video-editing software, such as Adobe Premier or Final Cut Pro.

Budgeting your vlog money

If you have absolutely nothing to start out with, you can expect your foray into videoblogging to cost about $3000, including the cost of a new computer and a simple MiniDV digital camcorder, plus an ongoing expense of about $50 per month for a broadband Internet connection. If you have a fairly recent computer and a camcorder that has a FireWire cable, you can get started right away for nothing but the cost of your Internet connection.

The following items are necessary for videoblogging, so you'll absolutely have to buy these (or have purchased them in the past):

✔ **The camera.** Your best option for videoblogging is a MiniDV camcorder with a FireWire cable, because you'll have the easiest time getting the video off of it and onto your computer. Camcorders that use FireWire have been made since around the year 2000, so your camcorder doesn't need to be brand new to work. If your video camera is analog, you'll need an external converter that converts analog data into digital and then feeds it into your computer; such converters cost $150 to $200 and up. With some MiniDV camcorders selling for under $300, you may find it more cost-effective to upgrade than to struggle with the converter. Some cameras record directly to a file — whether on DVD or media card — without requiring FireWire; many are equipped with USB.

USB camcorders will not capture to iMovie on the Mac.

✔ **The Internet connection.** Dial-up isn't a great choice for videobloggers. It's not impossible to videoblog with a dial-up connection, but it's hard. If your only option is dial-up at home, look for other places you can post from, such as cafés and libraries. *Ask first* to make sure they don't mind you using their faster connection for videoblogging.

✔ **The computer.** If your computer is more than about five years old, it's going to frustrate your vlogging efforts. You'll need a lot of hard drive space while you edit — at least 10GB free when you want to work on a video. Also, make sure your computer has a FireWire port. FireWire and USB have similar-looking plugs, but they are not the same.

✔ **Tripods, camera cases, extra batteries.** You can get a short, inexpensive tripod for less than $5, and they're invaluable for setting up a still shot and for getting a good angle on the camera while you're in the frame.

If your equipment is a few years old but the camera does have FireWire, and you're planning an upgrade path, consider upgrading to a larger hard drive first, then a better computer, then a better camera — and then work on the optional items. The hard drive will become crucial once you have more than a few videoblog entries saved — and the computer speed will make a huge difference in how frustrated you get while editing video and posting files. A better camera has a huge effect on your video, and you might think that's the most important place to start. It's not. Especially when you're starting, your enjoyment of the experience is far more important than how well your camera handles lighting problems.

Here's some optional equipment to consider on your upgrade path:

✔ **Improved editing software**. High-end programs include Final Cut Pro, Adobe Premiere, and QuickTime Pro. QuickTime Pro is actually a good upgrade to buy early — since you can use it to export to more video file formats — and it's inexpensive. Final Cut Pro and Adobe Premiere are good options when you want special effects in your video.

✔ **Sound hardware.** Microphones, booms, windsocks — these are all optional accessories for your videoblog. If you end up filming in noisy situations, you will want an external mic sooner rather than later, but be wary — microphones can be very inexpensive, but can quickly add up when you go for quality.

✔ **Audio software.** Music and video go together so well, you might want some audio editing software to go along with your video editors. GarageBand is Apple's music editing program, and it comes with iLife (which also includes iMovie, if you don't already have it).

✔ **Second camera.** A second camcorder, a webcam, or a digital camera that shoots video as well as stills can be a very handy addition to your vlogging toolbox, but it's entirely optional. For myself, I have a webcam, a digital camera with video, the camcorder, and a cell phone with video camera built in. I use the cell phone for tiny moblog posts, the webcam for videoconferences, and the digital camera when I'm going hiking and want to take video of the trip — it's lighter than the camcorder, and I probably would have brought it with me anyway, to take pictures.

Whatever you decide to do with your videoblog, there will be some expenses you can't quite get away from. Vlogging is a terrific hobby, but many vloggers are also turning it into a more professional arena. If you're interested in a career as a videoblogger or doing any kind of digital video work for pay, your vlogging toolbox is an investment, not just an expense.

Budgeting your time

Videoblogging eats time. Between planning your next vlog, filming it, attending events, downloading the video from your camera to your computer, editing the video, posting it, and then communicating with other videobloggers and watching their videos . . . well, it can quickly turn into a full-time job!

Budget the amount of time you spend on this newfound passion. If you find yourself attending events and only taking a small amount of video, reconsider the event coverage vlog as an option for you. Set a timer to check how long it takes you to import a video and edit it to your own satisfaction.

If you're having trouble keeping control over your time, consider these time-saving ideas:

✔ **Don't use music.** Searching for music that won't land you in legal hot water is time-consuming. Unless you already listen to music podcasts that feature royalty-free or Creative Commons music — and are already familiar with songs and bands you'd like to use — don't add musical soundtracks to your videoblogs. Just be yourself.

Of course, if you compose your own music, there's nothing to keep you from using it in your vlog. Some singer-songwriters already create videoblog entries that feature and promote their music.

✔ **Avoid fancy titles and transitions.** In your first videoblogs, experiment with titles and transitions to find ones that you like, but once you're comfortable with them, use them consistently. The most common transitions I use are cross-fades and fade-outs, because they're seamless. People are used to these scene transitions, so they hardly notice them.

✔ **Consider buying a faster computer or upgrading to a faster Internet connection.** A slow computer means slower video editing; likewise, a slow Internet connection means long waits when you upload your videos and download other videoblogs.

✔ **Use an RSS aggregator.** Watch videoblogs in an RSS aggregator program (discussed in Chapter 2), so the video files download while you're away from your computer.

✔ **Change your format.** If it takes you forever to make a vlog entry on your preferred topic, change the topic or format to something less formal, more fun for you.

✔ **Plan your vlog entry in advance.** If you already know you want certain clips to appear in a specific sequence, you can just grab the clips, put them together, put any transitions you like, and you're done.

Sometimes managing time for videoblogging is more a problem with managing time in general. If you're the kind of person who never has time for anything, you might just need to sit back and take stock of what's really important to you. If you're videoblogging because you want to capture and share your kids' lives with their grandparents, consider posting your videos on a monthly basis, and set aside a block of time each month to work on it. If your kids are old enough, get them involved in vlogging by having them edit the videos themselves.

Taking on an assistant can help for other vlogs as well — if you're camera-shy, you can enlist someone to be the face of your vlog. If you're the kind of person who just loves to play with the technical side of things, you could get someone else to shoot the video for you. Motion pictures are always collaborative efforts — videoblogs can be, too. (Read more about working with other people in Chapters 7 and 15.)

Planning the Content for Your Videoblog

A videoblog can be many things. It can be a personal diary, done in video. It can be news coverage, political commentary, or artistic expression. It can be a commercial promotional tool. When you create the blog that you're going to use for your videoblog, think about what your vlog will do or be. It's okay if you don't know — you can just think of it as a personal diary of someone learning about and starting a videoblog.

Planned vlogs and "reality vlogs"

There are many ways to make videoblogs, but in the planning stage, you can either go with a planned videoblog, or an unplanned vlog. An unplanned vlog is like a reality TV show — you set up the camera, put the personalities in front of the lens, and shoot video until you run out of tape, time, or patience. Then you go to the video editing stage where you look through all the video you shot and piece it together to tell the story you want to tell. You might have planned the story in advance, or you might decide on a storyline to fit the footage you have available.

Reality vlogs

If you make a reality vlog, you don't have to put as much planning into your vlog before you shoot, but you will need to be more organized and thoughtful about what goes into the video after you're done. Every second that doesn't move the storyline forward will end up on the cutting-room floor, so be prepared to edit heavily.

When you create a reality vlog, you should keep an eye out for one thing: scenes and clips that are meaningful. What's meaningful? Well, if you shoot a day's worth of video and want to post a vlog called "My Day," then the five hours you spent vegging out in front of the TV can be distilled into about six seconds of glassy-eyed staring. That filler time doesn't have much meaning unless you want to post a vlog called "how I watch TV." However, if your day included a trip to the grocery store, a walk in the park, and climbing on the roof of your house to clean out the gutters, then you have three distinct scenes that you can include in the vlog post. They establish the milestones of your day, and change the setting and action enough that your viewers won't get too bored.

In addition, your reality vlog might have a plotline. The most common story to tell in a vlog is "this is how I spent my time," but yours could be something different, more complicated, or more emotionally dramatic. Ryanne Hodson (http://ryanedit.blogspot.com) has a video of herself weeping over a hard-drive crash and subsequent loss of all her digital video. Her partner Jay, knowing she wouldn't want to lose that emotional honesty, captured her distress on film and Ryanne later posted it to her videoblog. The story is simple, but the anguish and drama is very effective.

Moments of extreme emotions make good storylines, as long as you stay sensitive to the people involved. You can also evoke positive emotions, by filming the funny moments in your day and posting them, or by touching on your audience's sensitive side. Even though he didn't post it as a videoblog, Mike Potter, winner of the 2006 CellFlix competition (www.cellflixfestival.org), did that with his video "Cheat," in which an elderly subject talks about how he "cheats" at a game with his wife, so he can get a few extra kisses. The short film, shot entirely with a cell phone, is quick, effective, and absolutely charming.

Pre-planned vlogs

A videoblog that has a purpose and a plan takes some time and forethought, but usually results in a more polished, targeted vlog. If you want your videoblog to attract a specific audience, you will need to make and post videos that interest the people you have in mind.

Some examples of videoblogs with a purpose are

- **Rocketboom:** A daily news show with a humorous slant. (www.rocketboom.com)

- **IceNRye's Geocaching Videoblog:** A long-format videoblog (40-minute episodes) about geocaching and dog training in Canada. (`http://icenrye.blogspot.com`)
- **Cherub:** A parody of a popular vampire TV series, and one of the few all-fiction vlogs (`www.cautionzero.net/cherub`)
- **Crash Test Kitchen:** A cooking show (`www.crashtestkitchen.com`)
- **Net Video:** A vlog from Net Video, a technology TV show from Australia (`www.netvideo.com.au`)

Even though most of the videoblogs I watch are off-the-cuff reality vlogs, I really appreciate the extra effort that goes into a planned videoblog. I think as videoblogging matures, there will be more of these targeted vlogs available, which will certainly make vlogging an even more viable delivery medium for anyone's message.

Low-tech tools for good videoblogs

The following three tools are just a few ways you can make better videoblogs without investing in more hardware and software. All three are ways to use the most important tool in your videoblog — your mind. How you organize information in your videoblog will determine how good it is to your viewers. If your vlog is very chaotic, with little bits and topics being mentioned that don't have much connection to the rest of the vlog, you'll have a hard time keeping anyone's attention unless the vlog adds value in some other way, by being funny or sexy.

A video journal

Yes, your videoblog is your journal, in a sense. But you can also keep a record of your videography so you'll know what worked and what didn't. When you shoot a video, write down some details about the shot within a few hours, so you'll have the information during editing, and when you review your clips later. You can keep a small spiral-bound notebook in your camera bag for this, or use any recording device you like.

Include the following in your notes:

- Where and when the video was taken. Include time of day.
- Who is in the video. You'll need this for the credits. Include musicians playing in the background. Pay special attention to who has given permission to be filmed — and who hasn't — for your edit.
- Assistants helping you with the shot.
- If the shot was taken outdoors, describe what the weather was like. For example, include how much cloud cover there was.

- ✔ If the shot was taken indoors, describe what kind of lighting was available (fluorescent, incandescent, sunlight, low-light).

- ✔ Ambient noise, such as people talking in a bar or restaurant.

- ✔ What equipment you used — your standard camcorder, or a different camera? Also note any sound equipment, such as if you used a microphone.

- ✔ Any camera special effects you used. Some cameras have built-in special effects, such as widescreen or night vision.

- ✔ Details that struck you as interesting while you shot the video, such as a memorable quote or a shot angle you really liked.

When you post your videoblog entry, you can choose to add the video notes to your blog post, or just keep them private in a notebook or in a text file on your hard drive.

You'll need notes when you edit and post your videoblog, so you can give credit where it's due. Notes also help you remember (and zero in on) clips you thought were particularly good or interesting.

In addition, you should go back and review your past videoblogs every couple of months to see what you did then that you've since changed, or if there's a particular effect you got without even realizing it and want to re-capture now. Your notes help make your vlogging more deliberate.

Outlining

If you have an idea for your videoblog's content, write it down. Having a plan or statement of your vlog's purpose will help you keep it focused and interesting to its target audience. Then, as you plan your first videoblog entry, think about what you want to say in it. What's the story you have to tell here? If you can, write an outline for the vlog post.

Here's an example outline for a videoblog post I made called "Hiking and Camping with Johnnyb":

> Intro: ID with fade-in
>
> Clip1: "We're going hiking" from cell phone, use picture-in-picture over a shot — still or video — of the trees
>
> Clip2: Slideshow of photos from the trip
>
> > Add voiceover describing what happened
>
> Clip3: Salamander footage, talk about encountering wildlife
>
> Clip4: Footage of the lesson of the hike
>
> Outro: Music credit

The videoblog in question is tightly formatted — each clip has footage and photos from a hike of some kind, with a miniature lesson or hiking and camping tip from Johnnyb, the host of the show. With only four clips of video plus a slideshow, this is a short vlog post.

In this particular case, I wrote the outline after I shot the video, so I could include all the footage I had. If you outline a videoblog post in advance, you may need to edit your outline later if you caught a really great moment or scene out of the blue. For instance, in this vlog post, I couldn't have anticipated finding a salamander and getting it on film.

Storyboarding

The outline is a general, scene-by-scene listing of what content will go into the videoblog. A *storyboard* is a way to plan out a vlog. In it, you will actually draw pictures to plan the shots you want to capture. A storyboard resembles a comic strip — it has several pictures lined up to tell the story. For more about creating and using storyboards, as well as an example of a storyboard, check out Chapter 8 — and the tear-out Cheat Sheet, which provides a mini-storyboard for you to carry in your notebook or camera bag.

Storyboarding is useful when you want to compose your shots carefully to get a particular effect and to use the language of film to express more than the flat storyline. Note, however, that it can take time to develop this technique, and it's even less forgiving than outlines for capturing impromptu moments.

Preparing and Presenting a Vlog

This chapter talks a lot about why people make videoblogs, and how to plan a vlog, but at this point you might be thinking, "Great, but how do I *do* it? How do I make a videoblog?" That question is answered in greater detail in the rest of this book (particularly Chapter 4, which takes you through the steps to create and post your first videoblog entry), but here is an overview of the process of creating a vlog entry and posting it:

1. **Download the raw video from your camera or source to your computer.**

2. **Edit the video clips in a video-editing program and convert the edited video to a Web-ready file format.**

3. **Post the video to an RSS-enabled blog on the Internet.**

Videoblog creation and editing

First, you shoot your video. You can do this with any camera, as long as you can somehow get the video from the camera onto your computer's hard drive. Shoot any subject you like — as long as it's legal — and *get permission* if you're going to interview someone and then post it to the Internet.

When you edit the video, you use video-editing software to take the footage from your camera and to cut the video scenes until each segment (called a *clip*) is short enough to tell the story without dragging too much. You put these clips in order with your video-editing software, usually by using some kind of timeline view. You can also add still photographs at this point. You might add titles and transitions between clips to make them flow more smoothly, or you could leave the video in more of a raw state.

Chapter 10 has more information on editing your video.

Videoblog files and compatibility

When you have finished creating your vlog entry, editing it, and adding the transitions and music, the next step is to compress the file into a format for the Internet. If you're using a Windows machine, you'll most likely publish a Windows Media file. If you're on a Mac, it'll be some type of QuickTime or MPEG-4 file.

Although Windows Media Player was available for the Mac until 2006, Microsoft recently discontinued support for it on the Mac. QuickTime is still available for both Windows and Mac, as are Flash and Real Media. When new features become available in your preferred file format, get a friend to test them out using another platform (Windows if you're on a Mac, or vice versa).

The common file formats that are viewable on Mac, Windows, *and* Linux are MPEG-4 and AVI — which isn't recommended for videoblogs because it's usually an uncompressed video format.

In Chapter 12, you get a closer look at file types and compression.

Chapter 2

I Vant to Vatch Your Vlog

*V*ideoblogs don't just show up on your computer, though it would be really cool if they did. You have to find videoblogs and download the vlog entries before you can watch them. Chapter 1 shows where you can hunt up some videoblogs to watch; this chapter talks about how to download and watch 'em.

Most computers made in the last five years can play a movie. In Windows, you have the Windows Media Player. Macintosh has QuickTime. Both programs have players for the other platforms available, so you can watch Windows Media Player movies on a Mac and QuickTime movies on a PC.

However, since videoblogging came about after the most recent generation of multimedia computers made it to market, new tools have been developed that are specifically geared to watching videoblogs. Take, for example, syndicated video content — and the new iPod that can play video as well as music. But even before Apple launched its latest moneymaker, great strides had been made in developing viewer software for all kinds of online video content.

As videoblogging matures, watch for more options to come out. It won't be long before every blogging Web site or program offers some kind of media-blogging option, and every new Internet connection comes bundled with software to subscribe to and watch videoblogs. Life in the future — gotta love it.

Video File Players

At their most basic, videoblogs are collections of video files, posted to the Internet using a method that makes it easy to update content (such as a blog) quickly. Therefore the most basic tools you'll need for watching videoblogs are the software programs that let you play those video files.

Not all video files are the same — video files come in a variety of file formats. (See Chapter 12 for more about video-file formats.) Just as there are some files you can't open with your Web browser, video players can only open and play files of a certain file format. Currently, that's true of most video file formats — they're proprietary in one way or another and are therefore locked into their own players.

The main reason that video-file formats are all different has to do with compression. When you post a video to the Internet, you have to compress it, or the file will be too big for anyone to download and watch. The tradeoff that gets you a smaller file size is a reduction in image quality, but more advanced compression schemes retain as much quality as possible while still getting the file size down to something manageable. With current compression rates, you can get a two-minute video down to 5MB of space, with only a small loss of quality. Without compression, the same movie takes up 440MB! Sure, it's DVD-quality video that you can play full-screen, but very few people will wait five hours to download a two-minute video of your life (or mine, for that matter).

The Big Three of video-file formats are for Windows Media Player (`.wmv` and `.wmf`), QuickTime (`.mov` and `.mp4`), and Flash (`.swf`). You'll notice that Windows Media Player and QuickTime have more than one file extension (the `.whatever` at the end of a file name). Most of those file extensions represent different ways to compress a standard movie so it'll download faster.

There is one other factor in the maze of file formats and wondering whether you can play a video on your computer. Although the file format helps determine what player to use, there's also something called a *codec* that creates the actual compression for the video. Codecs can be very complicated: if a player doesn't support a particular codec, it can't play the video, even if the file format matches. This is why you might open a QuickTime video and not hear any sound, or launch a Windows Media File, only to get an error message. Codecs are explained in more detail in Chapter 12.

At this point, you might be wondering when I'm going to talk about your favorite streaming video technologies. Well, check out Chapter 12 for openers; there I talk about videoblogging as it relates to streaming and file-sharing technologies — but you should be aware that it's not typical to stream a videoblog. One of the things people like about videoblogs is that they can download them overnight, and then get a look at what video(s) they've download in the morning. With streaming, you have to be connected to your server at the same time you're watching the content; it's all present tense. If there are any connection hiccups in the way, you won't get to see the whole movie. On the other hand, streaming videos are good for downloading long videos because they let users skip to the end without downloading the whole movie. Streaming is also essential for live video broadcasts.

QuickTime and MPEG-4

QuickTime is Apple's video viewing program. The QuickTime basic viewer, shown in Figure 2-1, is free and available on both Windows and Mac platforms. The QuickTime Pro version, which lets you do all kinds of fun stuff (such as edit other people's videos) is available as a $29 upgrade.

Figure 2-1: QuickTime has limitations on the free version.

QuickTime is also the origin of the MPEG-4 file format, which has become a compression standard to compress video for the Internet. Because MPEG-4 is a standard, you can now get MPEG-4 viewing software for most platforms — including Linux — without being forced to use QuickTime if you don't want to. The most common open-source MPEG-4 viewer for Linux is MPlayer (`www.mplayerhq.hu`), which has plugins for nearly every file type conceivable.

Using QuickTime is pretty simple if you're familiar with a standard VCR or DVD player. You open a file using the File menu. There are controls at the bottom to play, rewind, and fast-forward the video. One bit of the interface is different from a DVD player's controls: A sliding bar at the bottom of the video lets you skip around quickly in the video.

Because Apple has made QuickTime available as a plugin, you can watch QuickTime movies from inside your Web browser, as shown in Figure 2-2.

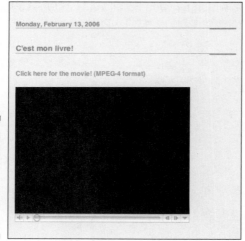

Monday, February 13, 2006

C'est mon livre!

Click here for the movie! (MPEG-4 format)

Figure 2-2:
QuickTime
can also
work as a
plugin in
your Web
browser.

When you install or upgrade QuickTime, you may need to enable the options to run it as a Web browser plugin to get this to work. No problem. Open QuickTime and follow these steps:

1. **Choose QuickTime Player⇨QuickTime Preferences to open the System Preferences related to QuickTime (shown in Figure 2-3).**

2. **Click the MIME Settings button to open the plugin settings.**

   These settings determine which file types from the Internet you want QuickTime to open.

Figure 2-3:
The System
Preferences
for
QuickTime.

3. **Make sure the video files you're most likely to encounter are checked, as shown in Figure 2-4.**

4. **Click OK, and then close the System Preferences.**

   QuickTime will be the default plugin for Safari, and for most Web browsers you might choose to install.

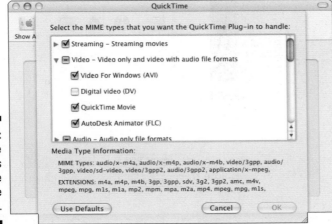

Figure 2-4:
Check the
video files
for the
QuickTime
plugin.

Windows Media Player

On Windows XP computers, the default video player is Windows Media Player, which plays, among other files, .wmv video files. Although most videobloggers use QuickTime for compressing their videos, there are quite a few Windows users out there as well — and some of them even use .wmv files, so it's helpful to have Windows Media Player in your toolbox when you go out to watch the vlogs.

Just as QuickTime is available for Windows, the Windows Media Player is available for Macintosh computers. Windows Media Player runs as a stand-alone application, as shown in Figure 2-5.

The interface is similar to QuickTime, with a standard File menu for opening files, and the play, rewind, and fast-forward buttons below the video window.

Windows Media Player lets you change the user interface using skins, which are available in QuickTime, but are not as common. You can change the way the Windows Media Player software looks, as shown in Figure 2-6.

To change the skins from Windows Media Player, select View➪Select Skin from the menu bar, and choose the skin you want to use. You can also download more skins from the Internet if you like.

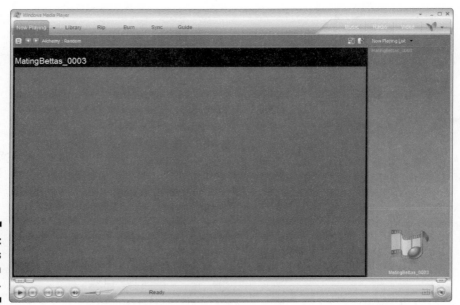

Figure 2-5:
Windows
Media
Player.

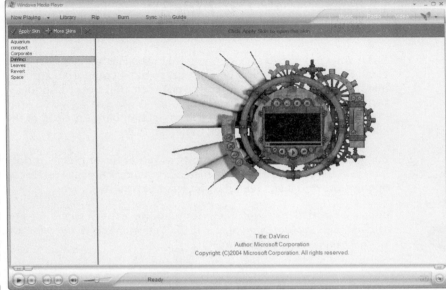

Figure 2-6:
Use the skins in Windows Media Player for a different look.

Flash Player

Shockwave Flash movies are a very attractive option for video files. The Macromedia Flash program is fairly easy to use, and the creator has a lot more control over how a Flash movie will display and play on the Internet. Many users have experience with interactive Flash animations, where the user can click the animation to have it do something or react to the user input. With a Flash movie, you can do the same thing. The creator of a Flash movie can even change how you watch it — say, make it impossible to rewind while you're watching the movie, or prevent you from saving the movie to your hard drive. Although Windows Movie Maker and QuickTime can also do this, the majority of people making video for these formats don't use it, whereas a surprising number of Flash creators do.

Personally, I'm not a fan of Flash movies for that very reason. I like to rewind movies when I'm watching them, so Flash's ability to disable the most basic VCR functions doesn't sit well. It's a bit like having 20 minutes of previews on a DVD and not being able to skip past them, if you know what I mean. It gives users the feeling that you don't trust them, as if the content is supposed to be more important than the user's ability to distinguish whether he or she *wants to watch the movie*. I think a lot of videobloggers are leery of giving that impression, so not many of them use Flash video in their vlogs. However, a lot of viral video Web sites and video-sharing communities (such as YouTube and Veoh) *do* use Flash for video, so it's probably here to stay.

But if you come across a videoblog that uses Flash, make sure you have the Flash Player. Flash is fairly ubiquitous, so most computers already have it installed. But if you don't, or you're not sure, pop over to Adobe, which now owns the whole Macromedia product line (www.macromedia.com) to download the free Flash Player. From the navigation bar at the top of the screen, click Downloads, and then click Get Flash Player.

Because the Flash Player is primarily a Web-browser plugin, it doesn't really have a standalone application. Instead, you launch your Web browser and open whatever Flash video file you want to watch.

Because Flash files are interactive, computer viruses sometimes masquerade as Flash files. *Do not open an* .swf *file that you receive in your e-mail from anyone you don't know and trust.*

Video-Enabled RSS Readers

After you have the video players installed, now it's time to make vlog-viewing painless. See, if you went out and visited every videoblog you wanted to watch every day, you would spend about ten hours a day downloading and waiting to watch the vlogs — leaving you no time at all to make your own vlogs. That's no fun! So what you need is some way to have your computer go out, grab the videos for you, and save them so you can watch them whenever you want to. Fortunately, that's the kind of tedious task that computers are great at doing.

Fortunately, several software programs already exist that do this for you. They rely on a technology called RSS, which stands for a lot of things, but Really Simple Syndication is a good way to think about it. RSS is a quick, easy way to take online content (such as blogs and videoblogs) and let people download the content into the RSS viewer of their choice. The syndicated content is called a *feed* because it works like a newsfeed or a stock ticker. (Lots more details about RSS appear in Chapter 13.)

You might also hear about Atom, which is a similar and related online syndication technology. Although I talk mainly about RSS in this book, if you have an Atom feed available, you can use that just as easily as RSS.

FireANT

FireANT, shown in Figure 2-7, is an RSS reader made by some of the pioneers of videoblogging. Because it's made by videobloggers *for* videobloggers — with videobloggers as beta testers — it is arguably the very best vlog RSS reader out there. It's what would happen if software developers went out and asked, "What would be the perfect RSS viewer for this type of medium?" — and then created it.

FireANT is available for both Windows and Macintosh computers. It plays any media file that your computer can play. You can subscribe to podcasts with it if you have an audio program that can play the podcast's audio file (usually .mp3), and you can even display PDF documents if you have a PDF reader such as Adobe Acrobat installed.

FireANT won't play files if you don't have a viewer installed. For instance, if you don't have Windows Media Player on your computer, FireANT won't be able to play .wmv files. Similarly, if you don't have QuickTime, it won't play .mov files. That's why I have sections on those programs first — you have to have them installed, or the rest of the stuff won't work.

Figure 2-7:
FireANT is a good choice for watching video RSS feeds.

You can download and install FireANT by visiting www.fireant.tv.

Subscribe to a Vlog in FireANT

When you first install FireANT, there are several popular videoblogs already in the list of Channels. This lets you get started and gives you an overview of videoblogging fast, but you might want to go out and find some videoblogs of your own to watch. With thousands of videoblogs available, there's bound to be something that sparks your interest.

Subscribing to a videoblog is easy in FireANT — just follow these steps:

1. **Find the videoblog you want to watch and copy the URL of its RSS feed to your Clipboard (press Ctrl+C for Windows or ⌘+C on the Mac).**

   If you don't have any idea where to start, use http://feeds.feedburner.com/vlogfordummies to subscribe to the videoblog for this book.

   The RSS Feed URL is not the same as the videoblog's URL. Typically, the RSS feed URL is a feedburner.com URL, or the URL will end in .rss or .xml.

2. **In FireANT, choose Channels⇨Add New Channel (or press Ctrl+N on Windows or ⌘+N on the Mac).**

   A tiny dialog box appears, enabling you to enter the URL for your chosen videoblog's RSS feed, as shown in Figure 2-8.

Figure 2-8:
Adding a
new
channel.

If you've copied anything to the Clipboard, it appears automatically in the dialog box. If you didn't copy the URL for the feed you want to watch, you can enter it manually here.

3. **Click the Add Channel button to add the videoblog.**

   The videoblog name will show up at the bottom of the list of Channels.

Getting New Videos in FireANT

To download new videos for a single feed, select the feed in the Channels panel and choose Channels⇨Refresh Channel from the menu bar (or press Ctrl+R on Windows or ⌘+R on the Mac). To refresh all the channels, select Channels⇨Refresh All Channels (or press Ctrl+Shift+R on Windows or

⌘+Shift+R on the Mac). It takes some time for FireANT to download all the videos, so be patient. The status bar at the bottom of the window tells you how much of the current video being downloaded is done.

Watching videos in FireANT

After you have refreshed a feed, you can double-click it in the Channels panel to switch to the Videos panel. That's where you find the available vlog entries displayed, as shown in Figure 2-9.

Figure 2-9:
The Videos panel shows the available videos downloaded for a feed.

You can play a vlog in the following ways:

- ✔ Double-click a vlog post to watch the video, or select it and press Ctrl+P on Windows or ⌘+P on the Mac.

- ✔ You can also select several vlog entries and press Ctrl+P on Windows or ⌘+P on the Mac to have all of them play one right after another.

- ✔ From the Channels tab, you can play all the new videos by pressing Ctrl+Shift+P on Windows or ⌘+Shift+P on the Mac, or by selecting Videos➪Play New Videos from the menu bar.

> ✔ Finally, you can also resize FireANT if you don't like the smaller video sizes. Although it's traditional to view Internet video in a small window, sometimes that just won't cut it. Certainly, if you want to watch vlog entries on your TV, it helps to set the video to play at the maximum size. To resize, select the size you want from the View menu.

Because videos are compressed on the Internet, when you resize a video to a larger-than-full size, the quality may suffer; the image may be blurry, or the action choppy.

Managing files in FireANT

With so much video out there, and such huge files, you may start to worry about disappearing hard-drive space! You can control how much hard drive space FireANT should use, and where the download directory should be, in the Preferences dialog box.

To manage files in FireANT, follow these steps:

1. **Choose FireANT⇨Preferences.**

   The FireANT Preferences dialog box appears, as shown in Figure 2-10.

2. **In the Automatic Cleanup of Downloaded Files section, decide whether you want to delete files after you play them.**

   Deleting the files keeps your hard drive from filling up, but it means you won't automatically save the videos you really like.

3. **If you do decide to delete the files, check the Wait until My Downloads Folder Reaches check box, and put a number in its GB field.**

   That's the number of gigabytes you want to reserve for your down-loaded videos. When your Downloads folder reaches that number, it starts deleting.

   Unplayed videos will not be deleted, even if your downloaded folder exceeds the number of gigabytes you set.

4. **Finally, you can change the Downloads Folder Location options to any folder on a hard drive that's connected to your computer.**

   For instance, I have an external hard drive with lots of space, so I use that for my downloaded videos.

Since the downloads folder contains all your video files, you can also open it directly if you want to watch a vlog entry without using FireANT to view it. FireANT provides the extra content from the vlog entry, such as text and extra tags, but if you just want to see the video separately (or you're planning to remix someone else's vlog entry into your own entries), you can find all the undeleted videos in your default downloads folder. This is another reason why it's good to know where that folder is by looking at the FireANT Preferences dialog box.

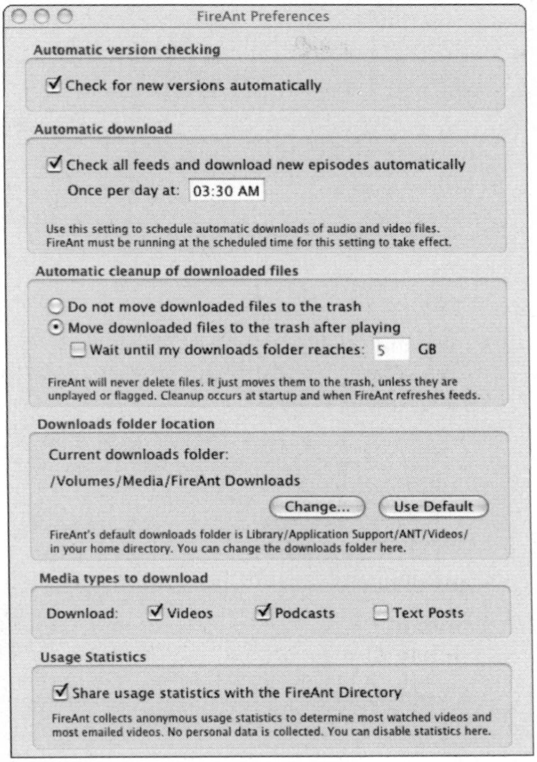

Figure 2-10:
The FireANT
Preferences
dialog box.

Also note that FireANT won't delete videos even if they've been played and moved to the trash folder. You can still retrieve them from the Trash or Recycling Bin if you want to.

Giving feedback in FireANT

FireANT offers you a way to give feedback to the vlogger who made any individual vlog entry as well as to the videoblogging community as a whole. It's not unique to FireANT, but FireANT has an easy interface for leaving comments.

You can leave a comment on any vlog entry for which the vlogger has enabled comments. Although some vloggers have disabled comments, most welcome feedback from the vlogging community.

To open the videoblog's page where you can leave a comment on that vlog entry, just click the Comment icon in the lower-right corner of the main viewing window, as shown in Figure 2-11. The comment page appears in your Web browser; there you can type in a comment about the videoblog entry.

Figure 2-11:
FireANT for
Windows
has a
slightly
different
interface
and
comments
link icon.

iTunes

When Apple added video support to iTunes along with podcast support, it was one of the best things to happen to videoblogging in a long time. iTunes is an excellent program, easy to use, and ubiquitous thanks to the iPod's popularity. With iTunes, you can subscribe to videoblogs and watch them in the same interface as you download music and sync it with your iPod. If you have a video-enabled iPod, you can even use iTunes to subscribe to a videoblog and watch it in iTunes or in your iPod, whichever you prefer (more about video and the iPod later in this chapter).

Videobloggers have to understand that Apple hasn't made videoblogging its first and main priority — or the core goal of the iTunes interface. So if you find the iTunes interface a little clunky for watching vlogs, it's because iTunes was made for music first, video second.

Apple has chosen to call videoblogs *video podcasts*. The videoblogging community on the whole, however, calls them *vlogs* or *videoblogs*, which is a more generic, non-brand-centric term.

Subscribing to a vlog in iTunes

You can subscribe to a videoblog's RSS feed in iTunes through the iTunes Music Store or directly in the iTunes interface by following these steps:

1. **To subscribe through the iTunes Music Store, launch iTunes and click the Music Store icon in the left panel.**

2. **Click the <u>Podcasts</u> link to open the podcast directory.**

3. **Click the Video Podcasts icon in the middle of the page to see what video podcasts are available.**

   You see a list of videoblogs featured in iTunes, or you can go back to the main iTunes interface and click Browse to navigate to the complete Podcast directory. If you know a specific videoblog you want to watch, you can search for it as well. Videoblogs aren't separated into their own directory in the iTunes Music Store, but you can hunt for them in the regular Podcast categories instead. (See Figure 2-12.)

4. **When you find a videoblog that interests you, click the Subscribe button to subscribe to it.**

Figure 2-12: The iTunes Music Store lets you browse categories for videoblogs.

Since the iTunes Music Store doesn't always have every videoblog out there, you may not be able to find what you're looking for. If you can't find the videoblog that you want to subscribe to by following the preceding steps, you can also directly subscribe to a feed from inside iTunes:

1. **Choose Advanced⇨Subscribe to Podcast from the menu bar.**

    The Subscribe to Podcast dialog box opens, as shown in Figure 2-13.

Figure 2-13: Subscribe to a videoblog manually in iTunes.

2. **Enter the URL for the videoblog's RSS feed in the URL text box.**

3. **Click OK to subscribe to that videoblog.**

    iTunes immediately starts downloading new videos from that feed. If you don't want to download the videos right away, you can close iTunes, or click the "X" icon in the iTunes song info window to stop the download.

Getting new vlog entries in iTunes

After you subscribe to a new videoblog, iTunes automatically checks it for new videos, but what about after that?

To get new vlog entries in iTunes, highlight the Podcasts icon in the Source panel and click the Update icon in the upper-right corner of iTunes. iTunes checks all your podcast feeds, including your videoblogs, for new content — and then downloads it.

If you highlight a particular feed in the list of podcasts and click the Update icon, iTunes will check and download only that feed.

You can also set iTunes to automatically download new podcasts in the iTunes preferences.

Watching vlogs in iTunes

Remember how I said that iTunes was made for listening to *music?* Here's where the iTunes interface falters when it comes to video. Many people, excited about watching videoblogs in iTunes, end up disappointed when they try to play a video and only the sound comes out. Never fear — you can play a video in iTunes by following these steps:

1. **Make sure the album artwork is turned on. If you don't see a Selected Song panel below the Source panel, choose Edit⇨Show Artwork from the menu bar to turn on the album art.**

   If you don't turn on the artwork, you won't be able to watch the movie!

2. **Click the Videos icon in the Source panel.**

   You'll see all the videoblog content you've downloaded appear in the main panel of iTunes.

3. **Double-click the video you want to watch.**

   It will play in the Selected Song album-artwork panel below the Source panel, as shown in Figure 2-14.

4. **If you want to watch the video in a separate window or at a larger size, single-click it with your mouse.**

   A separate window pops up, displaying the video as shown in Figure 2-15.

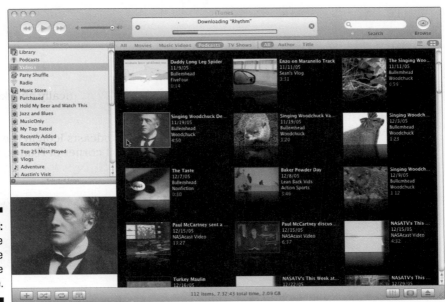

Figure 2-14: Watch the video in the Source pane.

Figure 2-15:
Single-click
the album
artwork to
display the
video in a
separate
window.

5. **You can resize the window by clicking-and-dragging the lower-right corner until it's the size you prefer.**

   You can also resize the video window with a menu; right-click or hold down the Control key and click anywhere on the window to pop open a context-sensitive menu. This menu lets you resize the window to half, normal, double, or full screen.

Managing files in iTunes

Some people have compared iTunes to a ravenous beast, viciously devouring your whole hard drive with all its music and video files. Personally, I think the comparison is unfair, unless you actually have to store all your music on your computer's primary hard drive. You'll notice that a second hard drive is one of the first upgrades I recommend for videobloggers. Get one large enough to store videos you're working on, as well as videoblogs, podcasts, and music in your iTunes library.

You can change where your iTunes files are stored by choosing iTunes⇨ Preferences to open the iTunes Preferences dialog box. Click the Advanced tab, and then click the General button to see where iTunes stores your music and video files and change that location if necessary.

Even after you've mastered using iTunes to subscribe to and play videoblogs, keep in mind that iTunes stores both audio and video files in the same location. It can be all too easy to lose control over your hard drive's storage space if you don't manage your podcast settings in iTunes.

To control how iTunes stores videoblogs and podcasts it downloads on your computer's hard drive, follow these steps:

1. **In iTunes, click the Podcasts icon and click the Settings button in the lower-right corner of iTunes.**

   The Podcasts Settings dialog box appears, as shown in Figure 2-16.

Figure 2-16: The Podcasts Settings dialog box also manages videoblog subscriptions in iTunes.

2. **Use the Keep option to tell iTunes how many *episodes* (vlog entries) to store before deleting them. The options are**

   - **All episodes:** All episodes you download will be saved. Use this setting only if you have a ton of storage space.

   - **All unplayed episodes:** Any episode you download will be saved until you play it, either in iTunes or your iPod. Episodes watched on your iPod won't be deleted until you sync your iPod.

   - **Most recent episode:** Only the last entry posted to the videoblog will be saved, whether you've seen them or not.

   - **Last 2 episodes:** The last two vlog entries will be saved.

   - **Last 3 episodes:** The last three vlog entries will be saved.

   - **Last 4 episodes:** The last four vlog entries will be saved (sensing a trend yet?)

   - **Last 5 episodes:** The last five vlog entries will be saved.

   - **Last 10 episodes:** The last ten vlog entries will be saved.

   The settings apply to all feeds equally. You cannot set one videoblog feed to save all entries and another feed to save only the unplayed entries.

3. **When you're done, click OK to save the settings.**

Worried about overloading your iPod? Don't — unless you have a video iPod, video files won't be copied to your iPod. iTunes is smart enough to know whether your iPod can play video files!

DTV

DTV is another standalone program for watching Internet video, but unlike FireANT or iPodderX, its focus isn't videoblogs — or even blogs. Instead, DTV's focus is on all Internet TV content — personal vlogs as well as more television-like videos. In addition to videoblogs, for instance, DTV also handles BitTorrent content, and video creators can use the Broadcast Machine to convert their videos to DTV's format for quick and easy publishing.

DTV calls all video RSS feeds *channels,* and has its own server-side software to make DTV channels out of your content. DTV can also be used to subscribe to and watch videoblogs, but it may not be able to display all the same description, artwork, and information for a vlog as for a channel. Also, some content that's available as DTV channels is not available outside DTV. (See Figure 2-17.)

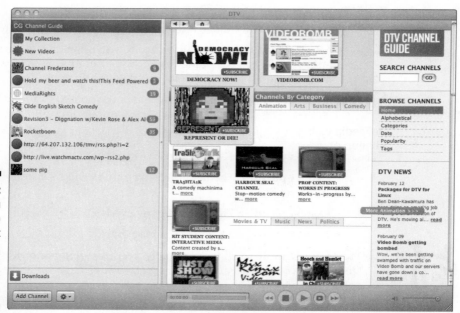

Figure 2-17: DTV lets you subscribe to feeds that have been set up as DTV Channels.

Web Browser Aggregator: MeFeedia

In an ideal world, you could watch videos from your Web browser, without having to go to every single videoblog's Web site, right? After all, if you can watch video in your Web browser anyway, you might as well watch it all in one window.

Unfortunately, creating such a site is not simple task, but one company has done it, and done it well. MeFeedia — another videoblogger-created Web site — has an index of over 3500 videoblogs (as of the writing of this book), which you can organize into a single feed, viewable in the MeFeedia Web site, or through a separate RSS feed of your very own. You can add that one RSS feed to your RSS reader if you want to use MeFeedia's interface for managing your subscriptions.

To use MeFeedia's feed reader features, first visit www.mefeedia.com and sign up for an account. You can still search MeFeedia for videoblogs you want to subscribe to, even if you decide not to use MeFeedia to subscribe to them.

Because MeFeedia is a Web-based RSS reader, you don't have to worry about storing incoming video on your hard drive. All the video files you watch will be stored in your Web browser's temporary cache — which automatically empties itself when it gets too full. However, you may want to make sure that cache has at least 20–30MB, in case you run into a very large file when you're watching vlogs in MeFeedia.

Subscribing to vlogs in MeFeedia

MeFeedia calls your subscriptions and recent vlog entries your *video queue* — a lineup of videos patiently waiting to be watched. Follow these steps to subscribe to a videoblog in MeFeedia:

1. **Click the link at the top of the MeFeedia Web site called Directory.**

2. **Search for videoblogs you want to add to MeFeedia using the search form.**

   MeFeedia's search engine is fairly generous about search terms, and will find results that are inside the description as well as the titles of feeds, as shown in Figure 2-18.

3. **Click the Subscribe button to add the feed to your subscriptions.**

Figure 2-18:
Search for
feeds that
interest you,
or just
search
terms you
find
intriguing.

Viewing vlogs in MeFeedia

MeFeedia shows only the last three entries in a feed. If you haven't caught up
on your vlogs recently — and don't want to miss anything — you might want
to visit each site individually, or use a different RSS reader for a one-time
download.

To view a videoblog entry in MeFeedia, follow these steps:

1. **Click the** <u>Watch</u> **link at the top of the MeFeedia site to view your video
   queue, shown in Figure 2-19.**

2. **In the left-hand navigation area, you'll see thumbnails of the recent
   videos in your subscribed feeds. Click one to open it, as shown in
   Figure 2-20.**

   Because MeFeedia doesn't download your videos for offline viewing, it
   may take a few minutes for each video to download before it can play in
   your Web browser.

Figure 2-19:
The video queue contains your new videos from your feeds.

3. **If the video doesn't play automatically, click the Play button in your video viewer plugin to play it.**

Videos will only auto-play if the video's creator has set it to play automatically.

Figure 2-20:
Click a thumbnail to open the video.

Tagging videos and leaving feedback in MeFeedia

In addition to serving as a vlog directory and RSS aggregator, MeFeedia provides a tagging service so you and other viewers can give individual vlog entries a tag. These tags are used to help categorize and search for content, not only in videoblogs, but in other areas of Web content as well.

To tag a vlog entry, follow these steps:

1. **Open the vlog entry you want to tag in your Queue.**

2. **Click the Tag This! icon below the movie.**

   The Tags field shows up, as shown in Figure 2-21.

3. **Enter the tag you want to add to the video in the text box and click the TAG! button.**

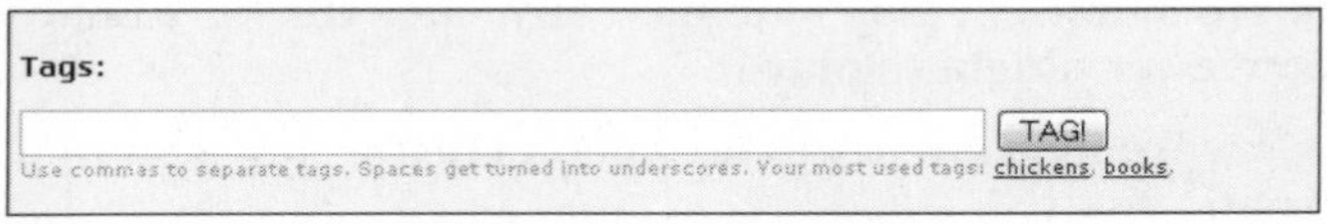

Figure 2-21:
Tag a
videoblog.

Tags:

[   ] [TAG!]

Use commas to separate tags. Spaces get turned into underscores. Your most used tags: chickens, books.

You can also bookmark a vlog entry by clicking the Add to Favs icon, or blog it using the Blog This icon, which lets you post about it to your blog or videoblog, if you have one configured in MeFeedia's settings.

Finally, the Leave a Comment link lets you give valuable feedback to the videoblogger who posted the entry. If they have comments enabled in their blog, you can click the Leave a Comment link to display a link to the vlog entry's comment page.

Vlogging away from the Computer

Sometimes, you just want to get away from it all. Especially your desk and the computer — if there's a sure-fire way to get a sore neck, it's watching a lot of movies on your desktop computer.

Fortunately, you don't have to feel chained to your desk to watch videoblogs. You can watch vlogs on your TV, video iPod, PlayStation Portable (PSP), or even your cellphone — provided you're willing to do a little work to make sure the videos show up and play correctly on your chosen device.

Watching vlogs on a TV isn't hard, but it does take a few extra A/V cables and no small amount of trial and error. You can find out more about how to get your videoblogs to play from your computer onto your television set at the *Videoblogging For Dummies* Web site at `http://www.mortaine.com/ vlogdummies`.

Going mobile with the iPod

Apple's iPod is one of *the* must-have geek toys of all time. In 20 years, the world will still be talking about the iPod and how it saved Apple's dwindling bottom line. As a music device, it's awesome. Good sound, very portable, and humongous storage capacity.

But as a video device? Well, that's the thing, isn't it? Neither iTunes nor the iPod were designed specifically for video. Industry pundits have asked "who wants to watch video on an iPod?" — and even Steve Jobs, founder and CEO of Apple, is even a little lukewarm about video on the iPod. That's probably because Jobs, like a lot of industry pundits, doesn't know much about videoblogs.

As you probably already noticed, vlogs aren't usually made for a widescreen or high-definition television. They're made for a smaller screen — and for short, fast downloads — ideal to watch on a 3-inch screen in your hand.

Downloading and playing videoblogs on your iPod

Since you can subscribe to videoblogs through iTunes, the easiest way to download vlogs to your iPod is to use the instructions for managing your vlogs in iTunes (see the earlier section, "Managing files in iTunes"), and then sync your iPod to iTunes.

However, you may want to configure your iPod to only download certain videoblogs, or to keep them for only a certain length of time. To set up your iPod's video options, follow these steps:

1. **Open iTunes, connect your iPod, and then choose iTunes➪Preferences to open the Preferences window.**

2. **Click the iPod icon in the Preferences window to show the iPod's options.**

3. **Click the Podcasts tab to show the podcasts options, as shown in Figure 2-22.**

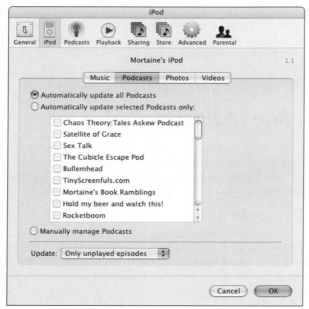

Figure 2-22:
The iPod dialog box lets you set up your iPod.

All your subscribed videoblogs appear in the iPod dialog box. If you want to limit which videoblogs get copied to your iPod, select *Automatically update selected Podcasts only* and check which videoblogs you want to include. Updating manually is not recommended; you'd have to drag and drop each video individually into your iPod.

4. **As you know by now, vlogs can take up a lot of space. Use the Update field to select how many episodes you want to update on your iPod:**

   • **All episodes:** All vlog entries downloaded from that videoblog will be copied to your iPod.

   • **Only checked episodes:** All entries that have a check mark next to them in the iTunes library will be copied to your iPod (shown in Figure 2-23).

   • **Only most recent episode:** Only the very most recent vlog entry will be copied to your iPod.

   • **Only unplayed episodes:** Only vlog entries that you haven't played yet will be copied. If you play an episode on your iPod, it will be marked played in iTunes and will be removed from your iPod. If you don't want your iPod to fill up with video, use this setting.

Figure 2-23:
Checking a vlog entry marks it as checked for purposes of updating your iPod.

The Videos tab lets you specify which video playlists to sync with your iPod. You only need to use this if you copy videos directly to your iPod without subscribing to them via iTunes.

If you have videos on your hard drive that you want to copy to your iPod without subscribing to a videoblog, just drag them onto the Library in iTunes and drop them. Don't drag them to the Videos category in the Source list; dragging them to the Library will add them to the Videos category automatically. You can then add them to playlists — just like any song in your collection.

Converting videos for the iPod

The iPod has a trimmed-down version of QuickTime on it, so you can play QuickTime movies on it — provided the movies fit into the iPod's limitations on size and quality.

If you use the instructions in Chapter 12 for creating your videoblog in MPEG-4 format, your vlog entries will already be iPod-ready!

Using your iPod to play video on your TV

To connect a video device to your TV, it needs three cables — two for audio, and one for video. The iPod has only one plug. Fortunately, Apple makes an inexpensive cable to plug your iPod into your TV (under $20 at the time of writing this book), and other manufacturers are following suit. The cable is shown in Figure 2-24.

The AV cable is a three-plug RCA connector. If your TV only has an S-Video input, you'll need an RCA-to-S-Video adapter, which, like most of these AV adapters, you can buy at your local Radio Shack or other electronics store.

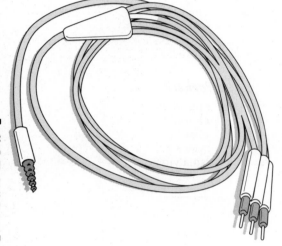

Figure 2-24: The Apple AV iPod cable connects your iPod to the TV.

You can also plug the universal dock into the TV and use it (and the optional remote controller) to watch movies on the TV. However, the universal dock is more expensive than the cable, and you'll still need the AV cable to get the universal dock to connect to your TV. It's not a bad setup if you want to have your iPod play all your videos on the TV, but the total price tag for the dock, cables, and remote is almost $90.

Playing videoblogs on other mobile media players, cellphones, and PDAs

Believe it or not, the iPod was not the first portable device that could play videoblogs. The PlayStation Portable (PSP) has long been able to play video away from home, and some cellphones can send and receive short video clips using multimedia messaging. Videobloggers even use a PocketPC device with a specialized RSS reader (FeederReader) to take their movies on the go.

Using a PlayStation Portable

The PSP is a nifty device with lots of features — most of which are designed for playing videogames and DVDs away from home. However, videobloggers have an array of tools for putting vlog entries onto a PSP.

For Windows, there's PSP Video 9 and Videora (`www.pspvideo9.com`), as shown in Figure 2-25. Videora enables you to set up RSS feeds and convert video to the right format for transferring to your PSP device.

For the Mac, use PSPWare (`www.nullriver.com`) to convert your vlog entries to PSP format. If you use FireANT to download your videos, you can drag and drop them from the FireANT Downloads directory straight into the PSPWare window, as shown in Figure 2-26.

Using FeederReader on the PocketPC

Just when you might be wondering when you might find another "by the vloggers for the vloggers" application, this time for mobile devices, along comes FeederReader for the Pocket PC. It's a video-enabled RSS reader for Pocket PC (Windows Mobile) devices such as handhelds and SmartPhones — written by Greg Smith, who is also a videoblogger.

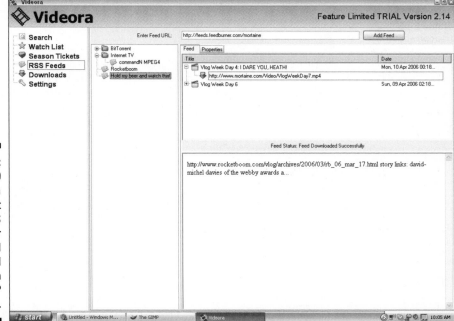

Figure 2-25:
PSP Video 9 with Videora lets you set up RSS feeds for download and conversion to PSP format.

FeederReader comes as a CAB file, which you copy to the mobile device and install as usual. Once it's installed, click its icon to launch it. (See Figure 2-27.) You'll be prompted to set up FeederReader with some default RSS feeds.

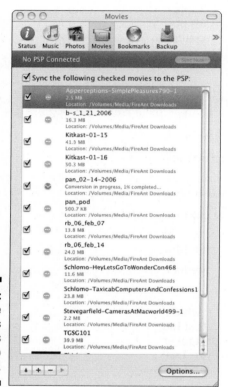

Figure 2-26: PSPWare converts and syncs videos to your PSP.

Figure 2-27: Feeder Reader's interface.

From the interface, there are two main panels. The top panel shows the feeds you're subscribed to; the bottom panel shows the current entry. You can click the Notepad icon near the bottom to hide the feeds when you watch vlogs.

To subscribe to a feed, click the Tools menu and select Add RSS Feed. You'll have to enter the feed manually, so pay attention for any typos. When you have the feed added, follow these steps:

1. **Dock the device and start ActiveSync so it can use your computer's Internet connection.**

   If your mobile device has its own network connection, such as a wireless connection, then use that instead.

2. **Highlight the feed with your stylus.**

3. **Choose Do⇨Update Channel to start updating the feed and downloading videos.**

4. **When you're done, click the vlog entry to open it in the lower panel.**

5. **Click the notepad icon to hide the feeds and just watch the current video.**

6. **Click the large video space at the bottom of the entry.**

   That's the attached video. Media Player will launch and show you the movie.

With PocketPC, your options for which videoblogs you subscribe to are much more limited, and you may find that individual vlog entries just won't play if the creator has used Flash or certain encoding options that aren't compatible with the Pocket PC's media player. Trial and error will help you navigate these bumps in the road, as will the community of FeederReader users in the online user forums for the software.

 If you have FireANT installed, you can export your feeds from FireANT as an OPML list by choosing Channels⇨Export Channels, and then import them into FeederReader by choosing Tools⇨Import OPML Channels to transfer your feed URLs quickly onto your device.

Watching videoblogs on your cellphone

Every cellphone carrier varies, so it's impossible to give precise instructions for watching videoblogs on your cellphone. Fortunately, there is a standard file format (called *3G*) for video and multimedia files on cellphones.

Most videoblogs aren't in 3G format, so you'll need to do a bit of manual conversion to get your vlog entries onto your phone. You'll also need QuickTime Pro, which has a 3G file format export option available.

To convert a video file to 3G format using QuickTime, follow these steps:

1. **Download and save the vlog entry file to your hard drive.**

   The easiest way to do this is to use FireANT to subscribe and download your vlogs for offline viewing.

2. **Open the vlog entries in QuickTime Pro.**

3. **For each vlog entry, select File⇨Export from the menu bar in QuickTime Pro.**

   The Save Exported File As dialog box appears.

4. **In the Export drop-down list, select Movie to 3G to save the movie in a cellphone-ready format, as shown in Figure 2-28.**

5. **Choose a location on your hard drive to store the movies, click OK, and wait for the file to export.**

6. **In your e-mail program, e-mail each vlog entry to your cellphone's SMS address.**

   The SMS address is usually your cellphone number at your cellphone-service carrier's gateway. You may need to send each file individually in order for your phone to view them properly.

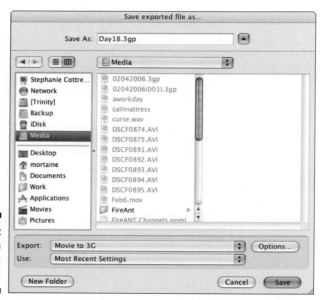

Figure 2-28:
Export each
entry to 3G
format.

You may also be able to transfer videos to your cellphone via Bluetooth, if both your cellphone and your computer are Bluetooth-enabled. Transferring over Bluetooth can save time as well as connection fees.

Even though there isn't a program out there that does this automatically (at least, as I'm writing this book), it can't be all that long before there's a simple interface to convert and e-mail movies to a cellphone. Use your favorite search engine to search for programs or services that offer this conversion automatically.

Remember that your phone has limited storage space. Make sure your video files don't eat your cellphone's entire memory. A 3G video compresses down pretty small (about ⅛ the size of a compressed vlog entry with the same content), but if you have a lot of them, they will add up! If you run out of space, your phone might have a separate storage card you can store videos to. If you're out of space, you just won't be able to transfer the video, of course.

Chapter 3

Stocking Your Toolbox

The videoblogger's toolbox is the set of tools that helps him or her create really great videoblog entries. At its most basic, that toolbox consists of a computer with an Internet connection and a camera capable of recording video and transferring the video to a computer. Other items in a videoblogger's toolbox include the software for editing your video, extra camera equipment (such as lights, tripods, and microphones), and improved computer hardware.

In this chapter, I show you what options you have when you're gathering the equipment for your videoblogger's toolbox.

Picking Out Camera Equipment

If you don't already own a camera capable of capturing video (be it a camcorder, digital camera, video-capable cellphone, or even a webcam), you need to buy or borrow a video camera. (It's possible to make a videoblog without a video camera by using still pictures, animation, scanned artwork, and screen captures to compose movies. However, most vloggers use some flavor of a video camera to record their vlog entries.) The following sections describe the features and options you want to look for when you're shopping for a camera to record videos for your vlog.

Digital camcorders

A digital video camera can range in price from a couple hundred dollars to several thousand dollars. For a personal videoblog, you generally don't need the power and picture quality of a high-end camera. It's an informal medium, so for most purposes, a consumer-range camera will do fine.

The most important thing to think about when looking for a digital camcorder is how you're going to use it. What kinds of video will you be shooting? If you frequently find yourself recording video at soccer games, for instance, then you will want a camera that films high-speed action well. If you're a coffeeshop concert-goer, and you want a camcorder with good low-light quality and great sound.

Most people do not think they will be in low-light situations often enough to consider a camcorder's low-light performance, but in fact, the majority of video you shoot is probably indoors, with indirect lighting. Cameras that perform well in low-light situations perform just as well in good lighting, so if you can afford a camera with good low-light recording quality, buy it.

When you shop for a digital video camera, you'll find that the chip used to capture the image — called a CCD (charge-coupled device) — makes a difference in quality. The CCD collects the light from the lens and converts it to a digital signal. The larger the CCD, the more light your camcorder collects, and the better the picture quality. The CCD is referred to by size in fractions of an inch. That means that a ⅙ CCD is smaller than a ¼ CCD. Some camcorders have more than one CCD. In fact, a camcorder with three CCDs (which collect red, green, and blue light separately) results in better overall color separation and can mean the difference between the video being grainy in low light and a professional-looking video.

Another thing to look for is a good zoom lens. There are two types of zoom: optical and digital. The most important thing to look at is the optical zoom. By and large, digital zoom does very little to help your video — it makes the image look more blurry than it needs to be. An optical zoom can be 10 to 30X, which means the image will seem to be ten to 30 times closer to the subject. However, read product reviews carefully. When you zoom in on a subject, camcorders become very prone to *camera shake,* where your camera is more sensitive to motion as a result of the zoomed-in lens.

Take a MiniDV tape with you to the store when you shop for camcorders and test each one before you buy. If you have a friend with a MiniDV camcorder, have them play back the tape to check the quality of the sound and picture.

Consider upgrading the battery when you buy the camera as well. Most camcorder batteries are only good for 30–60 minutes. Buy whatever extended battery is available for the camera — you'll be glad you did when you're on a weekend trip, don't have the charger, but have 8 hours of battery life to play with!

The essential accessories you'll want to buy along with your camcorder are the following:

- A larger media card, if the camcorder uses one
- Extra tapes
- Extended battery
- A tripod
- A padded carrying case

An optional protective item is a UV lens filter. If the camcorder can accept add-on lenses, think about getting one of these basic filters. They're clear and don't really have any impact on the quality of your video — but they're cheap protection. If your camcorder is hit on the front, or if you take it into an environment that would otherwise scratch the lens, it's a $20 UV filter that gets damaged, not the camcorder's lens.

Digital cameras

Many digital cameras have a video or movie mode available, which can film anywhere from a few seconds to a couple of minutes of digital video. If you're looking for a digital camera to use to record video, look for a camera with these features:

- Capable of zooming when recording video
- Front-mounted microphone
- External microphone jack
- Tripod mount
- USB connection and cable
- Removable media card

When you shop for a digital camera, read the online reviews and go to the manufacturer's Web site to read the camera's user manual. Many digital camera reviews don't really discuss the limitations of the camera's video feature, because reviewers care about still picture quality. The manual, however, will tell you what you can and can't do with the video mode, and will usually tell you how many minutes of video you can shoot with a given memory card size.

When it comes right down to it, though, digital cameras take photos very well, but they don't really make great video cameras. Don't let that stop you from considering your digital camera as a backup camera for video — when you're low on tape and the digital camera can get an extra 4 or 5 minutes of footage, sometimes that's all you need.

The shopping list for a digital camera accessories is very similar to that for the camcorder:

- A media card with a large amount of memory
- (Optional) A media card reader
- Extra batteries or rechargeable batteries and a charger
- A tripod
- A protective case

Depending on what kind of digital camera you buy, you may be able to buy a UV lens filter, which will protect the camera's lens from accidental damage.

Cellphones

With the new generation of video-enabled cellphones and the development of 3GP, the standardized cellphone video format, you can videoblog on the go when you're away from the computer or even the camcorder.

The limitations so far with 3GP are pretty restrictive, so this is one of those formats that requires you to be more creative under technical constraints:

- 3GP videos are small — about half the screen size of an iPod-ready video.
- Cellphones typically can't store or edit more than about 30 seconds of video at a time.
- iPods can't view 3GP videos (at the time of this writing), so viewers have to convert your moblog entries and manually add them to the iPod.
- Cellphones don't usually have a secondary light source — make sure your shot is well lit before you begin.
- The quality of the video is such that close-ups work best, and faraway shots look grainy.
- Close-up audio sounds much better than sounds recorded at a distance.

So, consider those constraints. This particular tool is great for very specific types of footage — close up, personal, short, intimate clips that don't necessarily tell a whole story.

Cellphones are also great camouflage for candid videoblogging. Just angle your head, hold the phone up to your ear, and periodically nod and grunt into the mouthpiece, like you're absently listening to your mother talk about her new curtains. Of course, if you do this without permission or in a banned place (like a locker room!) you can land yourself in legal hot water, so make sure you have the right to vlog before whipping out the phone.

Naturally, you don't want to consider a video cellphone without also looking at your cellular service. If you already have cellular service, you may not want to change service providers, especially if you're happy with your carrier and coverage, or you're in the middle of a service contract. If you are happy with your carrier, then you'll need to limit your search for a video cellphone to phones that are compatible with your carrier or your service plan.

If you are thinking of switching providers, then your options are wide open. Naturally, you should do all the things you normally would when selecting a cellphone provider, including borrowing a friend's cellphone from the same provider and checking the signal at home and at your workplace. In addition, make sure that the phone you borrow gets both the standard cellular signal as well as whatever signal you might need to take advantage of the video on your phone. On some carriers, that's the same signal, but on others, like Cingular, it's two separate signals — one for the bars and the other to represent the digital/data signal.

When you shop for a video-enabled cellphone, look for the following features:

- **Shoots 3GP video.** This is the new standard for cellphone video; it can be imported into iMovie and Windows Movie Maker. Alternatively, a video cellphone that supports MPEG-4 or QuickTime would also work.

- **Has a good data signal strength.** You will probably send your video files via multimedia messaging or e-mail, so make sure the phone has a strong signal for that in your most common locations.

- **Microphone on the camera side of the phone.** The microphone will pick up what's in front of it, not what's behind it. If the microphone for your phone is the mouthpiece, and the camera is on the back, then the microphone will record poor audio from your video subject.

- **Memory card for storage.** Many cellphones now can take a memory card that you can use to store video files.

- **Multimedia service.** Some carriers and plans charge extra for multimedia messages. Find out what it will cost you to videoblog with your cellphone.

- **Bluetooth.** If you don't want to pay the extra multimedia service costs, Bluetooth connectivity is a good way to get your videos out of your phone and onto your computer without using the network. You'll need a Bluetooth-equipped computer as well. (Check out www.bluetooth.com for details.)

- **Videoblogging software.** This one is optional. Currently, Lifebook is available for Cingular phones and TypePad customers. Lifebook enables you to post video and pictures from your cellphone without having to connect to a computer or use an e-mail gateway.

✔ **Video-editing software.** It's not required, but it is handy to be able to add a soundtrack and splice in your intro and outro without having to transfer the video to your computer.

✔ **Scratch-resistant screen.** Video cellphones get scratched pretty easily. Get a scratch-resistant screen, or buy an iPod screen protector and cut it down to size.

Finding the Right Microphone

Half the equation in a good videoblogs is the sound. (After all, talkies put the silent film out of style in the 1930s.) But a surprisingly common problem in videoblogs is great video, but poor sound. The audio can be muddy, or too quiet, or drowned out by nearby noise or crowds.

Your brain filters out the unnecessary information you hear, such as the background noise from other people's conversations in a restaurant. When you film that same restaurant, however, your video camera *can't* filter out that background noise. As a result, you might have a terrific interview that is ruined by a loud conversation at a nearby table.

Even when the noises nearby are not particularly loud, they can be distracting. Consider, for example, when you're filming a club event or activity. Your video camera is set up somewhere convenient, but it just happens to be at a table with a fidgety child. Even if the kid doesn't say anything, the noise of him or her shifting around, sighing, chewing ice cubes in boredom, and generally being fidgety, will wind up in your audio.

So how do you get rid of all that noise? A good microphone will do 90 percent of that work for you; software can handle the remaining 10 percent.

Microphones, like every electronic thing in the world, need electricity (power) to work. Most microphones run on what's called plug-in power, in which the audio jack in your camcorder or audio device also supplies the power for the microphone. Some microphones, however, need an external power supply. They can be powered by the accessory shoe on your camcorder (if the shoe is *hot* — that is, electrically connected) or by an external battery pack (such as with a lapel microphone). When you buy the microphone, don't assume that it's self-powered or powered by the audio plug. Check first.

Directional microphones

Microphones can generally be broken down into a few specific types and features:

- ✔ **Unidirectional microphones** pick up sound from one direction. If you are standing in front of the microphone and speaking, then the microphone picks up your voice.

- ✔ **Omnidirectional microphones** pick up sound from all around them. Except for a very rare spot (usually toward the back of the microphone), these mics get sound from everywhere.

For most video applications, you want a unidirectional microphone. Why? Because most of the time, you'll be filming someone speaking. For individual speakers, unidirectional mics are best. They duplicate that filtering that people naturally do when there's a lot of ambient noise. When a unidirectional mic also has noise-canceling features, it dampens the ambient noise as well, making for superior audio.

Use an omnidirectional mic when you want to record sound from multiple sources all at the same time. An omnidirectional microphone is useful for recording conversations — with a unidirectional mic, you would have to move the microphone to point at each person as he or she is speaking. Also, if you want to record live music events, you should get an omnidirectional microphone. An omnidirectional mic will pick up sound from the different instruments more or less evenly, while a unidirectional mic will only pick up the instrument directly in front of it.

Built-in microphones

For most environments, the microphone that came built into your video camera will probably suffice. Some camcorder mics, of course, have poor audio quality, something that you're most likely to discover when you've shot an hour of video and only belatedly realize the sound is too quiet to hear.

Built-in microphones come in a couple of styles. The most common is a front-mounted microphone somewhere on the front of the camera. It might be labeled, have a grille pattern on it (as in Figure 3-1), or it might show up only as a tiny hole in the body of your camcorder (the mic is tucked in there).

Other built-in microphones are located somewhere on the back of the camcorder, but probably look like the tiny-hole style. The problem with rear-mounted microphones is that they're not facing the same direction as the lens. As a result, the loudest audio will be from behind the camera, while the video is from in front of the camera. This happens with front-mounted microphones as well, but not as much.

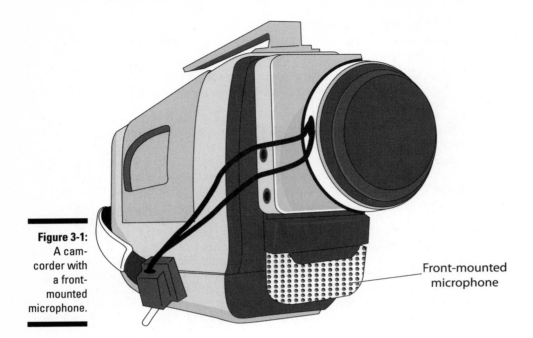

Figure 3-1:
A camcorder with a front-mounted microphone.

Front-mounted microphone

In the higher-end cameras, you may find a shotgun microphone built into or mounted on the camera, as shown in Figure 3-2. This model looks like an honest-to-goodness microphone, not just a little hole on the side of your camcorder. Frequently, the microphone has a wind sock on it as well. This type of microphone is more commonly an external accessory microphone, but some of the higher-end camcorders have them built in.

Most built-in microphones are unidirectional. In addition, the built-in microphone may be what's called a *zoom microphone* that increases the noise-canceling function and increases volume when you zoom in on someone, so it appears that both the video image *and* audio get closer.

External mics

External microphones plug into your camcorder's audio ports and let you record audio along with your video without having to rely on the built-in microphone for your camera. When your camcorder's audio is substandard, this is a good way to improve it cheaply and with minimal hassle.

You have a lot of options for an external microphone. You can pick up a unidirectional mic at Radio Shack, for instance, for about $25. This kind of mic is very simple. You usually need an adapter for it — standard microphones use a large (quarter-inch) plug instead of the ⅛-inch plug that your camcorder most likely came with. Get a wind sock for the mic, make yourself a microphone flag, and you're in business!

Shotgun microphone

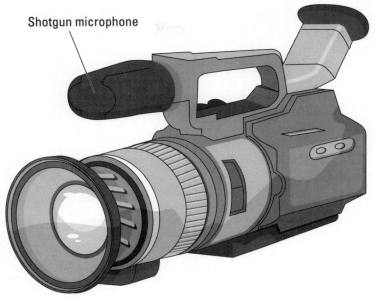

Figure 3-2:
A cam-
corder with
a built-in
shotgun
microphone.

If you really want high-quality audio, you'll need professional-grade equip-ment, which uses a type of connector called *XLR*. Since your camcorder may not have XLR connections, you'll need another adapter, or an external audio recorder (which you then synchronize to your film when editing). Wind sock? Flag? No, I'm not talking about a nylon thing that hangs on the porch. A *wind sock* (also called a *wind screen*) is a small piece of foam that goes over the end of the microphone, as shown in Figure 3-3. If it's bright orange, it gives the microphone that classic "Mr. Microphone" look. Otherwise, it just cuts down the noise for wind and air currents and generally makes for better sound quality.

Make a microphone flag

A microphone flag is that little box-around-the-mic that you sometimes see on network news reports where the reporter is on the scene doing interviews. They're common in press con-ferences, where you'll find a podium with many microphones, all identified by microphone flags.

If you use an external microphone, a micro-phone flag can add a touch of class (or whimsy)

to your videoblog. And they're fairly easy to make! You'll need a printer (or artistic skill) and a block of floral moldable foam. You can get the foam at a craft store — you want the stuff that's easily molded to fit your shape.

You can find more instructions at `www.mortaine.com/vlogdummies`.

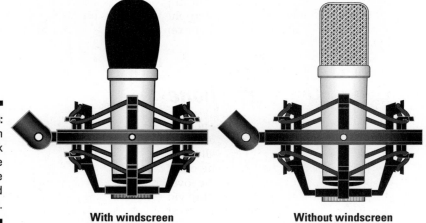

Figure 3-3:
A foam
wind sock
protects the
microphone
from wind
noises.

With windscreen   **Without windscreen**

The *microphone flag* (see the sidebar "Make a microphone flag") is the little box with a logo that you see near the top of a microphone when TV reporters interview people on camera. Microphone flags are handy because, even if someone nabs your video, it'll always be obvious what station (or, in this case, videoblog) was really responsible for the interview.

In addition to the simple Radio Shack–style mic, you can get a more sophisticated microphone that mounts to the accessory shoe of your camcorder — a standardized slot for mounting accessories such as microphones and lights to your camera. Many camcorders come with them, though most people go through their whole lives without ever using the accessory shoe on the camcorder. If your camera's built-in microphone is adequate, you may never even need the accessory shoe.

On the accessory shoe, you can mount a *shotgun microphone,* which is a unidirectional mic that will pickup better sound. This is essentially identical to a camera with a built-in shotgun microphone, but you purchase the microphone separately from the camera. A good microphone may cost anywhere from $150 up to several thousand dollars. With a shotgun microphone, always get a wind sock to cover the pickup end of the microphone and prevent wind noise.

Finally, you can buy a *lapel microphone.* This is a small microphone that pins or clips to the speaker's clothing and usually has a wireless transmitter to send the sound to a receiver. The receiver may be plugged into the video camera and pass the audio directly onto the tape, or it may be a separate device. If it's a separate device, you'll need to edit your video carefully to synchronize audio and video so the appropriate on-screen lips are in sync with the audible words. Lapel microphones are not cheap, but if you do a lot of interviews or film many speaker events, they may be just the thing you need.

Computer microphones

So, if you have a good microphone on your video, why on earth would you ever need a microphone for your computer? Well, you might not. But sooner or later, one of several things will happen. You will shoot a video, only to discover that the sound didn't come out right, and you won't be able to shoot it again. You'll need to record a voiceover to fix the sound. Or you may want to do a screencast, where you capture video of your computer screen and narrate it. Or you have something fun to show, and want to narrate that. Or you shoot a series of still photos and put them together in a slideshow. Or maybe you join the videoblogging community and participate in one of the weekly videoconference chats. Whatever the reason, sooner or later you will find yourself needing to add audio to your movie without using the camcorder.

Always get a noise-cancelling microphone for computer use. This will remove most of the noise that your computer makes. Most computer mics are unidirectional, and some are very sensitive. Try it out in advance to make sure the pickup is pointed at your mouth, as illustrated in Figure 3-4.

Pickup points
at your mouth

Figure 3-4:
Set up your noise-cancelling microphone carefully.

After you have your computer microphone set up, make sure you've selected it in the System Preferences (Mac) or Control Panel (Windows). For PCs, the selection may be automatic when you plug in a USB microphone. Mac users may need to go into the System Preferences (Apple Menu⇨System Preferences) and select the microphone in the Choose a Device for Sound Input list, as shown in Figure 3-5.

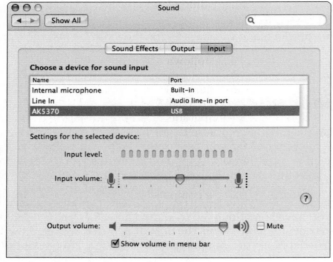

Figure 3-5:
Select the
correct
microphone
in the Sound
dialog box.

Getting Your Computer in Order

At the beginning of this chapter, I said that the two main components for videoblogging are your video camera and your computer. I talk about the video equipment and microphones earlier in this chapter. Now I discuss that box of chips and circuits that is such a ubiquitous part of modern life.

This book is heavily slanted towards the Macintosh because, not surprisingly, Macintosh users have led the way in videoblogging. It isn't hard to figure out why, either: iMovie, which shipped free with the new generations of Macs, has offered desktop editing for video since 2000. Windows Movie Maker, however, didn't ship with Windows until Windows XP, so it lagged several years behind the video-editing craze among Mac users. (Microsoft doesn't have much to worry about, though — there are still more people viewing videoblogs in Windows than on Macs, and the number of Windows-based videobloggers continues to increase.)

The following sections discuss the important items your computer needs to have to make your videoblogging experience as fun and easy as possible.

Hardware considerations

You need a reasonably recent and fast computer to edit videos for your videoblog, preferably something made within the last three years. It should have Mac OS X or Windows XP installed, so you can take advantage of the latest generation of easy desktop video-editing software. Even if you have a fairly recent computer, you may find your video-editing chores will go faster if you upgrade your computer.

When you're looking for a new computer or upgrading your current system, look for biggest and best of the following items:

- ✔ **RAM (random-access memory):** Get as much RAM as you can afford, preferably 1GB or more. You'll need all that memory for editing video. Keep in mind that as you upgrade your computer's software, your need for RAM will increase; be sure to get enough to grow on.

- ✔ **A large hard drive:** Video takes up tons of hard drive space, so buy a bigger hard drive than you think you'll need. If you can, get a huge internal drive. You might find it's easiest to just buy an external hard drive after you get the rest of the computer set up and going. A 400GB hard drive isn't unreasonable for a videoblogger.

- ✔ **A FireWire port:** FireWire is the easiest way to transfer video from a digital camcorder to your computer.

- ✔ **A good video card and a large monitor:** A fast video card is helpful, as is a large monitor so you have plenty of room to work on your videos.

Good speakers are also helpful when you listen to your audio to improve the sound quality.

Video digitizers

If your camcorder doesn't have FireWire or USB, it's probably not a digital camcorder. That means your video is on an analog tape that your computer can't read. Computers read digital data, and older camcorders record analog data. Thus you'll need to get a video digitizer to convert your analog video data into digital video data.

Video digitizers cost a couple hundred dollars. They usually connect to your USB port on your computer, but older models can connect to serial ports as well. The essentials are that you connect the video camera to the digitizer using standard audio/video cables. Then you connect the digitizer to your computer using the USB port. You play the video from the camcorder to your computer and capture it using iMovie or Windows Movie Maker or whatever software came with the digitizer.

Since the digitizer costs about $200, and a new FireWire-capable camcorder costs about the same amount if you shop frugally, think very carefully about this particular purchase before you make it. If you don't have FireWire on your computer, or if you have some old beloved family footage that you absolutely want to store digitally, then a video digitizer might be worth the cost. Shop around, though. If you only have a few family videos, you may find it's less expensive to send them to a video-digitizing service and get them back on DVD. Then you don't have to go through all the trouble and expense of buying a digitizer for yourself.

Getting the Right Software

In addition to your computer hardware and camcorder, you need good video-editing software to get the job done right. In terms of how you experience and enjoy editing video, software is the core tool in your toolbox.

In the following sections, you'll find an overview of some of the most popular video-editing software out there. Software prices range from inexpensive (or included) software to professional-grade (and professionally-priced) products. Most of the programs are from the Macintosh side of editing. In the Windows world, you can generally find less expensive software with the same features. Because of the different ways Apple and Windows computers interact with graphics hardware, however, Macs are considered to be better at graphic arts. Unless you are a professional graphic artist or video editor, however, you probably won't notice the difference.

Apple's iMovie

When you buy a new Macintosh computer, it comes with iLife, a suite of programs that allow you to manage and edit various media types — from photos to music, movies, and DVDs. iMovie is the video-editing software included with iLife.

When you edit videos in iMovie, you import the video clips, either directly from your camcorder, or from a file copied from your digital camera or hard drive. You can also import music from iTunes and pictures from iPhoto during the editing process.

iMovie is a *nondestructive* video editor. That means it doesn't change your original video files when you make changes to the clip. Instead, it saves a record of what changes you made and applies that record when you use the clip in your movie. As a result, you can get to the original video files if you need to make a backup (strongly recommended) or if you want to quickly copy the video clip and use it somewhere else.

iMovie's features are pretty impressive for an almost-free product:

- ✔ Import from many sources and file formats
- ✔ Timeline-based editor as well as clip editor

- Many built-in transitions and titles
- Filters
- Two tracks for audio
- Import music from iTunes
- Built-in sound effects
- Record voiceovers directly from iMovie
- Add photos and photo effects
- Third-party filters and transitions are available
- Reuse clips and movies

One limitation of iMovie is that it uses QuickTime as its compression engine, so if something doesn't work in QuickTime, it's unlikely to be fixed in iMovie, and vice versa. Similarly, if you install a third-party transition or filter (called a *plugin*), it has to be 100% compatible with both iMovie and QuickTime, or the plugin you installed in iMovie will cause QuickTime to fail. This incompatibility issue is a big headache for folks who have bought hundreds of dollars worth of plugins for one version of iMovie, and then upgraded to a newer version iMovie — only to have the filters break, iMovie to stop working, and problems to crop up with QuickTime as well. If you install third-party plugins and you're having trouble with QuickTime, back up the plugins and remove them to see whether that fixes the problem.

If you didn't get iLife with your Mac, or your version is old and you want to upgrade, iLife costs about $179 per license.

Apple's Final Cut Pro

Final Cut Pro is the ultimate video-editing software. This is the tool for professional videographers and independent filmmakers. Final Cut Pro might be overkill for a beginner, but that's okay — unless you're a very wealthy beginner, you won't start with Final Cut Pro.

Final Cut Pro offers some features of particular interest to videobloggers:

- Conversion from nearly every video format
- Real-time effects and editing
- Multiple audio tracks/channels
- Filters, transitions, and titles
- Timeline viewer/editor
- Works with other Apple-based tools
- Plugins and third-party applications

At $1299, however, Final Cut Pro is not a beginner's tool. Don't buy this one unless you're moving into the world of professional video editing.

Apple QuickTime Pro

QuickTime Pro has several editing options available — it has almost as many features as iMovie. However, its interface for editing is much more complex than that of iMovie — basically, you have to do everything by hand and there is no simple Timeline or clip viewer to help you sort things out with a drag-and-drop interface.

One advantage to QuickTime Pro is that it can do certain effects for which iMovie needs a plugin. For example, QuickTime Pro can create picture-in-picture effects without trouble, and you can apply a mask to a QuickTime Pro movie so one image appears to play inside another image, as shown in Figure 3-6.

Additionally, QuickTime Pro has a wider range of conversion options, so you can open even a compressed video file and save it in an editable format.

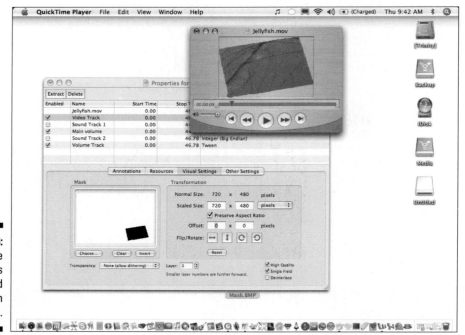

Figure 3-6: QuickTime Pro offers advanced effects such as masking.

QuickTime Pro is available for both Windows and Macintosh. It's an inexpensive upgrade (about $29) to the QuickTime Player. When you purchase the upgrade, you just receive a license key to unlock the Pro features of the software.

Adobe Premiere

Adobe Premiere Pro is another professionally-priced tool, and it's only available for Windows computers. For about $849, you can get the core Premier program, and for $1299, you can get it bundled with several other Adobe core video products, such as After Effects and Photoshop. If you don't need all the features of the Pro version, a cost-effective alternative is Adobe Premier Elements, which costs $99.

The Pro version is comparable to Final Cut Pro, both in features and in price. It's another powerhouse application that fits into its own suite of tools for making professional-quality videos. Adobe Premiere offers the following features:

- ✔ Conversion from nearly any video format
- ✔ Multiple audio and video tracks
- ✔ Title, transitions, and filters
- ✔ Third-party plugins
- ✔ Timeline viewer and editor

Premiere Elements, shown in Figure 3-7, is a pared-down version of Premiere for the home user. Like Final Cut Express for Mac users, it offers some of the advanced editing features of Premiere Pro, but without the high price tag.

Macromedia Flash

Macromedia Flash has been around for several years, but Macromedia was recently bought by Adobe, so you can expect development to take a new direction. Flash can create wonderful animations, but it can also be a powerful video-publishing medium as well. (See Figure 3-8.)

Figure 3-7:
Adobe
Premiere
Elements is
a cost-
effective
alternative
to pro-
fessional
editing
programs.

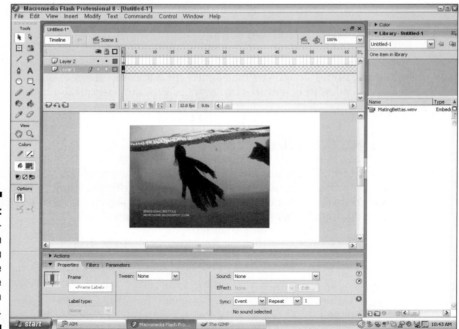

Figure 3-8:
Macro-
media Flash
lets you
create
interactive
files or Flash
videos.

Macromedia Flash offers two features that appeal to creators:

- ✓ **Interactivity:** This is the core strength of Flash. If you've spent any amount of time on the Internet, you've probably found some of amusing Flash games. Flash delivers the animations and interactivity with a smaller file size than most expect, because it stores most of its data as compact instructions to the Flash viewer.

- ✓ **Browser-only play:** It's difficult to save a Macromedia Flash file to your hard drive if the creator set it up to play only in the Web browser. Even if you (as a user) do save a Flash file to the hard drive, it's hard to do anything further with it; unless you also have Macromedia Flash, you can't really edit it.

Macromedia Flash doesn't really have a major competitor in the Web-based interactive animation market, but it's not the best choice for editing video. It's pretty hard to create an interactive video from film, so the main strength of the Flash video falls by the wayside for videobloggers. Macromedia Flash isn't really a video editor per se (it edits video, but that's not its main task); asking it to do a job it isn't made for seems rather inefficient.

However, if you enjoy making Flash animations or games, there is no rule that says a videoblog can't be a blog of Flash animation *and* games. In fact, several videobloggers have done this, including some terrific Internet comedians who use Flash to distort the visuals and animate the story to give it a more surreal feel and heighten the humor.

Macromedia Flash is available for both Windows and Macintosh, and retails for about $699. It's also available in many Web-development bundles, some of which make it more competitively priced.

Windows Movie Maker

Windows Movie Maker, shown in Figure 3-9, comes free with Windows XP and is at least as fully featured as iMovie. It's a good competitor in the desktop video-editing software market, but it's limited in the file formats available (`.wmv` and `.avi`). This means you have to run your edited video through a conversion program to make it compatible with standard video formats such as MPEG-4.

Windows Movie Maker lets you import video from your camera using either FireWire or USB, or from files on your hard drive. You can include still pictures and record voiceovers directly to the video, just as in iMovie. It has a Timeline Viewer interface. If you're on a Windows machine, it's a good tool to have. Not too many Windows users even know it's there, because it tends to be hidden in the Start menu under Accessories or Multimedia. Check carefully; this is a good video editor, especially when you're starting out.

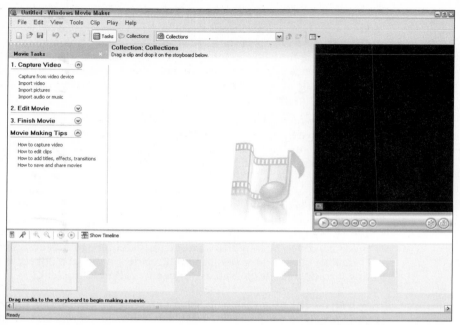

Figure 3-9:
Windows
Movie
Maker.

Affording It All

By now, you're probably wondering if you should have set aside a budget of several thousand dollars before picking up this book. Never fear: You can videoblog on a budget. Remember, you already have the most important tool in your vlog: you!

Use what you have

Before you run out and spend $3000 on equipment and software, look at what you already have on hand. Do you have a video camera, digital camera, or webcam?

For example, in 2000, I bought a pretty nice little Sony camcorder, which I used for digital video on a trip to Paris that year. I downloaded the videos to my iMac at the time — it was Mac OS 9, but it came with iMovie, which suited my purposes. I used the same video camera and iMovie (though a later version) until spring of 2006 — through almost a whole year of videoblogging.

Sure, the videoblog posts made with that camera may not be the highest quality, but they are video, they are a blog, and the creative content is what matters in my vlog, not necessarily the quality of the images.

My point is, if your camcorder and computer were made sometime in the last five years, you can probably use them to make your videoblog. If you don't have a camcorder, then by all means consider buying one — and use the advice earlier in this chapter to do so. Unless you're rich or an unrepentant spendthrift, start with what you have. If you find your tools limiting, then consider spending money on an upgrade. But don't give up on a usable piece of hardware just because it's not brand new!

A videoblog without video

For the next couple of minutes, pretend that you have a very limited amount of disposable income. Say you don't have a camcorder or the money to purchase one. Or perhaps you had a camcorder, but your homemade steadycam was a little less than steady, and your camcorder is now at the bottom of a ravine.

Suddenly, you may be faced with a creative challenge: How do you make a videoblog when you can't make a video? Don't be ridiculous! You have iMovie or Windows Movie Maker, don't you? You have digital photos, don't you? Or clipart? Or funny doodles you made during that boring lecture in high-school physics class? The video in a videoblog does not have to be filmed from real life. You can use still photos, drawings, and clipart to tell your story.

Consider some possibilities for a videoblog about an event. You can video the event, or you can take still shots throughout the event, put them together, and narrate the story. If you take the photos in rapid succession (one immediately after another), perhaps moving yourself or your subject only slightly, you can get an animation-like effect, not unlike one of those little flip-books you probably made when you were a kid.

Of course, you can also screencast from your computer, using screen capture software. Add a narration track, and you can tell a whole story — completely from what you see on your computer monitor throughout that day.

When you create this kind of videoless vlog, where you don't have the video recorded on a camcorder, you have to be more conscious of the story you want to tell. You have to plan it out more, and you may need help from some more artistic friends, but you can definitely tell it.

Funding for videoblogs

Since videoblogs cost money, you might be wondering whether there's a way to make money with them. After all, you're providing an important service, right? Why shouldn't you get some compensation for your time? Or at least some financial support so you can keep producing content?

The fact is that, like text blogs, only a few videoblogs bring in any money — and the chances that videoblogging will become a major way to make money for any particular individual are slim. There are, however, some ways to fund your videoblog — some of them easier than others:

- **Donations.** Perhaps the easiest, least commercial way to solicit financial support is to ask for some donations. Many users set up a PayPal donation link to receive payments, and RSS has a tag called `rel="payment"` to tell aggregators where you accept money. You can even request donations for a nonprofit or charity without alienating too many viewers. See Chapter 13 for more information on RSS.

- **Sponsorships.** If your videoblog is for a business or organization, then that business is your sponsor. Your vlog might be tangentially related to a business, but you could get it sponsored anyway. For instance, a company such as Chrysler might be persuaded to sponsor a car-review videoblog if doing so offers a business advantage. Make sure you disclose your financial affiliation in your videoblog, so viewers aren't surprised when reviews of your sponsor are less than objective.

- **Subscriptions.** An RSS subscription can be easy to set up, or you can use a paid subscription service that requires users to pay in advance for access to your RSS feed.

- **iTunes Music Store.** If your vlog has a big enough audience, you can arrange with Apple to charge for your videoblog subscription in the iTunes Music Store.

- **Web-site advertising on your blog.** Ads won't appear in your video when subscribers watch it in the RSS feed, but it's a small revenue source.

- **In-video advertising.** If your video has a natural tie-in with a product or service, consider selling ads in your videoblog.

- **Contests and film festivals.** Enter your best videoblog posts in film festivals and competitions. You may or may not win, but the feedback you get can really help you improve your vlog — and if there's a cash prize, all the better!

One such contest is the Cellflix film festival hosted by Ithaca College, which highlights films that are shot entirely on cellphones (though they can be edited on a computer). Visit `www.cellflixfestival.org` for details.

> ✔ **Grants.** When all else fails, or if you have an educational or artistic videoblog, submit a proposal to nonprofit grants and foundations, asking for funding to help you keep your vlog going. For more help with this approach, check out *Grant Writing For Dummies* by Beverly A. Browning or similar books on finding nonprofit funding.

Most people who get into videoblogging do so because they want to (a) have fun, (b) become famous, or (c) promote a service or product they already have. If you're in it for fun, forget about making money. It's not that money and fun are incompatible, but that you can have a lot more fun if you don't have to worry about breaking even. Just set a monthly budget for how much you want to spend on this hobby, and stick to it.

If fame is your aim, money attracts fame like bees to honey. Unfortunately, it's your money attracting the fame, not the other way around — you can end up spending a lot of time and money just promoting your videoblog. If you want to get famous without spending a lot of money, focus your efforts on being creative and coming up with great ideas for vlogs.

Finally, if your videoblog exists to promote a service or product, then you already have your revenue stream built into your vlog. Don't hide the fact that there's a financial relationship between your vlog and your financial enterprise — and aim for producing the most professional-looking videoblog you can. After all, this is your public, commercial face. Make sure it looks good!

Chapter 4

Recipe for a Vlog

. . . .

In This Chapter

▶ Creating your first video for your videoblog

▶ Getting video from your camera to your computer

▶ Editing video

▶ Saving your movie for your videoblog

▶ Posting your videoblog

. . . .

Ready to jump in with both feet? Dive off the board without looking? Hold your breath and take the plunge? In this chapter, that's exactly what you'll do — dive into creating and posting your first videoblog entry to the Internet!

It may seem like a bit much to take on all at once — there's a blog to set up, video work to be done, and hey, didn't someone say something about syndication? Sure — all those things, but the bare-bones basics *are* pretty basic: You. Video. Web.

The first post for nearly every videoblogger is the same — an introduction, with very simple editing — mainly to figure out how to do all this by doing some of it. When you finish this chapter, you will have joined the ranks of thousands of videobloggers — introducing yourself to the whole world!

Unscripted, Unedited You

The first ingredient in your videoblog recipe is to create a short digital video of yourself. You can do anything in this video — most people introduce themselves because the easiest subject to talk about — the one you know the absolute most about — is yourself.

Aw, SHOOT!

In Chapter 3, I mention that your video camera can be a digital camera or camcorder, but that whole videoblog process will be a lot easier if your camera takes digital video of some sort. (Saves you having to convert the images and buy the extra-large bottle of aspirin.)

Make sure your camcorder can actually record images as digital video. If it doesn't, head over to Chapter 5 to get a little help with wrestling the video onto your computer.

Follow these steps to set up your camera and get ready to record video:

1. **Get out your video camera and make sure it has a tape or card inside, depending on how it stores the video.**

2. **Next, set up your camera so the lens is pointing at you.**

   You can simply hold the camera in your hand, extend your arm, and point the lens at your face or (for a steadier picture) set the camera on a dresser and aim it in your general direction. If you have a tripod, screw the tripod mount into the base of the camera and set it up somewhere.

   Before you record, look through the viewfinder to figure out where to stand when you talk.

3. **If you're indoors, turn on whatever light you have in the room.**

4. **Press the Record button on your camera, walk over to your stage, and get started; you can cut the walking-on part later.**

   Some cameras have different modes (Camera, Playback, Monitor, and so on) and let you record only when you're in the Camera mode. If you're not sure, read the manual that came with your camera. If you lost the manual, check the manufacturer's Web site; many camera manufacturers have the user manuals online for you to download in case you've lost yours.

   Some cameras blink a light or make a small beeping noise while they're recording — some don't. Some have a configurable light so your target never knows whether they're being recorded (but then, neither do you). If yours is configurable, you might want to configure it to light up when you're recording. (You don't want your carefully planned videoblog entry to consist of "Okay, are we done? Yeah — I stopped recording now!") Again, you may need to check the manual for these functions, because their quirks vary widely between manufacturers.

5. **Smile!**

"Reality TV" that's real (what a concept)

Okay, you've got your camera. It's on and recording . . . . Now what?

Now, you TALK! Introduce yourself. Tell the world about your favorite color. Or your pet. Or your job. Or your hair. Or just your 30-second bio. Are you doing anything really cool with your life right now (besides reading this book and starting a videoblog)? If so, give your elevator speech! The world is ready to watch, and this is your 30 seconds to get the record straight from the get-go.

If you get nervous, don't look at the camera. Instead, put a photo of your best friend next to the camera and talk to him or her, as if you're sending a video postcard.

Don't take too long with this video. A 30-second spot is usually enough, though if you have a lot to say, you could go for up to a minute. Keep a clock handy if you need to stop yourself from rambling.

How much to reveal online?

One of the constant worries on the Internet, especially for those who blog or publish personal details online, is that nagging question, *How much is too much, and how much is safe to talk about?*

First, for safety reasons, you should always be aware of what you have said in your videoblog — as with any blog. When you talk about yourself, ask yourself whether you'd mind having a total stranger see this information.

Don't state your full, legal name, street address, or phone number when you videoblog, and never, *ever* give such information out about other people. (Some people choose to take risks with their online identities, but that is not your decision to make for someone else — nor theirs to make for you. Why invite creepy or dangerous situations?)

If you're a parent, try to be safe as well as sane. Children make natural videoblogging subjects, as well as natural videobloggers — they have an innate creativity to them, and any parent with a video camera has a ready-made clown just waiting for the limelight. However . . .

Remember that complete strangers might watch your videoblog — are you comfortable with that? For that matter, are you comfortable with people who are *not* strangers watching the details of your life with your child? Custody battles (for example) may become more and more complex as blogs and videoblogs become a way for absentee parents to look in on their kids' lives — and (often) find more issues to fight about.

When you're recording and editing your videoblogs, always keep three potential audiences in the back of your mind, and make sure you'd be comfortable with any or all of them watching your videoblog before you post it:

- A complete stranger
- An acquaintance or colleague whom you know casually or professionally
- A member of your family or a close friend

Are you *really* stuck? Okay, press Record and answer the following questions:

- ✔ What is your first name?
- ✔ What do you really like about your home?
- ✔ Who do you admire, and why?

When you have your 30 seconds of "reality TV," stop recording, because you're done. This very first videoblog entry is all about the quick-and-dirty post, not blindingly excellent staging and content.

From Camera to Computer

The next step is to get the contents of the camera onto your computer. For this, you'll need your camera's user manual again, and possibly a special cable for the purpose (it may have come with your camera).

If you used a webcam that was already attached to your computer, and the video was automatically saved to your hard drive, you've already got digital video in there, so you can skip this step.

Transferring movies from a digital camera

Most digital cameras come with a memory card or a cable, or both. The memory card is usually removable and can be inserted into a card reader that plugs into your computer. The card reader is a handy gadget, but you may have to buy it separately because it's never included with the camera. Some computers now come with a card reader built-in; check the computer and camera to make sure they both use the same cards.

Digicam over a cable

If your digital camera comes with a cable, you can plug it into the camera and plug the other end into your computer's USB or FireWire port.

If your camera has a FireWire cable and your computer doesn't have a FireWire card, you'll need to use a card reader to get the data off your camera.

Downloading the video to your computer is a quick (three-step) process:

1. **Make sure the digital camera is OFF when you start.**

2. **Plug one end of the cable into the camera, and the other end into your FireWire or USB plug on your computer.**

Figure 4-1 shows what FireWire connectors (both 4-pin and 6-pin connec-tors) look like. Figure 4-2 shows what USB cables look like.

3. Turn on the digital camera.

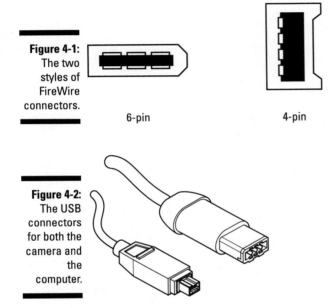

Figure 4-1:
The two
styles of
FireWire
connectors.

6-pin   4-pin

Figure 4-2:
The USB
connectors
for both the
camera and
the
computer.

Digicams with a card reader

If you have a card reader, you may find it a convenient way to transfer files to and from your camera. Since the card reader usually draws power from the computer, using the card reader will help keep you from going through camera batteries quite as often. Here's the standard drill:

1. Take the memory card out of your camera.

2. Put the card into your card reader, making sure it's facing the right direction.

3. Put the card reader into your computer's USB slot.

4. If the USB slot doesn't automatically detect the card reader after about a minute, pull out the reader and try again.

If your computer has a built-in card reader, just take the card out of the camera and put it into the reader slot.

Transferring the files: Macintosh steps

On the Macintosh, you can transfer files from a digital card fairly easily, but it's important to follow these directions to keep from corrupting your digital camera card by accident.

1. **Use a card reader or cable to connect your digital camera to your Macintosh computer.**

   At this point, iPhoto launches — which is your cue to download your photos onto your hard drive.

2. **Import the camera contents into iPhoto.**

   As of iLife 06, iPhoto can import video files to your Photo Library.

3. **Drag and drop to copy the movie onto your desktop or to a specified place on your hard drive.**

   When the file is done copying, eject the digital camera's memory card by clicking the eject icon next to it in the iPhoto Source panel.

If you have a version if iLife that is older than iLife 06, you can import movies from your digital camera card by using it like a hard drive:

1. **Connect the card reader or camera as normal.**

2. **Close iPhoto and launch the Finder.**

   iPhoto has designated your digital camera as a new drive; you'll need the Finder to (well, yeah) find it.

3. **Navigate to the new drive that has appeared on your desktop.**

   The new drive may be called "Untitled" or it may have a title, but either way, it's really your digital camera.

4. **Double-click the new drive icon so it opens as a folder.**

   This folder holds the digital-movie file you transferred to the computer.

5. **Using the Finder, navigate to the movie file you just created.**

   The file will likely have either an .avi or .mov file extension — and don't be surprised if it's humongous. (Pictures and sounds take up a lot of storage space — movies, being both, make for huge files.)

6. **Drag and drop the movie file to your desktop or hard drive.**

7. **When the file is done copying, eject the digital camera memory card by dragging and dropping its hard drive icon to the Trash.**

   This is the only way to remove the memory card safely. If you don't eject by dragging the drive image to the Trash, your memory card can become corrupted and lose its data.

Transferring the files: Windows steps

In Windows, transferring files from a card reader is fairly straightforward and doesn't run the same risks of data loss as on a Macintosh.

1. **Insert the memory card into your USB card reader or built-in reader**

2. **If necessary, plug the card reader into your computer's USB port.**

   You're prompted to open the new device, either as a folder or in Windows Media Player.

3. **Open the device as a folder.**

4. **Using Windows Explorer, navigate to the movie file you just created.**

   The file will likely have either an `.avi` or `.mov` file extension, and you'd better believe it'll be huge.

5. **Copy it onto your desktop or to a designated folder on your hard drive.**

6. **When the file is done copying, close the Explorer window.**

7. **Remove the USB card reader.**

   No fuss, no muss, no dragging of icons, no problem.

Connecting your camcorder

Like the camera, your camcorder will have some sort of cable to connect it to a computer. If it doesn't, you'll have to consult Chapter 3 (and the rest of this chapter) for the scoop on getting analog video off an older camcorder. If your camcorder is all-digital, it may have a memory card like the ones in digital cameras — in which case, you can follow the instructions for a digital camera instead. In general, that procedure looks like this:

1. **Make sure the camcorder is turned off.**

2. **Plug the camera cable into the camera and into the FireWire or USB plug on your computer.**

3. **Turn on the camera.**

Transferring video to a Macintosh

Mac OS X has a built-in program called iMovie that's designed to de-stress the process of editing your digital video. Here's how to use it to get digital video into your computer:

1. **If iMovie doesn't automatically launch when you plug in your camera and turn it on, double-click its icon to launch it.**

   Figure 4-3 gives you an idea of what shows up on-screen.

Figure 4-3:
When you plug in your camera, launch iMovie.

2. **Create a new project and name it** MyIntroduction.

Figure 4-4 shows what the result looks like.

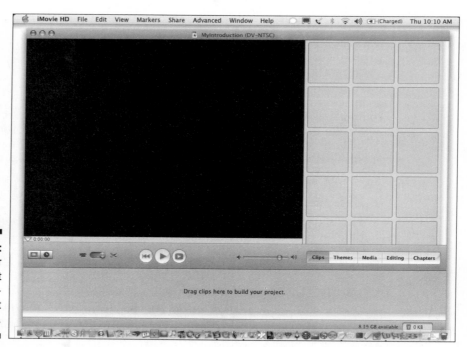

Figure 4-4:
Name your new project MyIntroduction to get started.

3. **Toggle the camera icon at the lower center of the screen to switch over to Import mode.**

   - If there's more than one mode on your camera, turn it to VCR or Playback mode before you import the video.

   - If iMovie displays a `Camera not found` message, make sure you turn the camera on and try double-clicking the camera icon again.

   The iMovie screen turns blue.

4. **Rewind the camera tape to the beginning of your clip.**

5. **Click the Import button to start transferring the video from your tape onto your computer.**

   While iMovie downloads your video, you will not be able to do anything else in iMovie. If you click any of your existing clips, the camera will stop importing video. Also, the video will play on-screen in real-time while it downloads, so you may want to temporarily mute the sound on your computer.

6. **When you reach the end of your clip, click the Stop button to stop downloading the video onto your computer.**

7. **Save the video project.**

8. **Toggle the camera icon to switch back to Edit mode. You can now turn off the camera.**

At this point, you'll have a clip (or perhaps more than one if you had a couple of takes in your shoot) in the right side of the iMovie screen. You might have a couple of garbage clips there, too — clips that were on the tape before or after your shot, which were imported by accident. Drag and drop those to the Trash — you won't need them.

Transferring video to Windows

Windows XP has slightly different connection concerns than Macintosh. Microsoft was a late player in the FireWire game, so Windows support for FireWire can be spotty. (Your camcorder manufacturer may have an updated FireWire driver for you to use in Windows; check the company Web site.)

If you cannot get Windows to see your camcorder when you plug it in as a FireWire device — even after installing any updated drivers — you may need to get a FireWire-to-USB adapter in order to use that camera with Windows.

When you have the camcorder working, you can transfer your digitally taped video onto your computer by following these steps.

1. **Plug in and turn on the camcorder.**

   Make sure the camcorder is on VCR setting and that you've rewound the tape to the start of your video.

2. **Launch Windows Movie Maker.**

3. **Select File⇨New Project.**

4. **Select File⇨Record from the menu.**

   The Video Capture wizard appears, as shown in Figure 4-5.

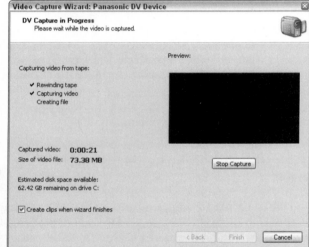

Figure 4-5:
The Video Capture wizard.

5. **If your camcorder is plugged in and configured correctly, select it from the Available Devices Window and click Next.**

6. **Choose a name for the video and select My Videos in the place to save it, and then click Next to continue.**

7. **Select the digital device format (DV-AVI), to preserve the highest quality of your video when you import it, and then click Next.**

8. **Select Capture the Entire Tape Automatically and make sure the Show Preview during Capture check box is marked. Click Next.**

   The video will be rewound and your camcorder will play the tape into Windows Movie Maker. (See Figure 4-6.)

9. **When your introduction video is over, click Stop Capture to stop recording.**

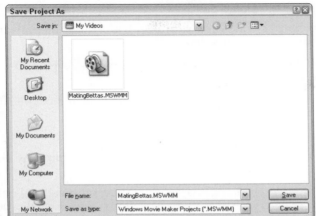

Figure 4-6:
The Video
Capture
wizard
capturing a
video to the
hard drive.

Transferring from an analog tape

(Analog? How twentieth-century.) Okay, if you must transfer your video from an analog tape — because you don't have a digital tape handy, or your camcorder is too old to record digitally — you need more technology than just a camera and a computer. Your computer needs a way to convert the analog video into a digital format, and that requires more than software. You need hardware — specifically, a *video-capture card*. Some newer video cards have a capture feature built in; if not, you may have to make a separate purchase at your computer store. While you're there, pick up some audio-in and audio-out cables and a video cable; they probably don't come with the computer. Here's a checklist of what you'll need to pull this off:

- ✔ Video capture card or external device
- ✔ Audio cables
- ✔ S-video cable compatible with the video capture card
- ✔ Your camcorder or a VCR that can play your tape.

Most consumer camcorders made before 1999 are analog-only. In 1999, Sony developed the affordable Digital8 video format for the non-pro market of videographers. Digital8 and Hi-8 tapes are still used heavily in camcorders today. If your camcorder takes Digital8 or Hi-8 tapes, it can record digital video, and you can use the steps to import digital video in the "Transferring video to a Macintosh" or "Transferring video to Windows" section.

When you have all the techno-goodies gathered, and the video-capture card installed and tested, the first step is obvious . . .

1. **Turn off the computer.**

   The idea here is to avoid moving electricity around till everything is connected.

2. **Plug the audio and video cables into your camcorder and your computer.**

   You'll probably need to use only one audio plug — most older cameras can't record in stereo.

3. **Turn on your computer and the camcorder or VCR.**

4. **Import the video just as you would for the digital tape (as described earlier in the chapter).**

   Remember that you have to press the actual, physical Play button on your camera or VCR; the software will not start your camera playing for you. Also, with an analog tape, you won't have the trash clips of extra material at the beginning or end of your shoot; those you'll have to edit out yourself. (Ah, vintage technology.)

5. **When you're done, be sure to turn off the camera; unplug the audio or video cables from the computer after it's off.**

Cutting the Video

The next step is to trim off any excess footage from your video. Since you're going for a shoot-and-post type of movie at this point, you don't have to get *too* involved in editing your video till it's all shiny and smooth. It's just you making a quick introduction. No need for fancy effects.

This exercise uses the basic programs that come with your Mac or with Windows XP. There are many other software programs for editing video, (Chapter 12 gives you a look at some good ones), but for a quick first video, these basic — and free — tools will do the job. (Hey, why not? I still use iMovie to edit my personal videoblog, and many videobloggers find it serves them perfectly well.)

Cutting in Macintosh's iMovie

Here's how to use your virtual cutting-room floor in iMovie:

1. **If you don't already have iMovie running, launch it now.**

   The most recent project opens. If it doesn't, and you created the MyIntroduction project described earlier, open that one. The project appears on-screen.

2. **Click the camera/editing icon (shown in Figure 4-7) to enter Edit mode.**

3. **Click the first clip in the right panel.**

   The video appears in the main iMovie panel.

4. **Click the Play icon to play the clip.**

   If it's not part of your movie, ignore it and move on to the next clip.

5. **Click and preview each clip, one by one, till you find the clip with your introduction on it.**

6. **Drag the clip with your intro onto the Timeline at the bottom of the screen (refer to Figure 4-7).**

   The first few seconds of your video are probably (in strictly practical terms) trash. They don't have any content, or they may show you struggling through the tangle of cables in the room to get into the camera's view. No problem; that stuff is going away in the next step.

7. **Play the clip until you get to the very beginning of your introduction.**

   You can drag the time marker if you want to navigate quickly through the clip to the starting point of your introduction.

8. **Select Edit➪Split Video at Playhead to cut the clip into two (pressing +T also splits the video).**

Figure 4-7:
Open the project in iMovie and switch to Edit mode.

The timeline   Camera/edit mode icon

9. **Click the clip you don't want and drag it back to the right panel (or onto the Trash icon if you want to delete it).**

   After you split a clip in two, both clips are highlighted. *Make sure you select only the one you want to remove.*

10. **Repeat Steps 1–9 at the end of your introduction clip.**

11. **Select the whole video and click the Play button.**

   Does it sound right? Is it you? Great!

12. **Save the project.**

Cutting in Windows Movie Maker

Windows Movie Maker comes with Windows XP and is a simple tool for creating and editing movies. Here's how to use it to edit your videoblog intro:

1. **Launch Windows Movie Maker if it's not already open.**

   It may be hiding in the Start Menu under Accessories. When it opens, it looks like Figure 4-8.

2. **Choose File⇨Open and navigate to open the project you created when you imported your video.**

   If this is your first, uncut video, you'll have only one clip, and you'll need to trim it down to just the introduction. That's what the next step sets up.

3. **Drag and drop the video clip into the storyboard at the bottom of the screen.**

   Okay, the first few seconds of your video are probably *trash* — irrelevant to the actual intro. You know — no content, getting settled into the camera's view, other distracting stuff you want to cut.

4. **Play the clip until you get to the very beginning of your introduction.**

   Better yet, drag the time marker to navigate through the clip to the starting point of your introduction.

5. **Choose Clip⇨Split (Shift+Ctrl+S) to split the clip in two.**

6. **Highlight the part of the clip that you want to remove and press the Delete key to remove it from your movie.**

7. **Repeat this split-and-delete sequence at the end of your movie clip.**

   You will not edit or change your original movie clips when you split or delete them in the project storyboard.

8. **When you're done editing, save your project.**

Figure 4-8:
Windows
Movie
Maker.

Saving Your Movie for Videoblogging

So far, this chapter shows you how to save movies as *projects* — essentially files with some editing tools — and they're just what you need to tweak your movies. But they don't work for *publishing* your videos to the Internet, which is the whole purpose of videoblogging. So the next step is to save your movie as a file that you can share with the whole World Wide Web.

This section skims over the finer details of compression and uses some very basic compression settings for saving your files. For more detailed compression options, see Chapter 12.

Saving your videoblog entry in iMovie

iMovie has a couple of options for saving your movie. In this section, I use the simplest one that meets the needs of a videoblog. So, without further ado . . .

1. **Open your project in iMovie if it's not already open.**

2. **Choose File➪Export from the menu.**

   The Export Movie dialog box opens, as shown in Figure 4-9.

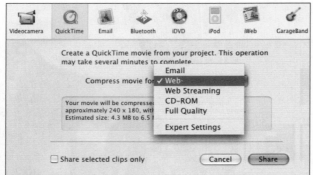

Figure 4-9:
The Export
Movie
dialog box in
iMovie.

3. **Select To QuickTime from the Export: field.**

4. **Select Web from the Formats field.**

5. **Click OK.**

   Doing so starts the process of exporting the movie.

6. **When prompted, save the movie file.**

   Might as well name it something practical: Save it as **MyIntroduction** in your Movies folder (see Figure 4-10).

Figure 4-10:
Save the
exported
movie file.

7. **Wait for the movie to finish exporting and getting saved.**

   When the export is complete and the file is saved, you have a movie named MyIntroduction.mov on your hard drive.

Saving your videoblog entry in Windows Movie Maker

In Windows Movie Maker, your compression and file-format options are similarly limited. But don't let that deter you — the Windows Media Viewer player is available for both Macintosh and Windows. And, of course, this is your first videoblog entry, so don't sweat it; you can always change file formats later if you wish. Here are the steps to follow:

1. **From Windows Movie Maker, select File⇨Save Movie.**

   This option exports the movie for Web viewing. The Save Movie wizard dutifully appears, as in Figure 4-11.

2. **Select Medium Quality from the Setting drop-down box.**

   On the Web, size matters: The smaller the file, the better. You want your videoblog entry to take up less than 10MB of space. It loads faster that way.

3. **Enter a name for your movie in the Title field.**

4. **Click OK.**

   You're immediately prompted for a filename and a location to save the file. Enter a name for your movie and click the Browse button to select a location for the file, and then click Next.

Figure 4-11:
The Save
Movie
wizard.

You can only save a file as a Windows Media Video File (with a `.wmv` extension) or uncompressed AVI (`.avi`) file formats in Windows Movie Maker.

5. **Wait while the movie is exported and compressed.**

When all that's done, Windows Movie Maker prompts you to view the movie.

6. **Click OK to watch your movie in Windows Media Player.**

Post It!

Okay, when you have something to post, the next order of business is to put it out there. For this section, you're going to need a place on the Internet where you can store your movie. Unless you already have a Web site and are comfortable uploading files to it, use the Web sites suggested here to upload and store your video files.

If you do have a Web site, you can use it as the place to which you upload your movie. You'll be able to link to the site from your videoblog, just as you can do with any other file on the Internet. (Skip ahead to the "Post the entry" section to read how to post your video to a blog.)

Get a free video-hosting account

Some of the best things in online life *are* free. For this first introduction post, I show you how to upload your video to the not-for-profit organization Internet Archive at `www.archive.org`. The reason I'm using the Internet Archive for this example is because they're free and, as a non-profit organization, they don't have any future plans to start charging for their services.

Now, if you are absolutely, mind-bendingly terrified of having your video posted to the Internet from now until forever, then you might want to find another host, or store your movie on your own Web server, and you'll find many good suggestions for those in Chapter 13. Because the Internet Archive's sole purpose is to provide a multimedia backup of the Internet, removing a file isn't instantaneous.

1. **Open your Web browser and go to `www.archive.org`.**

2. **Click the <u>Join Us</u> link.**

3. **Enter your e-mail address, a username, and a password, as shown in Figure 4-12.**

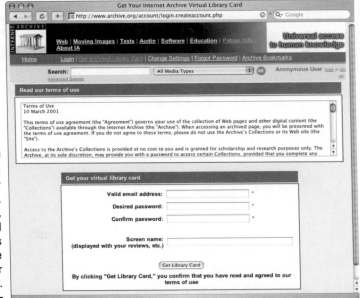

Figure 4-12:
Enter
username,
password,
and e-mail
address as
you create
your
account.

4. **Click the Get Library Card button.**

Your account is created and you're immediately logged in.

Upload your video

Okay, here goes. The door to the World Wide Web is open. All it lacks is your image. To take the next logical step, follow these steps:

1. **If you aren't already logged in to www.archive.org (or your chosen Web site) log in now.**

Go to www.archive.org/contribute.php to see your contributions to the archive.

2. **Click the link called <u>Create and upload a new movie or book</u> or go to www.archive.org/create.**

What's going on here is the creation of a new item for the archive, as shown in Figure 4-13.

3. **Enter the name of your movie (such as** My Introduction**) and click Create Item to continue.**

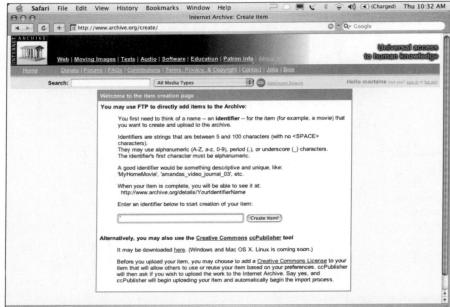

Figure 4-13:
Creating an
item in the
Internet
Archive.

4. **Follow the instructions for uploading files to your FTP space on `www.archive.org`.**

   • In Windows Internet Explorer, you open a window and then drag and drop the movie file into the designated space.

   • For other operating systems, use an FTP utility to upload your file to the archive.

5. **When you have finished uploading the file, click the `Click_here_When_Finished.htm` file in your FTP directory.**

6. **Click the link to your item details.**

   A dialog box opens, as shown in Figure 4-14; it prompts you to select a type of media.

7. **Select movies for the media type and Open Source Movies for the collection.**

8. **Click the Submit movie button to proceed.**

   You're prompted for more data about this movie file, as shown in Figure 4-15.

9. **The only piece of required information you're most likely to be missing is the title. Enter your movie's title in the appropriately named Title text box.**

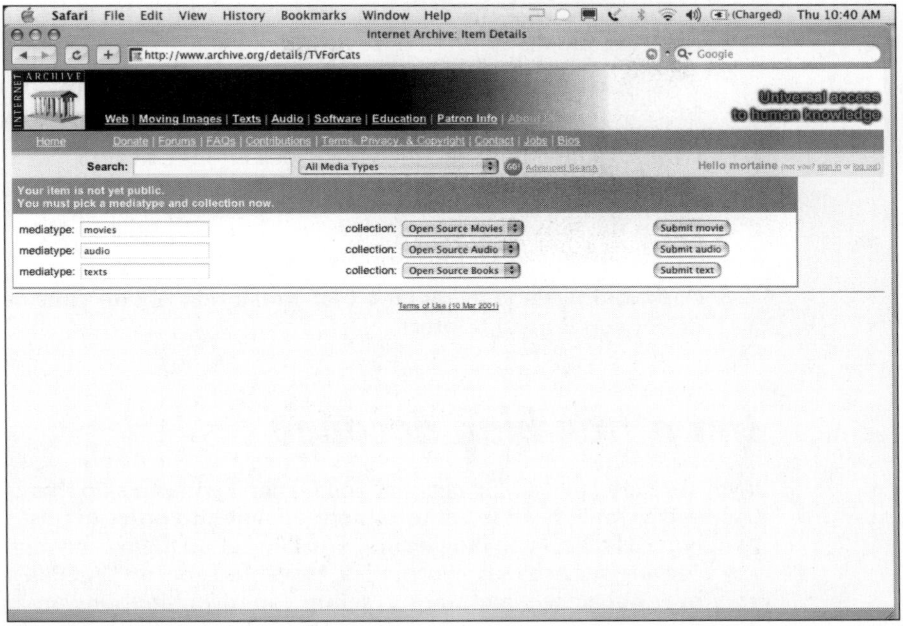

Figure 4-14:
Enter the
details for
your movie.

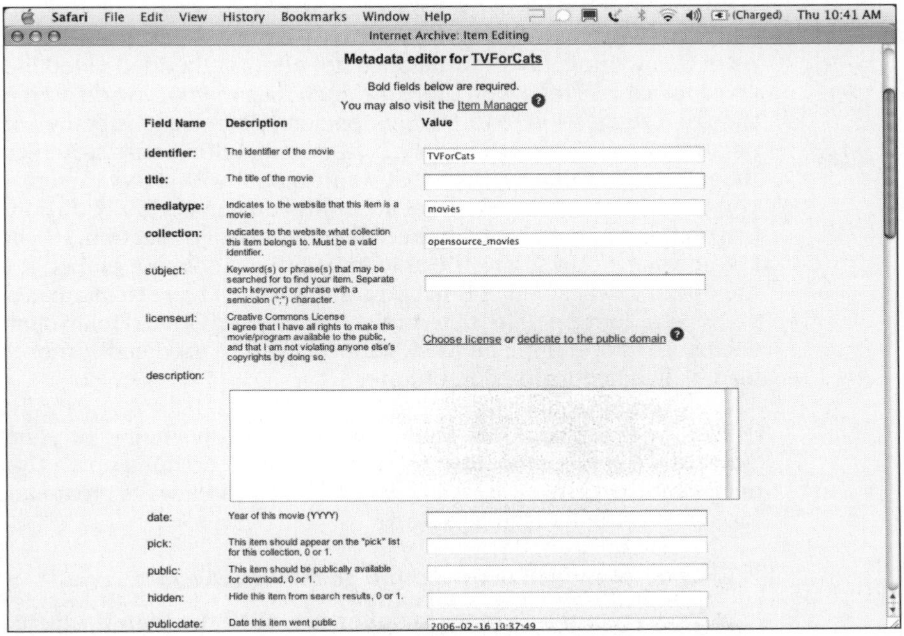

Figure 4-15:
Enter further
information
in the
metadata
editor.

10. **Scroll down and click the Submit button when you have finished entering the descriptive data for this video.**

    What you've just done, in strictly technical terms, is provide *metadata* (data about data). And here you thought you were describing a movie.

    With a click of a button, the video goes into the `archive.org` queue to be added to the public archive.

11. **When the movie is uploaded, return to the Details page to view its status and get a URL for your movie.**

12. **Copy and paste your movie's URL into a text file on your own hard drive; you'll need it later!**

Get a free blog account

If you already have a blog account somewhere, you can skip this task. Otherwise, you'll need to set up a blog account into order to post your videos to it. For this task, I use Blogger, but you can set up a blog account with nearly any blogging service (say, WordPress, Movable Type, or TypePad). If you have your own Web server and want to set up your own blog software on your server, you're free to do so, but doing that is beyond the scope of this chapter and this book. Check out *Blogging For Dummies* by Brad Hill (Wiley) if you want that much control over the blog part of your videoblog.

As of this writing, LiveJournal does not allow embedded video files, and the LiveJournal RSS feed won't include such files in your syndicated entries, though a suggestion to implement enclosures in feeds is being considered. As a result, even though I adore LiveJournal, I don't currently recommend them for a videoblog. (If you just want to post with a *link* to your video, and you already have a LiveJournal account, you can certainly do so using the instructions in the "Post a hyperlink to your video" section.) If you do go with LiveJournal, you will only be able to link to a video, not embed it using any of the options described in this book, and you will have to manually add the `rel="enclosure"` attribute in the link to your video. Finally, until the feed enclosure idea is implemented, you will need to use FeedBurner for your feed, which is described in Chapter 13.

One of the first things you should do is decide on a name for your videoblog. Since this is a personal introduction, don't get too hung up on the name. You may want to change it later anyway, and you can always create another blog for special videoblogging projects.

1. **Open your Web browser and go to www.blogger.com.**

2. **If you're not a Blogger member yet, click the <u>Sign Up Here</u> link.**

    If you are a Blogger member, you can simply log in and skip ahead to the blog-creation process. The next steps here are for new users.

3. **Choose a username and password, enter your e-mail address, and read and agree to the terms of service.**

4. **Click Continue to create your Blogger account.**

   You're prompted to create the blog itself, as shown in Figure 4-16.

5. **Enter a blog name (such as My Videoblog) and the address you wish to use.**

6. **Verify the captcha word and click the Continue arrow.**

7. **Select a Blogger template from the previews and click Continue.**

8. **When your blog is ready, click the Start Posting arrow.**

Post the entry

The last task in posting your first videoblog entry is to actually *post* the video into your blog so people can actually see it online. You can do this either as an embedded video or as a hyperlink.

If the blog service you use does not permit embedded files, you will need to post your movie as a hyperlink.

Figure 4-16: You are prompted to create a blog.

Post an embedded video

Have you ever gone to a Web page and been able to play a movie directly on-screen in the page? That's called *embedded video*. I have a personal liking for embedded videos because they mean one fewer Web page to download — and users can read the blog text and watch the video at the same time.

If you use embedded videos in your videoblog, make sure they don't play automatically. After all, it's probably best not to assume that everybody's system is up-to-date enough to handle something that fancy.

Try to limit your videoblog's display settings so that only one or two entries show up on-screen at a time. That way your users don't have to download ten movies every time they hit your videoblog's home page. In Blogger, set this up by first logging in:

1. **Click the Change Settings icon.**

2. **Click the Settings tab and the Formatting menu item.**

   The Formatting Settings page is also where you can change your post template. But don't worry about that right now — we'll cover posting templates in Chapter 6.

3. **Switch the number of days to display on a page to 1.**

   Unless you post more than once a day, you'll tend to only show one video at a time with this setting.

Here's the drill for posting an embedded video:

1. **Go to the Internet Archive, find the URL of your movie, and copy it to the Clipboard.**

   Make sure you copy the direct URL to the movie, not just the Web page that contains the movie.

2. **Log in to Blogger and navigate to the Dashboard.**

   The Dashboard shows all your blogs; Figure 4-17 shows how that looks.

3. **Click the plus icon next to the blog you created to hold your videoblog.**

   You will be taken to the Create Post page.

4. **Enter a title (such as** My First Videoblog Post**) in the Title field.**

5. **In the large text box, enter the following code:**

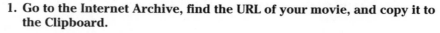

```
<object width="320" height="256" src="URL"
    autoplay ="false">
<embed src="URL" autoplay="no" height=240 width=320>
<noembed>
<a href="URL">Click here to play the movie!</a>
</noembed>
</object>
```

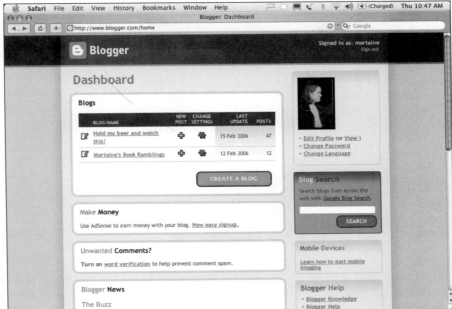

Figure 4-17:
Behold the
Blogger
Dashboard.

Replace *URL* with the actual URL of the movie at the Internet Archive. (But you knew that.)

6. **Click the Publish Post button to post your videoblog entry.**

7. **Click the <u>View</u> link on the confirmation page to view your videoblog entry.**

   With any luck, you should see your movie appear directly in the Web page. Figure 4-18 shows a Web page with an embedded video.

This particular method of displaying video in your videoblog will trigger a dialog box alert in current versions of Internet Explorer 6, which means a large number of your videoblog visitors won't see your video unless they click through the dialog box. See Chapter 13 for more details and a workaround using JavaScript. The hyperlink option in the next section will work in all versions of Internet Explorer.

Post a hyperlink to your video

The other way to post video into your blog is to post it *as a hyperlink*, either a plain-text hyperlink or as a linked image. To post your movie as a hyperlink, follow these steps:

1. **Go to the Internet Archive, find the URL of your movie, and copy it to the Clipboard.**

2. **Log in to Blogger and navigate to the Dashboard.**

Figure 4-18:
With embedded video, your videoblog is ready to play!

Refer to Figure 4-17 to see the Blogger Dashboard, which shows all your blogs.

3. Click the plus icon next to the blog you created for your videoblog.

You're taken to the Create Post page.

4. Enter a title (such as My First Videoblog Post**) in the Title field.**

5. In the large text box, enter the following code:

```
<a href="URL"> Click here to play the movie!</a>
```

Naturally, replace the *URL* shown here with the URL of the movie at the Internet Archive. With this method, you can use the main details page for the movie instead of a direct link if you wish.

6. Click the Publish Post button to post your vlog entry.

7. Click the <u>View</u> **link on the confirmation page to view your videoblog entry.**

The entry shows up on-screen as a hyperlink to your video on the Internet.

To save a frame of your video to use as the image, open it in your video editing program and navigate to the frame you want to use, using the timeline or preview. In iMovie, select File⇨Save Frame As and save the image as a JPEG. In Windows Movie Maker, select the option by choosing Tools⇨Take Picture from Preview and save the resulting image as a JPEG. Upload this file in addition to your video.

Avoiding technofrustration

Creating your first videoblog entry can take a really long time and be a lesson in frustration, but it doesn't have to be. As you've seen in this chapter, computers made in the last five years and current operating systems have the tools already available to capture your video and post it to the Internet in a format that other people can view. And once you get that first video online, the next one, and the one after that, will be easier, and pretty soon you'll want to get more and more creative with your content and presentation! That's what the rest of this book is all about.

A word about technology and frustration: Usually, if you find yourself tearing out your hair over something, it's either because you're overthinking the situation and making it more complicated than it needs to be, or it's because some other Web service isn't responding the

way it normally does. It can be very frustrating when you're new, because you just don't know if you're getting it wrong, or if something else isn't working. Take a deep breath, pick up your video camera, and get away from the computer for a few hours before you come back to the problem. Most problems will sort themselves out in the meantime, and the ones that don't will be easier to deal with when you've put some distance between yourself and the hassle.

Also, having friends really can help! Be sure to join the videoblogging communities mentioned in Chapter 14, and try to get to know a couple of other vloggers. Before you throw your camera or your computer out the window, send a question in to one of the communities. Chances are, some helpful Samaritan will have had the same problem and can help you troubleshoot and fix it.

Part II
Step Away from the Camera

In this part . . .

As with all good filmmaking, videoblogging is more than just pointing a camera at some action and letting it roll. It's about planning, and self-discovery.

In this part, you zero in on some behind-the-scenes techniques for making a better videoblog. You get some pointers about overcoming stage fright and writing a script for your vlog, as well as soliciting audience feedback from your viewers.

Chapter 5

Finding Your Voice and Audience

*T*he main reason people turn to blogging is to make their voices be heard — or in the case of videobloggers, *seen* and heard. Perhaps you already know who you want to reach with your videoblog, or maybe you have a message that you think the world should hear. Perhaps you're an expert on something and want to share your expertise. Or maybe your imagined audience is actually very small, consisting of just your friends and family who check your videoblog to see videos of your daily life. If you already have an audience in mind for your vlog, this chapter helps you target that audience and focus your vlog entries for that audience.

It's entirely possible, though, that you've come to videoblogging without any pre-existing ideas of what you want to say, or who you want to talk to. Perhaps you just want to express yourself, or you like playing around with the technology and want to see how far you can push it. You're in good company — a lot of videobloggers just like playing with the technology until they find something else to play with. It that's the case for you, this chapter helps you define an audience for your vlog.

Identifying Your Audience

One of the keys to successful communication — in any medium, forum, or venue — is to know your audience. Simply put, as a videoblogger, you are a speaker. You communicate to other people through your videoblog. The people who download your vlog entries, who spend time watching them, and who sometimes respond to you in your vlog's comments, are your audience.

Your audience can be very interactive, talking back through comments, engaging you in a vlogging dialog (where they post vlog entries about your vlog entries), or just dropping you frequent e-mails or finding you in chatrooms. But they can also be very mysterious, never commenting publicly about your vlog entries, or just being quiet in general about who they are and what they like about your vlog. You might wonder if they're even out there.

Figuring out who's watching can help you make decisions about what to vlog. For example, while I was writing this book, I made a vlog entry that didn't quite work. It was filmed at night, and was therefore grainy, and had a kind of hidden camera feel to it. It was a risk, different from my usual work, but something I wanted to try. My vlog was posted to two audiences — one that had background information about my inspiration, and the other consisting of videobloggers. The videobloggers didn't really say much about it (they can be so polite!), but the comments from the other group were much more blunt. (One such response was "What the heck was that?!?") To get such a strong negative reaction from that audience told me that the risk I'd taken had not paid off. I won't rule out a similar style in the future, but I will know in advance that it's a risk that my audience may not appreciate.

One way to find out who's watching your videoblog is to look at your server logs. *Server logs* are a record of every time someone tries to access a file on your Web server. Unfortunately, server logs only tell part of the story, but you can learn a lot about your audience, depending on what tools you use to mine the data in those logs. See Chapter 16 for more details about reading your server logs to find out how many people are visiting your vlog.

You don't have to sit back and wait for your audience to come to you before you decide who they are. You can decide in advance that you want to make your videoblog for an existing person, organization, or audience demographic. (A *demographic* is a profile of your target audience, including information like approximate age, income, gender, family situation, and interests.) In fact, if you identify your audience in advance, you can gear your message and your vlog entries towards that audience. Over time, you will find ways to effectively communicate with them.

Predefining the intended audience is a common practice. For a business, defining the audience in advance helps it create a product that the audience will want to buy. Predefining your audience for your videoblog can save you time, money, or video time. For instance, at the very beginning of this book, I set out the foolish assumptions of who I expect to be reading this book. It's not that the book can't be read by someone else, but that I started out acknowledging what must be outside the scope of the book.

For instance, if your audience consists of weekend car enthusiasts who like fixing their own cars, and you're going to do a videoblog about installing a lift on a Jeep, you know you don't have to spend time creating a video showing how you check tire pressure (unless you do it differently from everyone else on the planet). Because you've predefined your audience as car enthusiasts who know something about cars, at least the basics, you can assume if you say, "I checked the tire pressure already," your audience knows what that means.

One thing that helps in designing a communication project like a videoblog is to create a *model user profile* — a typical example of someone you would expect to have in your audience. The model user can be based on someone you know in real life, it can be a composite of several people, or it can just be a list of certain traits you expect most people in your audience to share.

Here are some things to ask yourself about the people you want to talk to in your vlog:

- **Why are they interested in my videoblog?** Usually, it's because your videoblog is going to be about something they like, perhaps a topic, political movement, or an aesthetic that they find intriguing.

- **How old are they?** You may have trouble figuring this one out, but if you can get a general idea, you'll be better off. For example, if you want to get the enormous market of Baby Boomers, you probably won't want vlog about college drinking games and trendy shows on the WB television network. Instead, you might aim for something more appealing to an audience of middle-aged and older folks, like a vlog about politics, health, or classic rock music.

- **Are they male or female?** Videobloggers are about evenly split between male and female, and there's no reason your audience won't be, too, unless you specifically choose to vlog a topic that tends to be more interesting to one gender or another. It doesn't mean you have to hang a sign on the front of your videoblog that says "No Boys Allowed" or "No Girls Allowed." Rather, you just know that in a gathering of a similar group of folks you'd find more men than women, or vice versa. If you think it's going to be evenly split, then never assume a gender for your audience when you vlog.

- **Do they work? What kind of jobs might they have?** If you're doing a professional videoblog, you can guess that most of your audience will have a job in the same industry or profession as you.

- **What level of education does my audience have?** This question is actually pretty important. Although art can be appreciated by anyone, how you deliver your art may be pretty esoteric. Additionally, if your videoblog is meant to teach people, then you automatically will have more knowledge than your audience.

- **What other interests do they have?** If you have a general, personal videoblog, you're eventually going to start vlogging your other hobbies. One personal vlog I know has a lot of entries about dog training and dog-agility trials — the vlog entries are fascinating and inspiring, but if the vlogger's audience had no interest in dogs, they'd want to skip over those entries.

✔ **Do I have any other common or shared experiences with my audience?** There's a wonderful and classic videoblog entry out on the Internet in which the vlogger took an old song from the children's show *The Electric Company* and videoblogged herself dancing and singing along to it. Other vloggers took it up and remixed it with themselves singing along as well. The project is now one of the more popular collaborative efforts — and if you had never watched *The Electric Company*, you might not understand why these vloggers were singing and dancing along, though you could still enjoy the vlogs. Some experiences are very culturally specific, and you can draw on those experiences in your videoblog — or (for that matter) use cultural differences as an opportunity to show your audience something new.

When you've answered these questions, or at least some of them, compile your answers into an example of your viewership — your model user. (You can make more than one profile if you have multiple audiences.)

You can give this model user a name if you like — it's easier to personify the model user if you do (which makes it easier to imagine talking to them directly) — or leave them nameless and just call them "my audience." When you're working on a vlog entry, review the entry before you post it — and imagine your model user watching it with you. Will he or she get it? Laugh at the funny parts? Connect with your point of view? If not, you don't have to scratch it and start over. After all, your videoblog is first and foremost *your* work. But it's good to know when you might be taking a risk that your vlog audience won't appreciate.

 You can ask the same questions if your model user is based on someone you know. In writing this book, I used a model user based on my own sister. She's interested in the subject because she has kids and relatives who live far away (like me). She's in the same age group as I am, is educated to the same level, but is not a big technology fan. Since I already know her other interests and cultural background, I know which jokes would tickle her funny bone and which ones would fall flat or seem inappropriate.

Targeting Your Audience

When you have a pretty clear idea of who you want to watch your videoblog, how do you get those folks to come through the virtual door?

Marketing and advertising companies have lived and died by this question. How do you get the customer or user to show up and to want what you have to offer? In the case of your videoblog, you're offering some interesting content that you yourself made. But how do you get people to watch it?

Most of the techniques I offer in this section apply to personal videoblogs. If you want to create a targeted, professional videoblog, you will need to adjust these suggestions to fit into your professional needs.

E-mailing the word out

You can start by putting the address to your videoblog in one of the most common Internet tools you use: your e-mail. No, I'm not suggesting that you spam anyone! But many people overlook the e-mail *signature* as a way to get the word out. If you're in any e-mail discussion groups, your signature can spread the word to hundreds, even thousands of people who are interested in some of the things you're interested in.

Here's an example of one of my signature files that does the job:

```
--
Stephanie Bryant, author, Videoblogging For Dummies
vlogfordummies@mortaine.com
Check out my vlog: http://mortaine.blogspot.com
```

 The online etiquette (or *netiquette*) rule for e-mail signatures (or *sig files*) is to keep it to four lines of plain text, and less than 72 characters wide, which was the width of an old dial-up terminal window. The key information to include is your videoblog address; your name (or online alias) is nice, too, but anyone receiving your e-mail will get your e-mail address already, so that part is a bonus.

Most e-mail programs have some way of storing a default signature file that will be automatically added any time you compose an e-mail message. The setting for your signature may be in your e-mail program's overall preferences (as shown in Figure 5-1), or it may be tied to your e-mail account as set up in your e-mail program. Check with your e-mail software's help system if you don't know how to add an e-mail signature.

Figure 5-1:
Signature files may be stored in the account options or your user preferences.

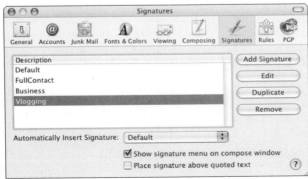

Listing your videoblog on the Web

Another way to promote your videoblog to your target audience is to list your-self in the common videoblog directories. There are several, but the must-use ones are Vlogdir (`www.vlogdir.com`), MeFeedia (`http://mefeedia.com`), and the Vlogmap (`www.vlogmap.org`), which is a geographical directory of videoblogs. Naturally, if there are Web directories specific to the geographic or topical areas covered by your videoblog, you should contact those to get listed as well.

Finally, you always want to list your videoblog in search engines, and check back periodically to make sure your videoblog still shows up. The easiest way to list yourself is to visit one of the search-engine listing Web sites, but the most effective way is to visit each search engine's home page and add your videoblog site to their engines directly. Google, MSN, Yahoo!, and AOL are the big four of search engines. Each has its own methods for ranking various Web sites — but don't get too hung up on how highly your vidoeblog gets ranked on a search result. Most videobloggers use the directories to find vlogs, and word of mouth is your most effective method for getting the word out.

Soliciting Feedback

One of the best ways to learn more about your audience members is to ask them to talk to you. You may have some idea of who you want to reach — you may even have specifically targeted a particular demographic — but unless you get direct, personal feedback from your viewers, you won't know what works and what doesn't work in your videoblog.

Comments

The most common way for your audience to give you feedback is to leave comments on an individual vlog entry. Most blogging sites offer a *reader commentary* feature that allows visitors to your blog to leave their thoughts and feedback in your videoblog. Figure 5-2 shows a comment screen in Blogger.

In some blogging sites, you'll need to specifically activate this feature; in others, it's on by default. Also, most blogging sites give you ways to set up some privacy options — for example, you can

 ✔ Extend comment privileges only to those users who are registered with that blogging site

 ✔ Screen unsolicited comments so they are still there but not visible to anyone but you

Figure 5-2:
You can
accept
comments,
screen
them, or
set up a
challenge to
catch
spambots.

✔ Prevent comments altogether

✔ Require unregistered users to pass a visual pattern-recognition test
(see Figure 5-2) before posting comments. (This feature helps keep
out *spambots* — those obnoxious automatic programs that send spam
to every valid address or online form that they can find.)

Most blogging sites can send you a copy of any comments you receive in
your videoblog to your e-mail address, so you don't have to compulsively
check your videoblog every ten minutes. (Not that you might not do that
anyway — videoblogging is pretty addictive — but you won't have to.)

Checking in with the vlogger community

The videoblogging community isn't huge compared to the rest of the Internet,
but it's getting larger every day. In under a year, the community grew from
a few dozen vloggers to over a thousand. Many vloggers participate in the
online group Videoblogging on Yahoo! Groups (`http://groups.yahoo.`
`com/group/videoblogging`), but you can also meet vloggers at real-world
vlogging events, independent film events, Vloggercon (`www.vloggercon.`
`com`), and more general blogging conferences. You can use the Vlogmap,
shown in Figure 5-3, to locate the vloggers who live near you, drop by their
vlogs, and introduce yourself.

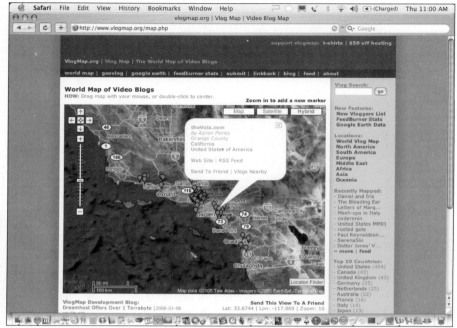

Figure 5-3:
Use the
Vlogmap to
find
vloggers
nearby.

There's more about joining and participating in the online videoblogging communities in Chapter 14.

Videobloggers are usually happy to give you feedback on your vlogs, but they're also perfectly happy providing the technology basics and letting you learn on your own what artistic and cinematic choices work best for you.

If you want hard-hitting criticism, you have to ask specifically for it, but be prepared not only for real critique, but *public* critique as well. You already know that vloggers aren't shy — you may ask for a critique, only to find your critique posted as a vlog entry on someone else's videoblog — and then syndicated around the world to hundreds of other viewers! It's also worth keeping in mind that harsh criticism is not necessarily any more valid than gentle criticism — and not everybody out there has figured that out.

Asking experts

There's one other place to get feedback: from experts in the topic that your vlog is about. If you have a profession-oriented videoblog, contact your colleagues and ask them what they think about your content.

When you ask an expert about your vlog entries, be specific about what kind of feedback you're looking for. For example, in a criminal-law vlog, you don't necessarily need the opinions of lawyers on whether a video shot is composed or edited well. Not that their opinions in such matters are invalid, but that your goal in asking them is to get more targeted feedback — say, on whether you've covered the right legal precedents and procedures.

When asking for feedback from experts, consider the following:

- ✔ **Be specific about the scope of critique that you want.** If you want an expert opinion on the legal advice you offered in your vlog entry, ask your lawyer colleagues to comment specifically on that.

- ✔ **Decide in advance if your experts are also audience members.** Sometimes there will be enough overlap that the expert opinion can help you understand what your audience is likely to think about your vlog entries.

- ✔ **Ask follow-up questions.** Whenever someone critiques your work, ask for clarification of things they liked, and if you took a risk in a particular entry, ask what they thought about it.

- ✔ **Also ask video experts.** You may know expert videographers and film-makers or meet them in the course of your videoblogging journeys. Ask them for their opinions on your vlog entries — not just the content, but also the style, composition, camerawork, lighting, and editing.

Self-Discovery through Vlogs

One of the most important audience members in your videoblog is yourself. If you don't like what you're doing in your vlog, you'll lose interest and stop doing it. Vlogging should never be a chore — it should be a fun way to interact with the world and make your own voice heard.

Expressing yourself

It's not surprising that a lot of vloggers are very expressive people. They're passionate about something and enjoy finding ways to talk about it. You will find, as you carry your video camera around more and more, that you want to record some things, and you avoid recording others.

For the pros in the news industry, it's standard always to look for a terrific scoop, the perfect shot, or a really great interview angle. But consider:

They're looking to grab prime-time attention because big advertising bucks are at stake. In videoblogging, you don't have to match your vlog entries to the demands of a network format. You don't even have to be particularly interesting, funny, or good in other conventional ways. I realize it's sacrilegious to say that, but it's true. Often the message you have to offer *is* more important than how you convey it. And sometimes what you might think boring is more fascinating to your audience than anything they might find on prime-time TV.

When you have a topic that really catches your interest, film it and post about it. You could find yourself vlogging a series of sermons from your church, or an artistic endeavor by a friend, or even a series of music jam sessions in a living room (like the Living Room Recital series posted to the Lean Back Vids videoblog). You might find yourself simply staring at the camera, ranting about your life, or posting a vlog entry about a couple of friends who are in love (with their consent, of course). If you're vlogging people playing published music, the Harry Fox Agency (www.harryfox.com) can help keep you copyright-friendly.

Learning from past vlogs

Although your videoblog is itself a type of diary, you can also keep a separate log or journal about your progress in videoblogging. By periodically reviewing your past vlog entries, you'll discover new techniques as well as new topics you want to explore.

Sometimes, as you sharpen your vlogging craft, you try out a technique that you don't quite have the skills to carry off yet. We've all been there. In one of my early vlog entries, for instance, I wanted to have video of someone speaking, cut to a voiceover over another visual clip, and then cut back to the person speaking again. I think I spent four hours trying to get the mouth and the words to synch back up at the end of the entry — and even when I did, the result looked clumsy and amateurish. I eventually ended up taking the effect out and putting in an additional video clip instead of cutting back to the speaker. Later on, when I finally discovered that iMovie could create the same effect without my having to synchronize the lips and words manually — and it was like a light bulb had gone on in my head.

At that point, I had the option of returning to my old entry and fixing it, or moving on and using the effect as I wished in later vlog entries. I chose not to edit the old entry, because I felt it was important for my personal videoblog to also show my development, however clumsy it might have been.

If you're looking to create a more profession-oriented videoblog, it's a good idea to review your old vlog entries periodically to make sure they're as professional and accurate as you can make them. For most subjects, review the content every six months.

When you review each vlog entry, either just after you post it or after some time has passed, consider these questions and answer them if you can:

- ✔ What is the idea expressed in this vlog entry?

- ✔ What resources did I have available?

- ✔ Were there any limitations I couldn't work around? Some limitations might include bad ambient lighting, interfering sound, or being unable to secure permission to film a subject or area.

- ✔ How do I want people to feel when they see this vlog entry?

- ✔ How do I feel when I watch it?

- ✔ How long did it take me to shoot and edit this entry? Did I enjoy that time?

- ✔ If I stumbled on this videoblog for the first time and this were the first entry I saw, would I want to see more?

- ✔ What did I do that was new in this entry?

- ✔ What risks did I take and how do I feel about the results?

- ✔ What other entries do I want to build from this one?

As you develop your technical skill and your own cinematic style, you will also develop a sense for what kind of artistic vision you want to create. Even if you don't view your videoblog as an artistic enterprise, don't neglect its value as a place for you to express yourself creatively.

Questioning your expectations

Your videoblog will surprise you. Your audience will surprise you. Heck, you will surprise yourself! It happens in every creative endeavor — all of a sudden, something you thought was going one way turns around and goes in another direction entirely — and you even end up liking it that way.

Sometimes you discover that you're better than you thought you were, or at least people are nicer than you expected, and say things that make you realize you've reached them. And sometimes you find that what you thought would be simple turns out to be very, very complicated — for example, when the topic sprouts lots of nuances, or the procedure you're recording calls for smaller, more detailed steps.

When you have such a constrained medium as a vlog entry, you'll find yourself struggling against your assumptions and expectations about film in general. Yep, you've got 'em; we all do — they're based on what we've seen in movies and television. The techniques that go into the average vlog entry are, in a word, basic; it's bothersome that even the cheesiest of effects, or the most basic of lighting setups, may be unavailable for use in your videos. Just remember that reality television has brought a whole new look to television — the slightly yellow cast of incandescent indoor lighting, for instance, is easily duplicated in videoblogs every day. Television journalists and documentary filmmakers do talking head interviews all the time without boring their audiences. Your videoblog will never be as boring as you might think (and it's worth remembering that the artist — in this case, vlogger — is often his or her own harshest critic). Okay, the vlog entry might be as engrossing as you think it is, either, but if you're interested and passionate about your subject, your audience will catch at least some of your enthusiasm.

For example, I recently watched a vlog entry that completely blew my mind. It was in funny vlogger Josh Leo's videoblog: He did a short entry about how he cuts up and eats an avocado. Let me state up front that there is no way I would even think of eating an avocado and making it into a videoblog entry. I mean — who thinks of that? Apparently Josh Leo does. Not only was Josh's vlog entry absolutely fascinating because he was meticulous and funny, but another vlogger posted a related entry (and linked to it in Josh's comments page) about how he eats a different fruit — a persimmon, I believe. I was astounded — two fruit-eating vlog posts in one day! Marvelous! (Wait a minute. Is an avocado a fruit? Oh well.)

Okay, seriously, if you're like most people, if someone walked up to you on the street and said, "I want to show you how to eat an avocado," you would walk quickly away. If "how to eat an avocado" showed up in your television lineup, you'd likely change the channel, expecting it to be boring. But when someone posts it up there on the Internet and takes a risk by eating an avocado in front of the world, just for the heck of it, it challenges what you expect out of good vlogging — and the freshness of the idea grabs hold of you and makes you want to say, "Hey! I do something unique and different! Let me show you!"

Look for those unique moments; they are what make your videoblog a unique expression of yourself.

Vlogging as small business promotion

Most of the early videobloggers are, in their hearts, teachers. They have something they want to teach the world — perhaps they want to teach it to sing! — and videoblogging is a compelling way to get their message across.

If you have a business, you're probably salivating at all the talk in this chapter about what amounts to target demographics and two-way communication. *Yes,* you're thinking. *That's what I want! I want to reach my customers and get more business!*

Well, you know how this works, right? You give them something for free to get them to come back for something else (preferably with a price tag). In this case, your freebie is your videoblog — specifically, what you share with them in your videoblog.

Consider, if you will, the day-to-day running of your business. Would it make a good story? Cable television has already proven that people are interested in watching the chaotic mess that is an upscale restaurant kitchen.

Perhaps you don't want to show the day-to-day business, or maybe you can't for privacy or legal reasons. What about your services or products? Is there something you can teach your customers about?

One of my friends is a lawyer for politically under-represented groups. He recently contacted me for advice on starting a videoblog. He wants to get the word out about his clients, but also about how to protect yourself legally if you're one of the disenfranchised. His videoblog audience will be both clients who can use some free, generalized advice, as well as activists working for the same causes. As a result, when he makes his vlog entries, he'll look for opportunities for his own citizen journalism as well as places where he can provide insight into the legal issues involved.

If you're really not sure how to talk about your business or what to say, I suggest doing something similar to the steps that I describe in Chapter 4. Get out the camera and set it up on a tripod or stable surface. Press the Record button. Stand in front of the camera and tell the world why you have this business, and what you like about it. Chances are you'll find yourself overwhelmed with ideas of things to talk about. Business owners tend to be passionate about what they do — share your passion and the vlog-entry topics will fall into place.

Chapter 6

Deciding on a Look and Feel

You don't have to go out of your way create a consistent look and feel for your videoblog. In a way, without even trying to, you'll make your videoblog unique and personal to your own image, whether you intend to or not. Part of the appeal of videoblogs is that people get to know you (or at least the *you* whom you present on-screen).

But if you find yourself feeling a bit like the wallflower at the party — not sure that anyone's even watching your vlogs or remembers who you are — consider pumping things up with a little self-branding.

Branding is a term used in business marketing quite a lot. It refers to the unique identification of a product in a customer's mind. When you think of certain foods, like ketchup, you might have a hard time separating your idea of ketchup from the taste and image of good ol' Heinz. How did that happen? How did Heinz become synonymous with ketchup? Among other things, through marketing — and branding.

Now, I'm not going to suggest that you need to be the Heinz ketchup of videoblogging. Far from it. But a little bit of consistency in how your vlog entries look will help your viewers remember who created them — and whose videoblog they should come visit more often.

Branding with Music and Graphics

The basic idea behind a look and feel is that you want to provide a consistent image for your audience or customer to identify. When they see or hear your brand, they'll think of you.

So what can you use to build your image? Hey, it's a videoblog! The world is your oyster. You can make your image stand out with elements such as the following:

- ✔ Sound bites
- ✔ Special graphics
- ✔ A repeated style of titling
- ✔ A simple color element that appears in every entry

The big Hollywood stars and directors have been doing this for years. For example, Arnold Schwarzenegger's "I'll be back" line is so famous, he's actually had to stop using it in movies (and campaign speeches). Another example that's a little less obvious is that nearly every Stephen Spielberg movie since *E.T.* has an image of the full moon in it. Spielberg made movie history with the famous scene with E.T. flying across the moon, and he's continued to use the image to remind the audience, "Hey, this is my work!"

Just remember that your image has to be unique and original. It's yours, not someone else's, so don't yank someone else's branding and use it for your own. Not only is it a breach of goodwill, you may run into legal hot water if you use someone else's trademark.

Creating a graphic or video logo for your videoblog

You can use graphics and logos in your videoblog to give a visual look and feel. But in addition to a graphic, you can also use a video clip as part of your look and feel. The visual part of your look and feel is the most important part; most viewers remember a visual cue more than they remember an audible one.

If your videoblog is for business, you might end up using the same look and feel for business cards and stationery — if you think you might go in that direction, use a simpler logo, so it'll print easier.

Whatever you decide on for your logo, you will want to save the graphic in a high-resolution format in case you want to edit the graphic later or for printed applications. Use a lower-resolution version of your logo for the Web site where you host your videoblog.

People don't always watch vlog entries from the Web site they're hosted on, so don't get obsessed by the look of your videoblog's Web page. A clean, simple page — with a couple of visual elements to remind users where they are — will suffice.

Using a still graphic or digital photo

For a still-graphic logo, first create your image in any graphic arts program (such as Photoshop, Paint Shop Pro, or the Gimp). Save the finished logo graphic as a PNG, GIF, or JPEG file so you can use it on the Web as well as in your videos.

If you're really stuck, you might ask a friend to make the graphic for you, or use a digital photo. Digital photos are easy to use and edit in iPhoto and other photo-editing software programs. Since you're using it in the context of your videoblog, you might find that a digital photo is an excellent choice. You can even grab a frame from one of your iMovie videos and save it to serve as a digital photo by following these steps:

1. **Open your iMovie project and use the scroll bar at the bottom to find the frame you want to use.**

2. **Select File⇨Save Frame As to save the frame as a graphic.**

   The Save As dialog box appears, as shown in Figure 6-1.

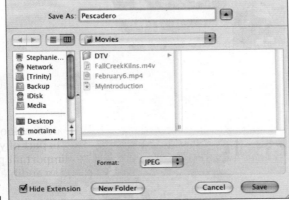

Figure 6-1:
Save an individual frame to use it as your Web graphic.

3. **Enter a name for the file in the Save As text box.**

4. **Select JPEG from the Format pop-up menu to determine the file type.**

   JPEG is the preferred format for digital photos on the Web.

5. **Uncheck the Hide Extension option.**

   Doing so ensures that the file type is visible with the filename.

6. **Click Save to save the picture.**

With the picture saved, you can then edit it in iPhoto or another photo-editing program, crop it down, or export it as a smaller, logo-sized picture.

Creating a video logo for your look and feel

For video logos, you can grab a good video clip from any video you've made. If you've made a video that serves as the introduction to your vlog (as described in Chapter 4), you may want to use part of that video for your video logo. When I created my vlog's look and feel, I dug up the very first video I'd posted to a blog — which happened to be a video of me having a drink at lunch. The clip was about 3 seconds long, which made it a perfect candidate for my vlog, which happened to be named after the beverage shown in the video clip.

To save a video clip in iMovie, your best bet is to create a new Project and import the video file you want to use, edit it, and save it. (See Chapter 10 for details on importing and editing video clips in iMovie.)

Your video logo is also a good place to experiment with a fun camera angle, a new filter on your editing software, or even animation (Figure 6-2). Although iMovie doesn't really support animation, Final Cut Pro, Adobe Premier, and Windows Movie Maker have some animation options you can play with.

Figure 6-2:
Use a video logo to give your vlog a unique look and feel!

When you're creating a video logo, keep the following tips in mind:

- ✔ Keep the video logo short — no more than 2 or 3 seconds in length.
- ✔ Aim for a personal touch. If you're not in the shot, put something representing you in it.
- ✔ Experiment with different styles, camera angles, and effects.

When you create a video logo, watch it all the way through and find one visual element that you really like about it. For instance, is there a particular color that you think is really striking in the clip? If you used an animation, is there a character in your animation that you can use in a still image? If you can't just grab a frame from the clip, you can still create a look and feel centered around a visual image in your clip — even if you have to shoot it separately with a digital camera.

Using music and sound

The second part of a look and feel for your videoblog is audible. How do you want your vlog to sound? What's your signature line, or music clip, or sound bite?

TV producers have included sound in their branding for as long as TV has been around, from the original *Mickey Mouse Club* song (and other TV show themes) to "Sit, Ubu, sit!" from Ubu Productions' outro and the signature "Grr. Argh." of Joss Whedon's studio Mutant Enemy.

Some ideas for using music and sound in your vlog logo:

- ✔ Record yourself saying your favorite quote, tagline, or catch-phrase.
- ✔ If you're a musician, record your own theme music.
- ✔ Search Creative Commons (http://creativecommons.org) to find music that you can more easily get permission for.
- ✔ Use sound-bite collections to find sounds you can remix into your own logo. Check for permission and licensing terms first.
- ✔ Record a family pet barking or meowing and mix it into your clip.
- ✔ As with the video logo, keep a sound bite short — no more than a couple of seconds.

Creative branding for your videoblog

Don't forget to be creative with your vlog's branding! If you have a theme to your videoblog, be it professional or otherwise, incorporate that theme into your video logo and Web site.

I tossed this out as an example earlier in this chapter, but imagine if all your early vlog entries included an image of one specific thing. Perhaps you always include a shot of your cat, or the color yellow, or a particular stuffed animal, or someone smiling. Pretty soon, you have a dozen vlog entries with that same image in them — and people start to identify your vlog with that image, even if all the posts were different. You could create a brand around the image of that thing — make it the centerpiece of your video logo and online identity.

Get creative with your look and feel as you start your videoblog! If you're at a complete loss, just make sure each vlog entry includes something made of your favorite color, just to keep it simple (the color might even appear just in the credits!) As soon as you start looking for things of that color in your videoblog, you'll start seeing that color around you more often, and then you'll pull out the camera and voila! An opportunity to vlog will have arisen!

A similar concept started early in the vlogging days, in a meme called "Green thing." In it, vloggers posted videos of a green thing received in the mail, but the vlogs were from all over, not just one person's vlog. If you start to include a flash of yellow or green or red or turquoise in each vlog entry you post, you can bet that eventually someone else will pick up on the idea — and may even include a flash of that same color in their vlog as homage to yours.

A *meme* is a piece of information or trend that spreads throughout a culture. In the online and blogging worlds, memes are like little fads that spring up and circulate. The most common blog memes are quizzes, such as personality tests or pseudo-tests, which tell the world a little something about a particular blogger. Memes often have a viral quality, and charge the meme participant to pass them on to someone else, like a chain letter. You can find some blog memes at The Daily Meme (`http://thedailymeme.com`).

Getting Repeatable Results with Templates

A *template* is a reusable framework that makes it easier to create standardized items like Web pages. In blogging terms, a template can be a basic layout for a blog site, or it can be an entry template, which is a bit of HTML code that you reuse to make each entry have a consistent feel to it.

The following code provides an example of an entry template you can use for your own vlog. This particular entry template is simply the HTML code that places a hyperlink to your video file. Note that you'll need to replace the URL shown here (`www.example.com/Video.mp4`) with your own videoblog file's location. If you use the Internet Archive or blip.tv — or any of the other turnkey videoblogging solutions discussed in Chapter 13 — the URL for your vlog entry will be generated automatically by those services when you upload your file. The URL will probably be considerably longer, too.

```
<a href="http://www.example.com/Video.mp4"
   rel="enclosure">
<br />Click here for the movie! (MPEG-4 format)</a>
```

In this template, the movie is linked from a basic text link that says "Click here for the movie!" The important detail here — for purposes of the RSS feed — is the bit that says `rel="enclosure"` because that tells the RSS aggregator (a program such as FeedBurner) to take the video file *as an enclosure* and include it in the feed.

You can also create an entry template that creates a link from an image by using the following code:

```
<a href="http://www.example.com/Video.mp4"
   rel="enclosure">
<img src="http://www.example.com/Video.jpeg"></a>
```

In this case, there are two files. One is the MPEG-4 video file, and the other is a JPEG image. The JPEG can be a captured frame out of the video, as mentioned earlier in this chapter. The graphic serves as a kind of placeholder for the movie.

I made an entry template that I use on the Blogger site; it makes it easy for me to post my videos — because I already know that the HTML code used to embed a video *works*. Blogger lets you save a blog-entry template on its site, so you don't even have to store the template as a text file on your hard drive (although you may want to anyway; it never hurts to have a backup).

To use an entry template in Blogger, follow these steps:

1. **Log in to your Blogger account and click the Change Settings icon next to your videoblog in your Blogger Dashboard.**

2. **If you're not already in the Settings tab, click it.**

3. **Click the <u>Formatting</u> link and scroll down the page to the Post Template field, as shown in Figure 6-3.**

Figure 6-3:
Enter your
template
into
Blogger's
Post
Template
field so you
can reuse it.

4. **Enter the HTML code for your template into the Post Template field.**

5. **Click Save Settings to save the template.**

   You may be prompted to republish your videoblog, but this isn't strictly necessary.

For other blog services, you can set up your template and just save it to your hard drive as a text file that you can edit later as needed.

In all cases, when you actually post your vlog entries, be sure to edit the text *before* posting so your vlog entry will point to the correct URL.

Creating Recognizable Intros and Outros

The earlier sections in this chapter discuss branding your Web site and your videoblog by using your own logo within them — but where do you *put* the video logo, anyway? And how else do you tell people that this is your work?

Intros, outros, titles, ID tags, and credits are all terms for small clips of video that stamp your vlog entries with your brand image.

Some vloggers call the opening titles and closing credits *intros* and *outros,* respectively, because they're short clips that frame the overall vlog entry. Keep in mind, however, that the terms *intro* and *outro* have a specific meaning in broadcast journalism — they refer to the anchor or reporter's introduction before — and conclusion after — a news piece. The small tag identifying a production company at the end of a show is called the *ID tag*.

Making titles and credits

Titles and credits are the most recognizable part of your videoblog's look and feel. Since your titles and credits appear inside your video, not just on your Web site, they'll be seen by anyone who watches your video through your RSS feed.

Titles, credits, and subtitles all serve different purposes, depending on where they're used:

- **In television,** opening titles tell you the name of the show, the producers, and usually the stars. The opening credits often run into the actual show content. A common sequence until recently was to show the opening titles, then cut to commercial, then start the show, with the rest of the credits (including guest stars for the episode) laid over the beginning of episode. The closing credits, which never overlap the end of the show, tend to get distorted by the television network, which resizes closing credit reels so they can show teasers of upcoming shows in the next time slot. Subtitles are used for clarification, translation, or services for the deaf, as well as to identify people or places referred to in the news.

- **In movies,** the opening titles and credits can run into the rest of the movie, but rarely do. The movie may open with a scene, cut to the opening title and credits, and then return to a new scene. Most of the time, though, the opening title and credit sequence appears before the opening sequence to the movie. Subtitles are almost universally reserved for translations of foreign languages. Closing credits are almost always a scrolling block of text that lists the starring actors, followed by the crew, then production companies and specialists.

- **In videoblogs,** it's common to have an opening title, often animated, and some kind of closing credits at the end of the vlog. The closing credits are far from universal, however — and many vloggers dispense with them entirely, preferring to give a short ID tag of the videoblog site instead. In the case of a corporate vlog, this would be a good place to have sponsor logos as well.

Using titles and subtitles

Titles and subtitles are two ways to get text onto your videoblog's screen. With titles, the text is the main element on-screen — as an identifier, a scene break, or even as commentary. Subtitles, on the other hand, go in the lower third of the video image. When you use subtitles, make sure you set the font size large enough to be readable, even if you're saving your vlogs at a typically small screen size (usually 320 x 240 pixels).

The following list provides some tips for using titles and subtitles effectively in your videos:

- ✔ **Don't use white text over a black screen.** Put the opening titles over the video itself or over your opening sequence animation or video clip, as shown in Figure 6-4.

- ✔ **Use a large font so people can read the title or subtitle text.** That goes for the closing credits, too!

- ✔ **Opening titles should be short and to the point.**

Figure 6-4: Run your titles and opening credits over the vlog so your viewers stay to watch.

✔ **Sometimes you'll want to include a title in the middle of a video.** Do this to signal scene changes, as shown in Figure 6-5.

✔ **Include titles or subtitles over the video any time someone you're interviewing says a URL or e-mail address.** Give the URL on-screen in large letters so viewers can see it and remember it.

✔ **Pay attention to your audience's needs.** For a video I made for my 7-year-old nephew when he was learning to read, I included a subtitle of an animal's common name (such as "Shark") every time that animal appeared in the video.

✔ **For any instructional show, it's common to put important technical details on-screen.** For example, if you're doing a cooking show, list the ingredients and their amounts on-screen in subtitles so viewers can read and jot them down.

✔ **Use subtitles to compensate for subjects who mumble on camera.** This technique is often used in reality TV shows.

Figure 6-5: Include subtitles to signal a scene change and to highlight the subject matter.

✔ **Use subtitles for humorous effect.** For example, you might provide a translation from what was actually said to what you think was meant.

✔ **Use subtitles creatively.** For example, you can add text-only commentary to a video segment — say, to explain or contrast silently with what's being shown.

Crediting your assistants, musicians, and subjects

Movies are one of the few artistic media that are almost always the result of hundreds of people's hard work and dedication. If you don't believe me, look at the long list of credits at the end of any movie — any actor with a speaking part and every crew member who had a hand in the making of that movie appears in the closing credits. (That's why they're so long!)

But videoblogs! Ah, videoblogs might be the work of 50 people — or just one. Rocketboom, the flagship videoblog out on the Internet, is the work of two key people, with correspondents and helpers all over the world. If your videoblog is just your own, then you only need to credit yourself, which you might do simply by including a URL to your blog and bio in the closing sequence of each vlog entry. Or you might want to point out the folks who helped you make your personal vlog dreams come true.

✔ End credits can be text over black, if you don't mind people not reading them. When viewers see a screen go black and text scroll onto the screen, they think the movie is over and they turn it off or switch to the next vlog.

✔ Keep it short. If you have more than 4 people involved in your production, post a URL to your movie's credits and leave it at that.

✔ Sometimes you're obligated to include a person's name in the credits, depending on the terms of your release forms and permissions agreements.

Not everyone wants credit — or, for that matter, on-screen notoriety. Always ask any vlogging subjects if they mind being named (and/ or filmed!).

✔ Ask your vlogging subjects how they want their names to appear in the vlog entry, and whether they require credit in the end credits. Some subjects are generous with their on-camera presence, but reticent about their online identities — and you can invite them to use a vlogging stage name if it makes them more comfortable.

Reusing opening titles and closing tags

The options for getting your look and feel into your videoblog include using the following in all your vlog entries:

✔ The opening title sequence, logos, or animation

✔ The vlog's opening credits

✔ Creative subtitling

✔ Themed content (whether subject matter or simply a visual element)

✔ Closing credits

✔ ID tags after the closing credits

Of these, the opening credits and closing tag are the most reusable clips you can create to make your look and feel consistent; you won't need to change them to reflect the content in a specific vlog entry. So it makes sense to spend the most time on getting them right.

The opening title and closing tag serve more or less the same function; it's rare to find a videoblogger using both of them extensively. Most vloggers use either an opening title *or* a closing tag, and then put any credits specific to the vlog entry at the other end. So, if you have an opening title sequence, you might roll the credits at the end of the video — listing any musical contributions, guest appearances, or Web sites mentioned in that specific post. That kind of setup gives your vlog a very movie-like feel. If you have a closing tag at the end, you could put the credits at the beginning — which would give you a more TV-like setup.

Adding an opening or closing clip in iMovie

Once you've created your opening or closing clip, you'll need to add it to each videoblog entry before you post it.

Make a backup of your opening or closing clip on a safe media (such as a DVD-ROM). That way, you know you'll always have a copy that you can import it into your vlog entries.

To add your clip to your movie in iMovie, follow these steps. (Note that you don't have to save your opening or closing clip to MPEG-4 or compress it in any way.)

1. **From iMovie, select File⇨Import.**

2. **Navigate to the movie file.**

   If you created the movie in iMovie, you'll find the iMovie project file, the Media folder, and a `.mov` file of the same name as the project, as shown in Figure 6-6.

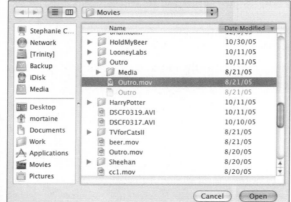

Figure 6-6:
Import your
opening or
closing clip
to iMovie.

3. **Select the .mov version of your clip and click Open.**

   The QuickTime video of your clip will import to the Clips section of
   iMovie, as shown in Figure 6-7.

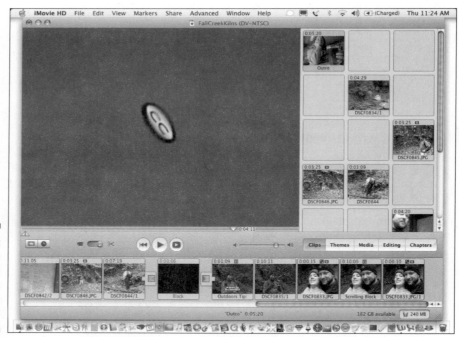

Figure 6-7:
The
imported
clip appears
in the Clips
pane.

Your opening or closing clip will not import with all its sub-clips intact — you won't be able to edit it as if it were a normal iMovie project. However, you will still be able to edit its original project, if you want to change the original and re-import it later.

4. **Make sure you are in the clip viewer mode of iMovie by clicking the clip viewer icon.**

5. **Drag the opening or closing clip to the beginning or end of the movie, as shown in Figure 6-8.**

Figure 6-8:
Drag the closing clip into place in the timeline.

6. **Remember to save your project after you import the clip (⌘+S).**

Keeping it short and sweet

The key to remember is that the shorter your reusable credits or ID clip is, the better. The longer your make that clip, the more likely people are to stop watching your vlog just because they think the intro is too long.

Here's an example: I listen to podcasts, of course, and I recently timed one of my favorite podcast's introductory sound clips. It was 30 seconds long — the time of an average commercial on television. In 30 seconds, I can get a drink of water. I can brush or floss my teeth (not very well).But more to the point, in 30 seconds, I can change the channel! Now, this particular podcast is usually just as long as my commute, so I'll listen to the 30 seconds of noise just so I can hear the rest of the show. But if my hands weren't on the wheel, I'd fast-forward right through it!

Any time your vlog isn't providing something immediate that your viewers value a lot, it's wasted time for them. Your videoblog's look and feel, though important to you and to your online identity, is not very valuable to your viewers after the first time they see it.

Of course, there is one sure-fire way around that — vary the clip every time you use it. *The Simpsons* does this with the couch sequence in the opening credits — there isn't a *Simpsons* fan alive who hasn't said "Rewind — I didn't see the couch!" at some point. Running gags and creativity go a long way towards adding value to your vlog!

Now, there are some viewers who would love to have longer vlogs to watch, up to 10 minutes or more. But those folks aren't talking about putting in a 30-second opening title sequence — they want 10 minutes of real, honest-to-goodness vlog *content*, and that's a lot of time to fill.

How long will your audience watch your video clip? About as long as it takes them to reach for the mouse button and click the fast-forward button, or use their mobile device's interface to skip ahead (and for the computer or device to respond). In other words, about one to four seconds.

Yep — you read that right. You have less than four seconds to push your video logo image at the viewer. If it takes just about as long to let your titles run as it does to fast-forward, then your audience will leave the button alone and receive your brand impression.

If you want an ideal workaround to beat the fast-forward button, get your video logo to be short enough so you can fit the credits into the *same* four seconds. That way, by the time your audience has realized the opening credits are over, the video logo really will *be* over, and the content will be rolling!

Always preview your vlog entry before posting it to make sure it flows well. This is especially true when you've recently added an identifying clip to your vlog, so you can test out how long the video logo seems to be and whether it seems to drag.

So, to keep your video logo short and sweet, keep the following in mind:

- ✔ Trim it down to one idea or image or animation plus your URL.
- ✔ Consider varying your video logo slightly each time so viewers will want to watch.
- ✔ Keep your video logo to under four seconds long.
- ✔ Use animation to keep viewer interest engaged.
- ✔ Insert a sound bite or music to reinforce the brand impression, even if the user looks away for a moment.

Chapter 7

Putting Yourself in the Limelight

. . . .

In This Chapter

▶ Understanding and overcoming stage fright — and vid fright

▶ Getting comfortable vlogging with yourself on screen

▶ Turning the camera away from yourself

▶ Working with actors and interview subjects

. . . .

*N*ot everyone is a natural in front of the camera, including many videobloggers. This chapter talks about becoming comfortable in front of the camera, and how to get other people comfortable as well.

Understanding Vid Fright

Vid fright is another word for stage fright in front of a camera. It's a little different from traditional stage fright — after all, you can't actually see your audience — but it's a very similar response.

Where vid fright comes from

Vid fright — and stage fright — comes from fear, which is a very primitive emotional response to certain types of stress. For instance, a lot of people get stage fright because they are afraid of looking stupid in front of a lot of people, or they're scared of what they see as exposure to confrontation ("If I open my mouth, everyone will realize what a fraud I am!"). There are very few naturally comfortable public speakers in the world; even the most comfortable speakers have an emotional response to speaking, though they become more energized, rather than frozen when it happens.

One of the best tips for overcoming stage fright is to somehow humanize your audience, either by selecting two or three individuals to look at while you speak, or by visualizing them all looking or acting in ways that are even more embarrassing than the way you feel.

Vid fright has an additional dimension — you cannot see your audience, just the cold, staring lens of the camera. Okay, that might be comforting if you don't like talking to people — but if your strategy for overcoming stage fright is to humanize your audience, that's really hard when your audience is represented by a machine. I'm a comfortable public speaker and enjoy talking to large groups of people, but the first time I stared into that glassy lens, I said, "umm . . ." and froze up. It took three takes to get my 30-second introduction out. But take heart — here's the good news:

✔ For lots of folks, talking into a camera lens gets easier with practice.

✔ Videoblogs aren't live events. Even if you absolutely freeze up the first time, you can keep going, and edit the clip later.

After you've made a short introduction video (as described in Chapter 4), you never again have to put yourself on that side of the lens again if you really don't want to. For that matter, a large number of photographers and cinematographers are in the business *because* they're camera-shy. If you're the one holding the camera, you don't have to be on screen.

Determining your comfort level in front of the lens

When an actor auditions for a role in a TV show or movie, he or she goes through a screen test to see how comfortable he or she is on-camera. Even reality TV shows perform screen tests, because if you cannot get comfortable with the lens, you won't be reliable enough to keep looking real (so to speak) during filming, and when filming a TV show or movie, every second costs money.

The best way to find out how comfortable you are is to just do it — so this section provides a series of screen tests to help you find out how comfortable you are when you're videoblogging. Unlike a screen test for a movie, however, the resulting video won't be subjected to nitpicking scrutiny (though you can do that later if you want to). That's because your audition isn't to see how confident you look, but rather how confident you *feel*.

After you finish with the screen test, take a moment to check yourself and rate how the experience made you feel. Use a simple 1–5 scale like this one:

1. This screen test left me cool as a cucumber — I could do that all day!

2. I have a lot of nervous energy, but I'm good to go again.

3. I'm okay, but I'd rather not do that again soon.

4. I need to lie down — that was exhausting and terrifying.

5. Where's the nearest hospital?

If the screen test you just performed made you feel uncomfortable, shaky, or worse, you know that's an area you need to work on to become more comfortable, or perhaps that's an area you may want to avoid entirely in your videoblog.

For some people, stage fright is so debilitating, it can cause actual physical reactions like panic attacks — and can exacerbate existing health conditions. If your reaction to the narration exercise in this chapter required you to lie down, you may want to consult a therapist for help in overcoming severe stage fright.

The following subsections describe the different types of screen tests you should try out to determine how you want to approach your videoblog.

Screen test: Narrating a videoblog

First, take your video camera and go find something to shoot — preferably not a human being. It could be your pet, or a nearby park, or something neat about your home. As you film it, narrate what you're filming and provide commentary about what you're showing the viewer.

When you turn the camera off, take a second and do a quick check of yourself. Is your heart racing? Did you sweat? Are you shaking? Do you want to just cry? Rate your reaction, using the 1–5 scale presented earlier (in the "Determining your comfort level in front of the lens" section).

If your reaction was a 4 or a 5 (extremely nervous and uncomfortable), then you'll want to stick to more introspective, artistic videoblog entries, or enlist a friend to serve as your videoblog's on-air talent, the way Amanda Congden serves as the host of Rocketboom (you never see the camera crew for Rocketboom).

Screen test: Getting in front of the camera by yourself

The next task is similar to the introduction described in Chapter 4 — and you can use that experience if you remember it well in this exercise. If not, just set up the camera and stand in front of it by yourself. Talk about something you did today (other than reading this book), or give a short review of a movie you saw or a book you read recently.

When you're done, turn off the camera, and rate how the experience made you feel, using the 1–5 scale presented in the "Determining your comfort level in front of the lens" section.

Again, if you're shaky or very uncomfortable, you might need to acclimate yourself to the camera, or resolve to never put *yourself* in front of the lens.

Screen test: Having a friend film your performance

The next step is to have a friend film you while you perform. Adding another human into the equation changes the dynamic. In some cases, you'll be more comfortable, because it's just like talking with a friend. In other cases, you'll be less comfortable, because now you have a witness to your embarrassment. Just pick someone you trust enough to hold your camera and ask them to film you. Find a spot that has something you can talk about — perhaps your favorite coffeeshop or your school — and talk about it for about 30 seconds. If you need inspiration, imagine that you're a news reporter doing a news piece on that location, and give the background story that your viewers would want to know ("This sleepy mountain town of Ben Lomond hides a secret treasure — this café, which locals claim offers a magical blend of coffee, water, and love . . .").

When you're done, ask yourself how you feel, and again rate your reaction using the 1–5 scale presented in the "Determining your comfort level in front of the lens" section. If you still couldn't get out of the 4–5 panic zone, even with a good friend filming you, it's time to take back the camera — you're not going to be on screen in your vlogs, not without a lot of time and rehearsal.

Screen test: Shooting a crowd

The last task is the largest amount of exposure, and potentially the more debilitating stage fright: filming someone else. For this, you'll need to take your camera out in public — a feat in itself, which may have you standing at the door, holding the camera bag, and thinking second thoughts.

Don't think. Just walk outside with the camera bag in hand. Take this in little steps:

1. **Take your camcorder out to a public space in your home town, such as a park.**

   Worried about the legal issue of filming people? In the U.S., there's no expectation of privacy on a public street. Private property, including publicly accessible stores, can make rules that limit filming inside. And since you're not going to post this video to your vlog, you don't really need permission to film individuals (though if they ask you to turn away, you should be respectful of their desire for privacy). See Chapter 15 for information on when and how to ask for permission to film. If you're outside the United States, check your local laws on filming in public, because they may be different.

2. **Take the camera out of the bag.**

3. **Turn the camera on.**

   At this point, you're still looking around at the world, casually browsing around in what's happening.

4. **Bring the camera up to your eye and start filming the street.**

5. **After a few minutes, stop filming.**

6. **Check in with yourself.**

   Do you feel ridiculous? Are you shaking? Are you comfortable?

7. **Look around you.**

   People will always look at a video camera — usually to decide if there's a news story being filmed and if they can get on TV. But does anyone look angry or uncomfortable?

Once again, check in with the 1–5 comfort scale. How do you feel? If you're still completely wigged out by shooting in a public space, then you may prefer to just have yourself or a few friends appearing in your vlog entries.

Screen test: Interviewing a stranger

If someone on the location where you're shooting looks particularly interested, or if you've chosen a spot where there are street performers, go up to them and introduce yourself. Tell them you're shooting video for the Internet, and you'd like to do a short interview with them. If they agree, they have just become your interview subjects.

If you can't find anyone on the location where you took your crowd scene, leave the location and go find someone you know casually — say, the barista at your favorite coffeeshop, or someone you work with or attend school with.

Many street performers will be happy to oblige, especially if there's a possibility of greater exposure — make sure you get information on where they perform regularly, or jot down their Web sites. If you end up using the interview in your videoblog, you want to tell viewers where they can see this performance as well.

Either set the camera on a stable surface or tripod, or do a gonzo-style interview where you interview the performers from behind the camera. If you were very nervous during your screen test, use the gonzo-style interview.

Ask them their names, and what they do for a living. If you're interviewing performers, ask them about their art and performance — what they love about it, or why they do it. If your interview subjects are just ordinary bystanders, ask them about a local issue, such as the school system, or ask them to tell you about something they care about. Feel free to prompt them. ("You're here at the Mushroom Festival — what exactly is it about fungus that you find so fascinating?")

Be prepared for a lot of sideways, nervous glances, shrugged shoulders, and "I don't know" kinds of answers. That's okay — in this particular exercise you're not really trying to fix their stage fright, just your own. (Later in this chapter, I talk about how to make your interview subjects more comfortable.)

When you stop filming, thank your subject and tell them where your videoblog can be found, but explain that you don't yet know whether you'll use this footage. That gives your subject the chance to say "I don't want you to use it" — or it can provide a graceful way out if the person didn't seem to understand that you were talking about a *video for the Internet* when you asked for an interview.

If you want to interview children, always talk to their parents first — and get their permission before you start. Be very clear about what you're doing and why. Very little scares parents more than a strange person with a video camera walking up to their six-year-old child to chat.

After you've left your subject, check in with yourself again. Are you nervous? How did you like talking to strangers? It's a given that you'll be nervous, but did you find the experience fun at the same time? How do you feel afterward?

If you're like most people, the interview was the hardest of all the screen tests. If you fell into it naturally, however, or if you found it fun to be like a journalist, consider doing interviews as part of your videoblog on a regular basis, and see Chapter 15 for more ideas on videoblogging with other people. Although a videoblog can be all about your life, it's also fun to use it as a showcase for other people, events, and local color.

Getting Comfortable On-Camera

If you were uncomfortable in your screen test, but not debilitated, you can take some steps to improve your speaking skills and become more comfortable and confident in front of the camera.

The suggestions here are just a start to becoming a more confident on-screen personality, but if you find yourself enjoying public speaking, even when you're nervous, you can use your videoblogging habit to train yourself for more public speaking gigs and events.

In all these suggestions, the key is to be prepared when you go in front of the camera lens. Being prepared means you know what you want to say and how to say it. You're confident that your appearance is acceptable (we're not models here), and that you are very familiar with your subject matter. The key to all public speaking, including videoblogging, is to be prepared enough that you no longer have to worry about your delivery and content, but you can instead focus on the technical aspects of the shoot (such as lighting, sound, camera angles, and camera stability), or the technological ones (editing your movie after you import it into iMovie or Windows Movie Maker).

Having a script

A *script* is the word-for-word text of what you're going to say when you're recording. You write it well in advance, and it helps to practice it aloud. The advantage of scripts is that you can edit the words until they're just right, and when you read or recite them, you won't be as nervous. If you practice your script in advance, you might even eliminate all the "ums" and "ers" that creep into people's language when they're expounding verbally and pause to think.

Use a script when

- ✔ You're planning an interview with a subject and you want to have your questions prepared in advance.
- ✔ You're filming yourself giving a speech.
- ✔ You're narrating a shoot that was pre-planned.
- ✔ You're planning to edit in a voiceover after the shoot is done.

Most videobloggers don't work from a word-for-word script. A script isn't appropriate when the situation might change, or when you're doing a very informal videoblog, such as a personal diary. You never want to script your interview subjects' responses, though you can script your questions. Leave enough leeway, though, that if the subject says something particularly interesting, you can spontaneously ask a follow-up question before moving onto the next scripted question.

When you write a vlog script, keep it short. Less than one page of text is sufficient. Keep your points concise, and use bulleted lists and bold text to highlight the key words and phrases you need to know.

If you decide to do spontaneous interviews centered around a theme, you might want to write a script of common interview questions. For instance, one theme for my videoblog is to do vlog posts of people talking about their passions. Other vloggers have other themes, such as technology interviews.

Here's a sample interview script:

> Hi, I'm here today with [NAME], who has been doing [ACTIVITY] for [DURATION]. Tell me, what got you into this exciting activity? [Wait for answer.]

And did you have to learn anything to do this? How did you learn, or did someone teach you? [Wait]

Tell me about the tools and equipment you use for [ACTIVITY]. [Wait]

What would you say, in a nutshell, is your favorite thing about [ACTIVITY]? [Wait]

Great! Do you have a Web site about [ACTIVITY] you want to promote?

For a technology interview, you might include details like what kind of system the technology runs on, what it does, and how much it costs.

If it's appropriate, ask your subjects to tell you what they really like about the interviewing topic. If you want to provide a more complete pros and cons viewpoint, you can also ask them what they don't like — or what they wish they could change — about the interviewing topic. When people enjoy something and are passionate about it, their faces light up and their smiles become contagious. That's good video.

In Chapter 8, I talk more about structuring your vlog entries to tell a story, using storyboards and scripts.

Practicing in front of the camera

Practice makes perfect! With the camera on or off, you can rehearse your camera-readiness by keeping the lens pointed at you as you go about your daily business.

The camera lens can be a very daunting companion. Its glossy, black eye can seem menacing at first. And then when you turn it around and play it back — terror!

But there's hope. For starters, you can (and should) spend time practicing in front of the camera. This is, after all, your new audience when you communicate with your videoblog viewers. It's the eye you have to look into when you talk.

One way to overcome shyness around the video camera is to watch videoblogs. In particular, vlogging pioneers Michael Verdi (www.michaelverdi.com) and Ryanne Hodson (http://ryanedit.blogspot.com) both have excellent on-camera presences. For instance, you'll always see Michael Verdi making eye contact with the camera lens, and he tends to hold the camera close enough that you almost feel like he's standing right next to you, chatting amiably about events in his life and in the world.

Okay, this may sound a little weird, but trust me, it works: To practice this kind of eye-contact video, hold the camera at arm's length with the lens pointing at you — and just talk to it. Think of it as a hand puppet or a stuffed animal, or even a pet. It's not intelligent, and it won't talk back to you. But it does pay attention by recording — and later on, you can get feedback from it by watching the video.

To get accustomed to talking to the camera, follow these tips:

- Carry your camera around with you at all times.
- Put your camera, with the lens cap off, on the table in front of you when you eat meals.
- Plan a videoblogging project that will take more than a couple of days — say, watching how many dirty dishes have to pile up before your roommate (or *somebody*) washes them, or videoblogging a bad haircut as it grows out.
- Record 30 seconds of video every day for a week.
- Record 30 seconds of video every hour for a full day. Edit these together into a "Day in My Life" vlog entry.
- Record five seconds of every person in your life. Ask them to record you for a few seconds, too.
- When you're ready to make a videoblog entry, record it at least twice before you edit and post it. You'll be able to splice different segments together to get a vlog entry that sounds right.

When push comes to shove, though, there is no substitute for practice. And practice means just sitting yourself down and doing whatever you need to do to get comfortable with vlogging, over and over again, until you're finished with your project and more at home with the whole idea of doing a videoblog.

Physical preparation for going on-camera

When an athlete prepares for an event, he or she trains in advance, dresses in appropriate clothing, stretches, and psyches up just before the starting gun. Your vlog is like any human performance, be it an athletic competition, a dramatic performance, or a boardroom meeting. You have a series of tools and rituals that you can perform to help yourself get into the right mindset, as well as to prepare your body physically for the event.

Just as you would train for an athletic event, you must physically prepare for recording your vlog. Physical preparations for yourself can be as simple as taking a deep breath just before you hit the Record button, or as complex as preparing a specialized costume, props, and scenery.

I cover setting and scenery in Chapter 8; for now, just focus on your own body and preparing it for your vlog. First, look at your appearance. Even if you're not especially self-conscious, you may (if you're like most people) have that horrified moment when you look at yourself in the video and scream "Oh, my God, I look like THAT?!" Worry not — the camera really *does* add ten pounds to everybody because it's a two-dimensional representation of a three-dimensional object. And besides, nobody cares about your weight in videoblogging. While appearances do matter somewhat (okay, sure, some shallow viewers prefer to watch only those people who fit their ideals of beauty — but why would the rest of us need *their* attention?), most videoblogs succeed on the merit of their content, not on the relative cuteness of their on-screen talent.

However, you can take a few basic steps to make yourself look good on-camera anyway. After all, people will pay more attention to you if you look like you care about and respect them enough to perform basic hygiene on yourself, brush your hair, and wear clothes that didn't come from the bottom of the laundry pile.

Which brings me to costuming. Now, I loved costumes when I was a kid, but now that I'm older, I prefer function over form. When you're vlogging, you may need to move around more than you normally would, to catch a particular angle, or to move around obstacles and other people. Make sure you dress for comfort, but if you plan on appearing in the shot, dress appropriately as well. Your wardrobe will be determined by your personal tastes, of course, but also by your videoblog's theme and content. A rock-music-review vlogger usually wouldn't bother with a boardroom suit and tie; the owner of a legal-advice vlog shouldn't wear flip-flops on-camera when recording video.

Don't wear horizontal stripes on-camera. Fine stripes interfere with the digital camera's imaging and create weird swirly patterns called *Moiré patterns* that can distract your viewers.

Green-screen and blue-screen technologies are high-tech ways to import a new background into a video by having the actor perform in front of a mono-chromatic surface. If you experiment with these technologies, make sure that whoever's on-camera avoids wearing colors of clothing that match the background! Any body parts covered by clothing that's the same color as the background tend to disappear in the final movie; the camera is fooled into looking right through them.

In addition to setting, props, and costuming, there's the simple act of warming up. Your voice is an instrument — like any organic tool, it should be warmed up before you use it. Yawn repeatedly to stretch your mouth muscles, and practice out loud what you want to say — or at least your talking points — before you turn on the camera. If your vlog has action in it — and what would be the point of a video without action? — warm up the rest of your body with some simple stretches.

Even stars have a warm-up routine. For example, before every performance, Judy Garland would run around the stage, to give herself the breathless, rosy-cheeked façade that became her signature style.

Going incognito

Earlier in this chapter, I talked about going out and recording a crowd scene. Sometimes you may want to use a little stealth when doing this, particularly if you find that your vlogging subjects stop acting natural when you pull out the camera.

One simple thing you can do is record your video on your digital camera, if it has a video feature. People will look at someone with a video camera — they may even stare or get nervous. But few people will look twice at photographer, apparently shooting away at the local scenery. When you're really in stealth mode, some cellular phones have a video option — pose yourself right and you can record as a hidden camera without anyone realizing you're not just chatting on your phone.

Another option is to go all-out with the tourist look. Tourists get overlooked everywhere, unless they look like tourists with money. If you have a simple camcorder and a loud shirt, you can get away with it. For this particular bit of urban camouflage, wear a pair of khaki pants, a fanny pack, and either a T-shirt with the name of the town you're in, or a loud Hawaiian shirt that just screams "I'm from out of town!" Unless you live in a town so small that everyone knows each other's first and middle names, nobody will know that you're not really a tourist.

Related to the tourist disguise is the backpacking student disguise. This one requires you to have as small a camera as possible, but it does have the advantage of letting you go for a week without shaving in preparation for your vlog. Just look as scruffy as you can, carry a beat-up camping backpack, wear hiking boots, and have your student ID (or something that looks like one) hanging on a keychain at your belt.

Of course, if you really *are* a photographer, or a tourist, or a backpacking student, taking your video camera along for the experience is not only a great way to vlog, but you're one step ahead of everyone else in looking inconspicuous when you vlog!

Remember: Stealth vlogging does not mean peeping, harassing, or breaking the law — and that getting caught may have consequences. Do not, for example, videoblog your friends in the locker room at school. Do *not* stealth-vlog children without their parents' permission — ever. Do not stealth-vlog bridges or high-rise buildings unless you enjoy having long conversations with members of law-enforcement agencies. *Do* obey signs in private spaces — such as locker rooms, bathrooms, and some stores — prohibiting use of cameras, and pay attention to local laws regarding what may and may not be filmed.

Psyching yourself up

More people are afraid of public speaking than of death. Although physical preparation can help, 95 percent of your preparation for facing the lens is mental. Psyching yourself up to vlog can make the difference between a nervous, um-filled videoblog and a clean, confident vlog you're proud of.

Some suggestions for mentally preparing yourself for your vlog:

- Repeat to yourself that you are knowledgeable and capable to speak on this subject.

- Look at your notes or script to refresh your memory, if you're doing a scripted vlog.

- Imagine that you're making a video to be sent only to your best friend, and no one else.

- Imagine yourself smiling as you post your great vlog entry.

- Go through some kind of physical preparation before every vlog post. The physical preparation will help put you in the right mindset.

- Pretend you are an actor or a great public speaker whom you admire. This is the "fake it till you make it" strategy, and it works!

- Above all: Relax! Do whatever you need to do to get five minutes of down time before you go before the camera. If you are relaxed, you'll seem more confident on screen.

Chances are, if you have only a normal level of stage fright in front of the camera lens, you won't be completely paralyzed when you have to make a vlog post. After you follow these tips, you'll be confident enough to post to your vlog regularly. And if you're still completely terrified, read the rest of this chapter and find out how to become an invisible videoblogger.

How to Get Out of the Lens

Many videoblogs never even show the person responsible for the vlog's content. They may be more abstract, or use gonzo camerawork, or film an event with a voiceover commentary for the viewer's benefit.

Filming events and activities

The most basic way to get yourself out of the action is to film an event or activity that doesn't require your participation. You can shoot anything from a birthday party to speeches, sports events, or tradeshow conventions.

For formal events, such as speeches and tradeshows, you may need special permission from the event organizers to shoot and publish video on your vlog. In some cases, you may need press credentials to shoot video, or a special waiver from the site's A/V union. A lot of videobloggers don't bother, but you'll have to judge the risk of not asking for permission against the ramifications of filming without permission *and* landing in some legal hot water. Public events — say, street fairs, rallies, and block parties — are fair game when it comes to filming, and public servants and political figures are not only fair game, they legally cannot *prevent* you from filming them in public.

Once you've settled any permissions issues you might have, get your camera bag in order. In it, you should have the essentials:

- ✔ Event tickets, passes, or press credentials, if necessary.

- ✔ Your camcorder (of course).

- ✔ Enough tape (other storage media) to cover the event, plus a little extra in case you lose a tape or find something to record on the way home.

- ✔ A spare battery for your camera, or your charger, and test the battery in advance to make sure it's fully charged!

- ✔ A small stack of release forms for interview subjects. (Chapter 15 has examples.)

Some nice-to-have items:

- ✔ Business cards that have the URL for your vlog. When people come and ask you what you're doing, you can give them one of your cards. A nice, professional-looking card can be reassuring.

- ✔ A tripod or monopod. This is actually more necessary than optional.

- ✔ An external microphone, if you have one (see Chapter 3).

- ✔ Your camcorder's user manual.

- ✔ Your interview scripts, if you plan on interviewing people.

When you've checked your gear and packed your bag, head off to the event!

Whenever you have a crowd of people, there are certain things that are easier — or harder — to shoot than others. Usually, it's very easy to find something to shoot — just look where everyone else is looking. Unfortunately, it's also harder to get a good shot. If you've ever been the person standing near the back of a crowd, trying to get on tiptoes just so you can see over the mountain masquerading as a human being in front of you, then you know what I mean. (Unfortunately, a lot of my event footage shows the backs of people's heads, with the audio of the event, or of the crowd.)

If you don't want your events to look like you've suddenly developed an interest in the backsides of people's hairstyles, you'll need some height. Ideally, you want to be at about the same height as the stage, or about a foot taller than everyone else in the crowd. This means you need your camera to be about 6½ to 7 feet above the ground.

Now, granted, there are some folks who are naturally gifted in this regard, and who tower over a crowd like, well, a tower. As envious as I am of their natural vlogging advantages, I do not have this particular advantage, being five-one in stocking feet. If, like me, you're not so gifted in the height department, you can carry a stepstool or (if you're really short) a small stepladder with you to events. Although this is conspicuous, you will find that professional videographers and photographers use stepladders all the time to gain a bit of height over the crowd.

Another tactic is to find nearby landscape features to stand on — those that *don't* have signs saying "Don't Even Think about Standing Here" (or equivalent). Some likely candidates are building steps (if they're available), retaining walls, or even the bases of columns and architecture. Just be careful not to fall and hurt yourself, and be aware that your camerawork will be shakier than normal if you have to hold onto a camcorder *and* a light pole while you work.

A tripod or monopod can also help you out. Some tripods can be set up to be taller than an average person's height. The disadvantage to a tripod is that the taller a tripod is, the wider its base must be. That means you'll need to clear more space in the crowd, and be wary of passers-by walking into your tripod supports. A monopod won't be as stable as a tripod, but the advantage is that a monopod's one leg takes up much less space in a crowd. For filming in a crowded event, you cannot beat a monopod.

The quick-and-dirty method of elevating your camcorder, of course, is to just press record and hold it over your head. You usually can't see the shot very well, and the tendency is to tilt the camcorder lens upward, rather than down. If elevating your camcorder in order to catch an event on a stage, hold the camcorder level. The lens will be close to stage level, and you won't need to adjust. If you need to catch action on the ground, your best bet is to climb onto something so you can actually see what you're doing — it's very difficult to hold the camcorder over your head and aim it up or down accurately.

Just be careful when holding the camcorder over your head. If you use the LCD screen to watch what you're filming while your head is tilted back, it's easy to get dizzy!

Providing voiceovers

A *voiceover* is nothing more than audio commentary superimposed over a video track. You can record the commentary while you shoot the video, or you can dub it in later, using your video-editing software.

The advantage to a voiceover is that you can give your vlog a personal touch, while still staying off-screen and out of the camera view. If you are a particularly nervous person in front of the camera, this can be an excellent way to mitigate your nervousness.

You can also do a voiceover without needing a tripod or assistant to hold the camera for you.

Since you can record a voiceover after you shoot the movie, it's a great opportunity to add comments or details that you forgot to narrate — or, in some cases, fix a bad audio track. I've done this, for example, when a couple of words were mumbled or garbled during recording.

In iMovie, you have a few audio options for voiceovers:

✔ You can use the audio from the video, which you can extract if you want to have a voiceover that goes over other video in your clips.

✔ You can import a sound track, perhaps something you recorded separately, from iTunes.

✔ You can record directly into iMovie. Figure 7-1 shows the audio tracks in iMovie.

Figure 7-1: iMovie lets you record and manipulate additional tracks over the existing audio.

Windows Movie Maker has a similar feature, and it even has a Narrate Movie option in the menu to let you quickly record from a microphone connected to your computer.

Going "gonzo"

Back in the 1970s, the late, great Hunter S. Thompson fathered a style of participatory journalism in which the cameraman was also the interviewer. This style of camerawork is called *gonzo* (no official relation to the Muppet), and now refers to any kind of camerawork in which the cameraman is somehow an active participant in the scene. When you see a sitcom where the actor suddenly turns to the lens and says something to the audience, that's a *monologue* or an *aside,* a dramatic form that's been around since before Shakespeare. But when the camera moves as if shaking its head, or the cameraman talks back or participates in the action, then it's gonzo.

Because the built-in microphone on a camera is closer to the cameraman's mouth than the interview subject's, you'll want to invest in an external microphone if you decide on a gonzo vlog.

You can use gonzo techniques when making your vlog entries. In fact, you can make your whole videoblog a gonzo experiment, where you go out in the world and interview people or play silly pranks (harmless ones, please), without ever showing your own face on-camera.

Gonzo camerawork is also frequently used in the adult entertainment industry, so searching for gonzo movies in a search engine can land you at some explicit Web sites. If that wasn't what you had in mind — or if you have some budding vloggers in your brood who don't need to see that stuff — you may want to adjust your browser's parental controls accordingly.

Working with Other People in Your Vlog

Unless your vlog is a video diary, where you simply record yourself, you're likely to record other people in your videos. The following sections provide tips about how to approach and work with other people when you're recording for your vlog — whether they're interview subjects, paid actors, experts, enthusiasts, and any other talent you might use in your vlog to make it interesting.

Finding actors

You can find actors through many avenues. First, of course, you'll probably ask your friends and family to participate in your videoblogging adventures.

Some won't be particularly keen to do so, and you should respect that. But others will leap at the chance to do silly things on-camera. Encourage that, but don't expect professionalism from your volunteers. After all, if you want them to be professional (strictly speaking), you have to give them something in return.

Another way to find actors is to advertise for them. It's helpful if you can offer an incentive — say, money — to your actors, which means you'll either need to bankroll some actors (in addition to your bandwidth, hosting, and camera equipment costs) or start asking for some revenue sources.

If you hire an actor at a rate that's reasonable for your location, you can reasonably expect the person to be somewhat professional. He or she should show up and do what you say to do (within limits). If your hired talent offers creative suggestions, that doesn't mean you have to adopt them every time. It's best not to expect the talent to be up to speed about vlogging, though it's cool if they are. Actors have a broad range of talents, but what you pay for is their delivery of your message. If you're putting together a vlog with a targeted message — say, a public-service announcement, or a vlog entry that tells people about your company's services — then hiring actors may be the perfect way to deliver the goods.

Finding and working with experts

However, there is also a source of free (or cheap) on-air talent that you can pursue. Okay, maybe you can't count on them being the best public speakers, but you *can* count on them knowing a lot about their subject matter. I'm talking, of course, about experts and enthusiasts.

An *expert* is someone who is highly knowledgeable about a particular subject matter, and has usually undergone specialized training to become a professional or an authority in a chosen field. Frequently, it's someone's life's work, usually a career, that produces that kind of knowledge. In the technology industry, you'll find experts in engineering roles, IT, and programming. In medicine, an expert would be a doctor or specialist, or a nurse with many years of experience.

Non-experts gravitate towards certain experts and ask their opinions because the knowledge the experts have is so specialized, and the non-expert doesn't even know where to begin to learn about the subject. Ask any doctor or lawyer, and they'll tell you that the most dreaded words they hear at a party aren't "The dog ate the hamburgers" but "Let me get your expert opinion on . . . "

For some of the more specialized professions, giving an expert opinion on a general or hypothetical situation is impossible — either because the expert doesn't know the details and so can't fully evaluate it, or because doing so will put the expert in legal jeopardy. This is why you hear a familiar disclaimer so often hear on medical call-in shows: "Go see your doctor." The expert giving the opinion knows when a hands-on evaluation is required.

However, when you do an interview with an expert, you can still learn a lot about that person's subject. You can ask about the types of misconceptions people have about the subject matter, and what's most enjoyable about this particular field. You can ask an expert to detail a process or procedure — for the technology experts, this is a particularly fun question, because they tend to be process-oriented problem-solvers.

You can find experts in the phone book, through speaker's bureaus, at professional organizations, in *Who's Who,* and in other directories of experts. In fact, you can find regularly updated directories for the legal and news industries if you want to locate expert witnesses, analysts, and spokespersons (and one good place to look is www.experts.com).

Finding and working with enthusiasts and fans

An *enthusiast* is generally someone who has a lot of interest in but less direct experience with a subject than an expert. An enthusiast may pursue a topic as a hobby, or may be starting out in the field and still learning. Frequently, the difference between an enthusiast and an expert is education and experience. An enthusiast may be a terrific pianist, for instance, but be unable to read sheet music. While such a person is still a fascinating subject to interview, usually you can't get a broad overview (or pro-level details) of the field in your interview. But enthusiasm is contagious, and that can make it fun.

You'll find enthusiasts at club meetings, events, classes (often taught by experts), sometimes even on the street or in cafés. I live in the kind of town where it's common to walk past musicians performing on the street. Without knowing whether they're experts in music, I can always tell that they're enthusiasts — because why would they put themselves out there like that if they didn't genuinely enjoy it? Interviewing a street performer is an excellent way to learn about performance art forms.

Although experts will sometimes expect a fee for an interview, real enthusiasts or hobbyists generally wouldn't think of it. If they're just starting out, or if the subject matter is just something they love, Internet exposure alone is a pretty good payoff. Frequently enthusiasts are more interested in spreading knowledge about their passion than getting paid to do so — and nothing spreads the word faster than a few hundred viewers watching them do what they love.

When you interview enthusiasts, ask them about how they became involved in this passion, or what they like best about it. Here is a great way to get them to open up, because the passion they feel will come through.

Interviewing the person on the street

You can also put everyday people on-camera. Not experts, actors, or enthusiasts, but what journalists used to call "the man on the street." You may have a local newspaper that offers some kind of street talk segment where interviewers poll local residents and ask them all the same question to see what kind of a variety in responses they'll receive.

You can do the same thing with a video camera, of course. Just walk up to a stranger, introduce yourself, and mention that you're filming for an Internet videoblog, and you wanted to ask this person a question. At this point, you may need to have a 10-second elevator speech prepared about what a vlog is (see Chapter 15 for help with preparing that). If the interview subject agrees to help, just turn on the camera and ask the question. Film the response, and you're done. Make sure you get the interview subject's name, so you can include it in your credits.

Get an on-air release or signed permission form from your interview subject. More on releases, including on-camera permissions, in Chapter 15.

Public events are another venue in which you can do these kinds of interviews, and you can use them to spice up event footage visually.

The best kinds of questions to ask are ones that don't have an easy or obvious answer. For instance, if you ask someone "Hey, how are you feeling today?" the chances are you're going to get a very bland answer: "Fine." But if you ask "How do you feel about the Patriot Act?" or "What do you think about the decision to close off this street to car traffic?" then you'll most likely get a broad variety of opinions and reactions.

Sometimes your man-or-woman-on-the-street won't know anything about a particular issue — for instance, your subject might not have known there were plans to close off the street at all. If that's the case, just state simply and factually the situation, and let the person give an opinion, but make note that this opinion was formed on the spot, and may not reflect the person's more considered views — in such cases, you may end up not using the footage.

Note, however, that if *everyone* confesses ignorance, you can turn the story into one about a lack of knowledge — perhaps even a lack of publicity about the issue. At that point, the ignorance of your fellow citizens, though a little discouraging for the civic-minded, becomes a symbol of the breakdown in communication between those making decisions and those who have to live with the consequences. (See? Even stuff that isn't there can be useful.)

Prepping your actors or interview subjects before shooting

Once you have your actors and interview subjects lined up, you'll want to review with them — *before* you press the Record button — what you plan to do.

When you work with actors, you give them a script in advance and ask them to act it out. It's helpful to offer cues for movement, but let the actors naturally find their own gestures and body language. If you force a particular way of moving onto an actor, the result may look unnatural and stilted. The actor may have questions to ask of you — what kind of microphone you're using, where the lens is, that sort of thing. If you've hired the actor, chances are you've done an audition or screen test in advance and know how confident the person is on-camera. If not, trust me, you'll find out.

When you interview non-actors — whether they're experts, enthusiasts, or ordinary folks — you have to explain more, but you don't have to write out a script or give direction on where to stand or walk.

Making people comfortable on-camera

You're not the only person who suffers from stage fright! When you interview a nervous subject, try to make the person comfortable by speaking calmly, and by taking your face away from the camera's viewfinder to make occasional eye contact. (Remember to smile encouragingly.)

If your interview subject freezes, don't hesitate to put the camera down and help the person recover. Your videoblog (for that matter, anybody's) is not so cosmically awesome that you need to give someone a panic attack! Show compassion for your interview subject, and hopefully you'll be rewarded not only with a swift recovery, but also with responses that show greater ease and confidence.

It is all right to capture a genuine emotional response from a subject, such as tears or laughter, but be sensitive to your subjects' feelings when you go to post the entry to the Internet. Check back with your subjects; explain that you love the honesty they conveyed, but you don't want to embarrass them. If someone is highly embarrassed, offer to edit the stronger emotional response toward something a bit more decorous. Frequently, the simple act of editing lets the viewing audience know that some kind of private moment was removed from the vlog — and that you respect that privacy.

Explain whether you plan to join your subject in the camera frame, or whether you'll be holding the camera while you interview. Tell your subjects where to stand. Tell them whether you want them to pause before answering a question (useful if you plan to film yourself asking the questions later and then editing the clips together). Tell them if you'll be introducing them first, and what you're using for audio (an external microphone, or the built-in microphone on the camera). Here's an example of the type of explanations and instructions you may give an interview subject:

> Okay, Bob. We're all set for the interview. If it's all right with you, I think it'd be good if you were standing in front of your T-shirt stand, because it's so colorful. Don't worry about the sign — I'll get footage of it later, and we'll make sure the URL gets into a subtitle. I'll put the camera on the tripod and join you, and then I'll start asking a few questions about the T-shirt stand and how it all got started. Pause before you answer so I can turn the microphone toward you; otherwise the sound won't pick up. Are you ready to go?

If "Bob" looks suddenly nervous, offer to get him some water and make sure he talks to you in a normal voice before you start filming. You certainly don't want him to have a panic attack on screen!

Chapter 8

Scripting the Show

I'm a writer by trade, so to me, there's a lot of fun in planning out and writing a script for a videoblog. Telling stories is endlessly fascinating to me, and I love listening to and watching stories told by others as well. But more importantly, I find that having a plan or a script results in a better story overall, and I'm more comfortable when filming. Try scripting a few vlogs by following the advice presented in this chapter and see if planning ahead works well for you.

Establishing a Plot and Setting

Video is a powerful medium for storytelling, for conveying a narrative to an audience. A *narrative* is the most basic form of providing information — it's a story, usually told in chronological order. Aristotle believed a story should have a beginning, middle, and end — and storytellers have successfully stuck to that formula for thousands of years.

A *story* can be any narration with a time sequence and (preferably) some sense of causality. Every narrative, from a children's fable to the lead story on the 6 o'clock news follows this basic structure.

Videoblogs, too, follow a narrative structure. The nature of the video medium is to run chronologically from beginning to end (unless the viewer chooses to rewind) — so it lends itself to chronologically organized narration.

Not all narratives stick to a strict first-to-last chronology. Flashbacks, foreshadowing, and background information are all ways to provide information about the story, but out of sequence to lend suspense, tension, and heighten the audience's interest.

As you plan your videoblogs and think about the stories you want to tell, think about the narration you want to build. Are you telling a story about your day? What's the culminating moment of the story (the climax)? Even though your videoblog will contain a single idea, you can express that idea as a very short narration — and that narration should be as complete as possible.

Deciding on a story to tell

Everyone has stories to tell. Human beings are in part defined by our use of language, and we use language to convey events as narratives. Every moment of your day is a part of your story.

This doesn't mean that every story is arrestingly *interesting*, or that it's automatically riveting to people other than the person experiencing it. For example, the antics of my cat, while fascinating to me, are interesting only to people who like to watch cats doing weird things. (If you're one of those people, browse over to Vlog Cats at `http://vlogcats.blogspot.com`.)

On the other hand, the news headlines contain many interesting stories (and a few duds), and they're interesting because they somehow affect our lives, or engage our imaginations. For instance, celebrity gossip and news is interesting because celebrities engage the imagination — people like to imagine what a celebrity's life is like, and how they themselves would act in the face of fame and fortune. Political news, on the other hand, is interesting because it affects our lives, by changing the nation in which we live.

Here are some examples of stories you could tell with a videoblog:

- ✔ For a personal vlog, tell (or show) an important event in your life, or a memory of an historical event.
- ✔ Also for a personal vlog, show a relatively unremarkable event that you enjoyed anyway, such as an afternoon at the park with your kids.
- ✔ For a technology vlog, explain how to do something technical and challenging.
- ✔ For a professional vlog, show snippets from your day at work.

Every videoblog entry tells a story, even if you don't intend it to. I've seen vlogs that I interpreted as one story, when other people wouldn't see it that way. Your viewers might read into your vlog a story that you didn't intend to put there.

Structuring a plotline

A *plot* is the basic building block of a narration. Plot determines the action of a piece — what happens first, what happens next, and how it all ends. For many people, plot is a very challenging part of the story, because it seems like it's the most contrived piece, but many people feel that if the plot isn't strong, the story will collapse.

Nothing could be further from the truth, however. Plot is only one component of your story, and even a basic plot can yield a compelling narrative. Take, for instance, the most basic love story: "Boy meets girl, boy loses girl, (optionally) boy finds girl again." This love-story plot has been used in nearly every great romantic story, from *Romeo and Juliet* to *Casablanca* to *Pretty Woman*. It is a very simple plot, yet all the complexity arises from the question *how?*

That one factor, *how?,* is what makes plots work. Viewers generally know how a story will end — if it's a drama or a tragedy, it will end unhappily for the protagonist. If it's a comedy or a romance, it will end in some positive way for the protagonist.

How also works to tell nonfiction stories and instructional narrations as well. For instance, if you make a videoblog entry about putting together a stereo system, and your videoblog just shows the cardboard box the stereo arrived in, followed by the stereo already put up, then your audience will get a very bare-bones story — a beginning and ending, but no middle. But if you film yourself putting the stereo together, complete with swearing and running out to the hardware store for the right cables, then they have a fuller sense of the story — they have the how.

You can even ask the question in reverse. It's not uncommon to have a lot of footage but no idea what story to tell with it — I find this is common when I've taken a camera with me to a party or for a day outing, such as to the beach. If you look at the footage, you will know how the plot unfolds, and you can determine then what plot you have in front of you.

A classic plot: The hero's journey

The hero's journey (or hero's quest) is one of the most basic plots in storytelling. It's the archetype plot, the stuff of legends, the backbone of most Western literature. It was analyzed and systemized in Joseph Campbell's book *The Hero with a Thousand Faces*. The hero's journey lends itself to stories that capture the imagination — and has for thousands of years.

Movies use the hero's quest plot heavily, bringing to life the legendary quests of everyone from Neo, the hero of *The Matrix,* to Frodo from the *Lord of the Rings* trilogy, to Flik, the hero of *A Bug's Life*.

The basic plot of the hero's journey is likely to look really familiar:

1. **The call to adventure:** The hero receives notice that everything must change.

2. **Refusal of the call:** The hero may refuse the initial call.

3. **The helper appears:** Some kind of assistant, in the form of a mentor or supernatural being, appears.

4. **The first threshold:** The hero crosses from the known world into the unknown.

5. **Initiation:** The hero undergoes a series of tests and meetings, usually in a series of three, which test and strengthen him.

6. **Ultimate boon:** The hero achieves the original goal of the quest.

7. **The return:** The hero returns to the previous world with the boon. Sometimes, he returns as a conqueror of the world of adventure, sometimes he refuses to return, he may have difficulty retaining the knowledge or wisdom from the adventure world, and sometimes he returns after being rescued.

If you are thinking about some kind of basic plotline for a videoblog, and you want to play on this structure, you could create a vlog detailing your heroic quest for a particular brand or type of potato chip — you set out on the quest, driven by your roommates or spouse (perhaps you even refused the call to adventure?), get in the car, overcome many obstacles, such as traffic and construction, to arrive at your destination. You are vexed by the absence of the favored brand, and must seek out a different store. Finally, at the third store, you achieve the ultimate boon — the desired potato chips! You set out to return, but here you encounter the final obstacle — will you successfully make it home with the potato chips, or will you instead eat them on the way home, returning empty-handed?

Granted, this is a silly example, and yet if you've never had this kind of mundane adventure, you probably have very accommodating taste buds. It's an adventure story that many viewers would sympathize with, and if you tell it well — and deliberately acknowledge the humor of using the same storytelling structure for your trip to the grocery store as Homer used for *The Odyssey* — then you will have the kind of vlog post that people really enjoy.

I'm going to use this example in the rest of this chapter, and I invite you do make your own vlog with a similar structure. You can change it around, too — the chips might be some other quest item, such as cheesy popcorn, a particular drill bit from a hardware store, or a grain of sand from an exotic beach.

Nonfiction plots

Nonfiction videoblogs — such as educational, historical, family video, or news vlogs — should also follow some kind of narrative structure. It's not uncommon for videoblogs to have a kind of unstructured, disorganized feeling to them, but looking carefully at your video and deciding on the plot will help you edit your vlogs down to the essential storyline.

Most nonfiction videoblogs tell a story in a chronological format. They start with the beginning and work through to the ending. Some vlogs, however, may change that around, using scenes or narration out of sequence to build or release dramatic tension.

For instance, it's common in news reporting to start with the ending — the outcome ("Alaska school back in session after scare") and then backtrack in time to explain the circumstances (". . . fifteen students were arrested after planning to disable the school's power and phone systems prior to an attack . . ."). This style or reporting comes from print journalism, in which the first line of the story is frequently the only thing a reader might read, so it must contain the entire story in a few words.

An historical videoblog, such as a personal history vlog or an educational video, might skip around in time. Since history has a known outcome, it's acceptable to acknowledge or reveal the ending early on (through a summary) and then fill in the background story.

Any process or procedural videoblog, such as a how-to or a cooking show, should always present the steps in chronological order. Since someone attempting to repeat the process has to follow the steps in order, if you present them out of sequence, your viewer won't be able to repeat your results. In how-to vlogs, the purpose of the vlog is to teach someone else how to do something, so repeatability is not only acceptable, but very important.

A plot in parts

You don't have to put your whole plot into one vlog post. If you want, you can break up a plotline into multiple posts, a sequence that viewers can download and watch one after another. In television, this is called a *story arc*. Most of the time, if you subdivide a larger plotline, the divisions will be smaller plots, self-contained with a beginning, middle, and end (though the end can be ambiguous, as with a cliffhanger).

If you have a story arc in progress, keep in mind that your audience is very likely to watch them out of order — so if the next vlog entry builds on the last one, try to make it clear in the vlog or the text of your post that your viewers should see the vlog before it. If it doesn't take a lot of time, you can also have a "previously on this vlog" series of clips at the beginning of your post. If you do that, however, remember that every second takes bandwidth, and try to respect your viewer's bandwidth and time as well as your own.

Storyboarding your plot

Here's where you get a bit farther into the storyboarding mentioned in Chapter 1. A *storyboard* is an outline of a plot, usually containing not just the story, but the series of shots you want to capture to tell that story.

Storyboards come from movie and particularly animation, and they frequently look like a comic strip; they consist of a series of drawings or sketches of how the director imagined the film unfolding visually.

Remember that a storyboard is to your video what an outline is to a book. It's just a bare-bones sketch of what you want to see in the finished product. Your drawings don't have to be particularly good or detailed — stick figures will do. You can even use clipart, if you're more comfortable that way, to place characters in the composition.

To create a storyboard, you'll need to have a general idea of your plot and script, your setting, and your characters. For the example below, we'll use the potato-chip quest mentioned earlier in the chapter.

When you have a plot, script, setting, and characters already, or at least a good sense of them, follow these steps:

1. Take a blank piece of plain, unlined paper and draw a series of boxes on it.

   The boxes should be about three inches on each side. Leave an inch or two below the boxes so you can write notes.

2. Write **opening credits** below the first box. You'll run the opening credits, if you have them, over the scene.

3. Draw your protagonist (a stick figure is fine if you're not great at drawing), and start off right away with the call to adventure.

   Below the box, you can also note which part of your script outline will be in this scene.

4. As soon as you switch settings or introduce a new character, move to a new box.

5. When you want to use a particular camera angle, storyboard it. This will help you find the angle later on when you start filming.

6. As the action speeds up, use more boxes.

7. The last two boxes are the story's climax and the denouement. See Figure 8-1 for an example of a completed storyboard.

Open Sequence:
At home. Kitchen. Roommate
wants chips.

Roommate begs for chips,
blackmails.

Driving to store.
Camera: Outside the car.→

→ Also wheel/driver-
side angle-
try both ways.

Grocery #1

Chips shelf, empty!

Grocery #2

No chips!

Get a helper:
Store manager

Grocery #3

Chips! (Checkout)

Driving back, thinking........

Figure 8-1:
You don't
have to be
an artist to
make a
storyboard.

About the roommate,
lounging around......

........Maybe.........

(Black) "Crunch"

The *denouement* is where the story releases tension after the climax. It's the hero returning from the quest, or the end of the sitcom episode where everyone stands around and laughs stupidly. In the potato-chip-quest outlined in this chapter, the denouement lends a bit of tension, perhaps even leading into a larger story arc, as the protagonist struggles with whether or not to eat the chips on the way home. If the outline had the protagonist returning to the house with the bag of chips, the denouement would completely defuse the tension, which is also a good ending. When you have had a very tense storyline (as in an action/thriller story), releasing all the tension brings the audience all the way through catharsis and returns them to emotional stasis. According to Aristotle, that's a good goal for any narrative.

To use the single-frame storyboard template provided on the Cheat Sheet to this book, just slip it under your paper and trace over it to make a frame and text lines. Or cut out storyboard frames from a piece of cardboard and keep it with your videoblogging notebook to quickly trace the lines.

Writing the Script

The script is another tool mentioned in Chapter 1 for creating good, well-organized videoblogs. Even though a script may feel confining at first, it's an excellent tool for getting the words to flow smoothly (believe it or not).

Developing a scene outline

A scene outline is a basic written description of each scene in your vlog, and what happens in it. For instance, the scene outline for the potato chip quest might look like this:

1. Roommate asks the hero for potato chips, specifying brand and flavor. Hero refuses, but is strong-armed into going out to get them.

2. Hero gets into car. Driving sequence: traffic, construction, slow-moving vehicles, and so on.

3. Grocery store #1: Chip aisle has nothing even close to desired chip.

4. Grocery store #2: Chip aisle has something similar, but not quite. Include interview with store manager asking about desired chip brand.

5. Grocery store #3: Victory! Checkout line montage.

6. Driving home with chips. The dilemma of to eat or not to eat is presented.

Writing a line-by-line script

A line-by-line script is a very good way to get around a lot of problems that come from spontaneous speaking and improvisation. A script means your speakers are less likely to say "um" and "ah" when they're nervous, and it means you can carefully construct the words used in your videoblog.

However, a line-by-line script is hard to deliver naturally. Most amateur actors (meaning most videobloggers) can't read a script and convey spontaneous emotions (like surprise) without seeming wooden. A script, therefore, is useful when you don't want your emotions to come out — for instance, when you're reading news headlines, or when you're giving a lesson.

In film, a script does not typically include a lot of stage direction, and it has no description. For this reason, scripts tend to be much shorter than, for example, a novel of the same content. This is also a major difference between a script and a scene outline or storyboard: The scene outline tells you what happens and when; the storyboard usually provides more visual detail for where the actors move and where the camera should be.

Scripts do contain the setting information, and may include a summary of some of the action. It is also common to abbreviate characters' names in a script. Character names are set all in caps, as are the limited stage directions.

An example script from the potato chip quest:

SCENE 1

[OPENS ON VIDEO-GAME SCREEN]

VOICEOVER (VO): I should have known today started out too good to be true. I'd spent the day playing video games, till about four o'clock when my roommate started bugging me.

ROOMMATE (RM): Hey, we're totally out of snacks. Can you run to the store for some white cheddar potato chips?

HERO (H): What? What's wrong with your legs?

RM: Ah, man. My car's totally outta gas. Pleease? I'm totally jonesing for white cheddar potato chips!

H: Arg! No way!

RM: You know, I'm not saying you have to do it, but I'll just remember this the next time your paycheck is late when the rent's due.

H: [GROWLS]

SCENE 2

CAR SCENE, TRAFFIC, CONSTRUCTION

VO: Of course it was rush hour, so I had to go out and fight traffic.

SCENE 3

GROCERY 1.

VO: And of course I get to the store and they don't have the darned chips.

SCENE 4

GROCERY 2.

VO: Nor the next store I tried. Even the store manager didn't know where they would be. I was so frustrated!

CUT TO: STORE MANAGER SHAKES HEAD SADLY

SCENE 5

GROCERY 3.

VO: Finally, I found the chips in the third place I went to. White cheddar potato chips! They're almost worth the drive!

CUT TO: CHECKOUT LINE

SCENE 6

IN THE CAR

VO: But then I was driving back to the house, I could almost smell the white cheddary goodness of the potato chips, and my mouth watered. And I thought about my roommate [CUT TO: ROOMMATE LOOKS DECADENT] lounging around in comfort, playing my video games and just waiting for me to return like a happy little domestic servant, with these delicious chips. And I thought: why? Why do I let him do this? Why am I always the one to get the chips?

FADE OUT.

In this script, the only physical actions defined are the settings and the store manager's action. All the rest of the physical activity is left up to the actors or the director of the vlog. This script also doesn't dictate how to deliver the lines, what emphasis to put on which words, or that the final monologue should be delivered while the speaker is eating potato chips.

A line-by-line script isn't necessary, of course. For voiceovers, it's very handy, because you can deliver the script without having to provide any visual acting — all the emotion is through your voice. When you actually have to be in front of the camera, however, you won't always be able to read the script — and that means memorizing your lines. Not everyone is good at memorization, so a line-by-line script is not the solution for every vlog.

Creating cue cards and cheat sheets

A cue card or cheat sheet provides a version of the script that actors can use while in front of the camera. Although actors can — and should — memorize lines before filming, cue cards and sheets can help those with less-than-perfect memorization skills deliver lines with greater ease.

A *cheat sheet* contains notes, sometimes a full script, of what the actor must say in front of the camera. It works best when the actor is very familiar with the material, and when holding a piece of paper up to glance at it isn't considered obtrusive. The one format in which a piece of paper is really accepted is the news broadcast. Broadcasters have had that cheat sheet in front of them for so long, no one considers it unusual to see, even when the broadcaster also uses a teleprompter. In fact, since many news programs run live, the cheat sheet duplicates the teleprompter in case of technical malfunction.

A *cue card* is a large card held up next to the camera to help the actor maintain eye contact with the camera while keeping the lines visible to the actor (but off camera) at eye level. The cue card often contains a line-by-line script in very large printed text, which is why you'll frequently see inexperienced actors appear to be *reading* their lines instead of *acting* them (this is common in product advertisements delivered by non-actors, such as sports stars).

When you create a cue card, pay special attention to the ends of the lines and the end of a card. The actor will naturally give a small pause at the end of a line if it seems like a natural phrase, so put conjunctions at the end of lines so the speaker knows there's more coming, and try to put the end of a sentence or phrase at the end of a line. Actors naturally give a complete end-of-sentence pause at the end of a cue card unless it is *abundantly* clear that the sentence continues on the next card. For instance, if the last word on a card is "and," the actor knows to draw out the word until the new cue card is up.

Check out these lines, for instance:

> AH, MAN.
>
> MY CAR'S TOTALLY OUTTA GAS.
>
> PLEEASE?
>
> I'M TOTALLY JONESING FOR
>
> WHITE CHEDDAR POTATO CHIPS!

If the last two lines instead read

> I'M TOTALLY JONESING
>
> FOR WHITE CHEDDAR
>
> POTATO CHIPS!

the actor would deliver it to sound like "I'm totally jonesing, for white cheddar, potato chips." It would sound like the end of the sentence was "white cheddar" until the actor got to the next line.

Building the poor man's teleprompter

Teleprompters have changed how people on television prepare to go on-camera, how they act when they're there, how politicians deliver speeches, and how news broadcasters read the news. A *teleprompter*, at its most basic, is an electronic cue card that scrolls the text of a speech to the actor without needing someone to hold and flip the cards as the actor reads them.

The basic technology behind a teleprompter is to project the script onto a transparent screen, with the camera lens behind the screen, so the words scroll in front of the camera lens. If you read from a screen and it's even a little offset from the camera lens, your eye movement will be noticeable.

Many people have created homemade teleprompters using a laptop computer and a piece of glass or plastic. The basic idea is to take a piece of transparent-but-reflective material (such as glossy plastic or glass) and position it to reflect the text on your screen back to you, as shown in the following figure.

The best position has proven to be to lay the laptop screen flat and put the glass at a 45-degree angle above it and directly in front of the camera. The reflection will appear in front of the camera, so when you or your actor reads the text, it will appear that your eyes make eye contact with the camera — and (therefore) with your viewing audience.

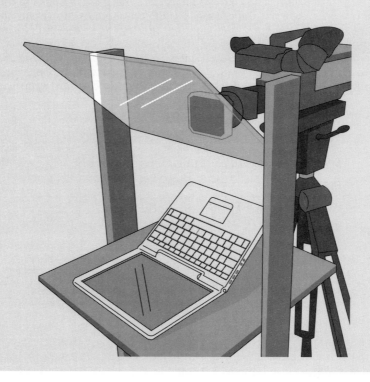

You then use software to flip the text on the screen, so when it's reversed in the reflective surface you can still read it, and enlarge and format it so it's easier to read. If you use your own word-processing program and just use software to flip the screen, you'll want to set the text size to be as large as possible, white text over black, and the column width should be no wider than three or four inches — any wider and your eyes will move noticeably as you read it.

Optionally, you can get scrolling software that will automatically scroll the text down for you. Teleprompter software is available that not only flips your script, but also scrolls for you; this software can range in cost from very inexpensive (under $50) to very expensive (over $500), depending on how many features you need and whether you also need it to play into a commercial teleprompter.

Some resources for building a home-made teleprompter are available at `www. creativepro.com/story/feature/ 22302.html` and `www.wallstreetfree thinker.com/otherstuff/Plasti Prompter/plastiprompter.htm`.

When using cue cards or cheat sheets, make sure to check them before you go on camera to be sure they're in the correct order. Write the number of the cue card on the back of the card. You may also find it helpful to write **FLIP AT (WORD)** on the back, specifying the word or phrase that the cue-card holder should watch for and use as the signal to switch cards. When you're holding cue cards, consider holding one card above the next, and then shifting them around as needed.

Practice in advance with the actor so you both know where the cue cards will be and how they'll be flipped.

Creating a Setting

Setting is a term used in writing and filmmaking to describe the place where a scene occurs. A setting may be as large as a geographical location (say, Paris, France) or it can be as small as the driver's seat of your car. Setting also includes the time of day and, sometimes, the season.

The setting has a huge impact on your videoblog. The setting affects the color, light, and sound that naturally occur in your videoblog entry. Although you can alter these slightly, if you try to film a graveyard night scene at three in the afternoon in a busy playground, your vlog won't be terribly convincing.

Selecting a setting and background

Most of the time, your setting will present itself naturally. You won't even have to think about it — because the setting becomes a major part of the reason for the videoblog.

However, when you have the option to select your setting, take as much care with this choice as you do with others in your vlog.

Look first at the available light — nothing affects your video's appearance as much as light; where visual appeal is concerned, it's the most important factor. The best lighting comes from the sun, but if natural lighting isn't available, a couple of good lamps will do the trick.

Next, open your ears and listen. Is there a lot of ambient noise? If you're filming in your house, is there a television playing in the background, or is the washing machine running? If so, turn off the TV and wait for the laundry to finish up the spin cycle. You want to limit the amount of noise that doesn't contribute to your vlog's content.

Limiting noise goes for visual noise as well. Remember that your videoblog might be seen by hundreds, perhaps thousands of people. That means you might need to do a little bit of tidying up and de-cluttering before turning on the camera. Put away the things you might not want a perfect stranger to see (like a pile of dirty laundry!). Having an uncluttered look in your videoblog will also take the focus away from your surroundings and put it back on your subject — the person speaking.

Filming on location

A *location shoot* is one for which you deliberately seek out a specific place as your setting, whether it's integral to the vlog content or not. Any time you need to go out to a new place for your vlog — such as to a convention center for a trade show — you're shooting on location.

When you shoot on location, you have less control over the lighting, noise, and clutter. Convention halls may be lit with fluorescent lights that wash out the faces and cause electronic noise in your equipment — and you may have to deal with a lot of babble and noise around you. A beach has the surf noise, something you simply cannot block out.

Look for ways to minimize the negative effects of the setting, by (say) moving into a hallway if the nearby noise is too loud, or by turning the camera so the microphone points away from the crowd. But don't neglect to include your setting's unique features in your vlog as well. If you vlog on the beach, get a good shot or two of the surf, and even though you may need to angle the camera to minimize the noise in the microphone, don't try to cancel it out completely.

Filming historical locations such as monuments or historic buildings works best when you move far enough away to view the whole structure — even if you also use close-ups and interior shots to highlight it in your vlog. You may need to go across a street or across a yard or park to get the whole structure in the shot.

Getting creative with settings

Use settings in your vlog creatively! Many videoblogs are defined by their settings — perhaps a vlog is always filmed from behind a desk, or perhaps it's filmed in Hawaii with gorgeous views of windswept beaches and bright blue ocean waters.

Spicing up an ordinary room

If you think your humdrum home is a little too . . . well . . . *humdrum* to be creative, think again! Now, I'm not going to get all Martha Stewart on you, but you can be very creative with the space you have to work with.

In addition to cleaning things up around your filming space, look at different ways to get creative with the space. Your background props tell a lot about you, especially if they're used in ways your audience wouldn't expect.

For example, suppose you did a videoblog that looked like it was just you, talking to the camera, occasionally cutting away to a photo or video you shot elsewhere, and then back again. More often than not, the results are kind of . . . ordinary, especially if your only setting for this talking-head shot is your living room sofa.

Now imagine the same vlog, but every time you cut away to a photo or video, something in the background changes when you cut back. Perhaps the photo hanging on the wall disappears and reappears, or gets replaced by something else. Suddenly your humdrum setting seems a little more whimsical and fantastic. What's more, people who watch your vlog carefully will feel rewarded when they realize that something is different!

Similarly, you can use color to set a particular mood or theme. For instance, if your videoblog is usually shot in your living room, you can drape a different colored blanket or sheet over the back of the couch to express your own emotions in the vlog. As viewers get to know your vlog, they'll start to recognize that when the blue blanket is on the couch, it means you're going to rant about something, and if they see the red blanket, they're in for a passionate vlog. Over time, you start finding your key mood colors outside when you take video of different spaces and color-code your footage to different emotional messages.

Liven up a setting

For some vlogs, the setting really is the meat of the vlog. For instance, travel vlogs — the entire purpose of the vlog is to highlight a new and different place.

Unfortunately, unless you are a very skilled videographer *and* narrator, travel vlogs can quickly turn into a boring slideshow of "my last vacation." So how do you liven it up?

Well, you can do something like what one videoblogger did: Where the Hell is Matt (www.wherethehellismatt.com) is the blog of a 29-year-old traveler who posts videos of himself dancing in the strange places he visits in his non-stop travels. Matt has a particular dancing style that looks a bit like someone intentionally tripping over his own two feet. Behind the dancing Matt is usually a landmark or other feature that his video highlights, something to give the video a sense of place (he also uses subtitles for this). In one clip from Kenya, a startled giraffe makes a cameo appearance, running off-screen. When the clips are all put together into one vlog, you realize that Matt has literally danced his way around the world — an impressive feat (and feet!).

Rocketboom mimicked the effect when host Amanda Congden went on a trip to Europe in August 2005. On her return, Rocketboom posted a video of her dancing in front of various sites in Russia, even getting passersby to participate in the dancing. If more videobloggers start dancing in their travel vlogs, it'll turn into an outright fad.

Of course, you don't have to liven up your travel vlog, but it does help to go beyond the landscapes. Bring your camera up to people and talk to them, if they're willing to be interviewed. Video some action, be it a public event or just the local wildlife doing its thing. Capture, if you can, the essence of your visit as much as you can.

Remember that your travel video will be more interesting if you are in it, so don't be reluctant to invest in a tripod (or recruit a traveling companion). And make sure you're in shape if you travel alone, so you can outrun any would-be thieves who might try to abscond with your camcorder while you dance in front of it.

Making common settings distinctive

In the potato chip quest vlog, the hero visits three different grocery stores to achieve his quest, and has five distinct settings (the home, the car, and the three grocery stores). And yet, if I don't pay attention to setting when I film, there will be very little to distinguish Grocery #1 from Grocery #3.

How, then, to make several similar settings distinctive?

- **Film both exterior and interior shots.** An exterior shot will show the name of the store, setting it apart from the previous store.
- **Film a transition scene.** A short clip back in the car en route from store to store tells the viewer that the hero is traveling between stores.
- **Emphasize the differences.** On the inside, a natural-food store looks different from a big chain store. Highlight those differences by zooming in on the organic foods in one, and the junk food aisle in the other.
- **Use subtitles.** It may seem cheesy, but subtitles work for pointing out a change in setting or emphasizing the passage of time.

Using green-screen technology

Everyone is familiar with green-screen and blue-screen technology, even if they don't realize it. When a TV weather reporter stands in front of a digital map and points out where the snow storms are, he or she is actually standing in front of a large piece of paper or a painted wall, usually green or blue. During the production of the video, a video editor keys to that shade of green from the video and makes it transparent in the video. The video of the weather reporter is then placed over the digital map to look like the reporter is standing in front of a dynamic weather map.

The effect is called *chroma-keying,* and many full-featured video-editing programs (such as Final Cut Pro) can do it. Additionally, there are plug-ins for simpler video editors such as iMovie; these provide inexpensive chroma-keying. Plug-ins for iMovie typically cost about $30–50 for a package containing several plug-ins, and you can find a directory of iMovie plug-ins at `http://imovie.pluginsworld.com`.

In digital video, green is used more than blue for this effect, though either is acceptable. The software itself can usually key any color you choose. Reds, yellows, oranges, and browns are never used because they appear in human skin tones, which the reporter or speaker usually has (since extraterrestrials with green or blue skin tones haven't broken into the videoblogging scene yet).

One basic thing to remember is that, if you use a green screen, do not wear green. Anything the same shade as the screen will appear transparent. The effect of having part of your torso appear transparent can range from merely humorous to downright embarrassing.

In the following example, the green-screen effect is achieved through an inexpensive plug-in designed for iMovie. The instructions for Final Cut Pro and Adobe Premier will vary, of course.

To install the plug-in, follow these steps:

1. **Point your browser to the following URL:**

   `www.stupendous-software.com`

2. **Click the Plugins tab at the top of the page, and scroll down until you see the Masks & Composites demo.**

3. **Click the <u>Demo</u> link to download the plug-ins, or purchase the full version of the filter set.**

4. **Unstuff the package and open the folder created (Masks & Compositing Demo).**

5. **Open the OSX folder.**

6. **Copy the SS Masks & Compositing file to your iMovie Plug-ins directory.**

   This folder is under your user home directory, in `Library/iMovie/Plug-ins`. If the folder doesn't exist, create it and then copy the SS Masks & Compositing file into it.

To film a blue (or green) screen and apply the effect, follow these steps:

1. **Get a blue or green screen to film in front of.**

   For this example, we'll use a blue screen. In some programs, you can pick the color to make transparent — but if you can't, contact a photography-supply store for the right shade of fabric or paint. You can also buy a blue or green screen inexpensively online.

2. **Film yourself standing about two feet in front of the screen, as in the clip displayed in iMovie in Figure 8-2.**

   Any closer and you get a reflection from the screen onto your skin, turning your skin blue or green and, after you apply the effect, transparent. Position your lights in front of you and pointing toward you to reduce the amount of reflected green or blue as well.

Figure 8-2:
A clip of myself in front of a blue screen.

3. **Film the background for this clip.**

   Unless you want to be out of proportion to the background, make sure it's roughly proportional to your blue-screen footage.

4. **In iMovie, edit the background and blue-screen clips so they're exactly the same length.**

5. **Put the blue-screen clip before the background in the timeline, as shown in the timeline in Figure 8-3.**

6. **Select the blue-screen clip from the Video FX tab, click the Blue Screen filter.**

   After the filter runs, the blue-screen effect will have been applied to your video.

You can use blue screens to selectively have the background appear behind the screened object. For example, you can use the same shade blue to mask out a window in a picture, and then put your video behind the picture. Though the picture will be still, the video will appear to play inside of it.

Figure 8-3: Place the clips in order in the timeline.

Developing Characters and Dialog

Characters are the people and personas who appear in your vlog. In a typical nonfiction vlog, a character is the same as the person performing — Amanda Congden plays herself on Rocketboom, Steve Garfield is Steve Garfield, and generally speaking, the vloggers are who they say they are.

However, your videoblog may have more characters in it than just yourself. For instance, any time you interview someone, you've added a character to your vlog. Any time people walk into your shot, they've inserted themselves into your vlog.

Selecting speakers and topics that zing

In composing a story, you have plot, setting, and character. Plot and setting can be very simple — *if* you have strong, interesting characters. People who stare blankly at the camera, or who don't have anything interesting to say, aren't great prospects for characters to put in a vlog (and they may be uncomfortable appearing in a video posted to the Internet, anyway).

Portraying people as characters

If a character is someone who appears in your vlog, picking an interesting character should be the most important step in making a fascinating vlog post. After all, the characters make or break any good story.

In a story, you have primary characters, secondary characters, and sometimes tertiary characters. *Primary characters* are the ones with the greatest complexity presented in the story. In a novel, the primary character is the protagonist, often also the point of view character or narrator. In a talk show, the primary character is the host. In a good murder mystery novel, the detective is a primary character, but so is the murderer (even if you don't know who that is until the end).

Secondary characters are the supporting cast. They are usually more two-dimensional than the primaries, but still have a role in the story. *Tertiary characters* are like the extras in Hollywood films, almost a part of the setting — the people who are there so the room isn't completely empty.

In the potato chip quest, there are three characters: the hero, the roommate, and the store manager. The store manager is a fairly uninteresting character — he's a secondary character in the story. The roommate, being the one who introduces conflict to the hero, might be considered either a primary or a secondary character, depending on whether you think the roommate is interesting enough. Most importantly, though, the hero is the primary character, the protagonist, and (at least in the voiceover script) the point-of-view character.

All this talk about characters might have you thinking that videoblogs are the same as movies and TV shows, where everyone is fictional. That's not true in a literal sense, but no matter how true-to-life your actors are, what you get on video cannot capture an entire person; what you have is a partial glimpse — a characterization. Since you can't even present yourself completely on screen, you become (in effect) a character in your vlog, too.

That doesn't mean you have to fictionalize anything, but it's a way of looking at your vlogs as a way to portray a person without having to get all the way into someone's life.

Give the people in your vlog an opportunity to show themselves off by doing interviews, filming them at their hobbies and passions, and becoming involved in their interests. Try to capture them in their most human moments, moments when they're emotionally honest with the world, or where they put themselves on the line, if you can.

Vlogging kids and pets

Children and pets are particularly difficult characters to bring to life. What usually happens is that the videoblogger is emotionally attached to the child or pet and films them, believing them to be the most interesting subject ever.

Now, if your videoblog's main purpose is so your parents can watch their grandkids grow up, then by all means, put thousands of videos of your kids up there — your target audience will be thrilled, and what do you care about anyone else? They're not your audience, so you can safely ignore them.

However, if you aren't emotionally attached to a child (or intellectually curious about early childhood development), watching videos of children toddling around is only fascinating for a short period of time. Watching kids scream their cute little heads off — even less so.

The same is true of pet videos — and I am as guilty as the next person of videoblogging my cat, let me tell you. In fact, one of my first videoblog entries was about my cat playing with yarn. I was amused by the viciousness with which he attacked a toy I'd made for him, so I filmed it, posted it to the Internet, and posted to a Web forum I frequent to ask for some feedback. The feedback I got? "No different from most other cat videos. Credits are longer than the video. Not worth the download." Although I was crushed by this seemingly harsh criticism, I came to realize that it was absolutely true. Although I am completely enamored of my cat, I realize that my audience won't be interested if I obsessively vlog his antics.

Now, both pets and kids do sometimes do things that are unusual and therefore interesting. Sometimes, a pet will have a particular trick, which does make an interesting vlog post. Kids really do say the darnedest things, and when you catch it on film, it's priceless. Look for those opportunities and vlog them. If you have kids and pets, consider these ideas for vlogs:

✔ Dedicate a vlog to your kids or pets — the audience you attract will be there specifically for your subject. (If you don't want strangers watching your kids, make a password-protected vlog for your friends and family to watch — full instructions are in *Building a Web Site For Dummies,* 2nd Edition, by David A. Crowder, and other basic Web site creation books.)

✔ Vlog the milestones, like first days of school.

✔ Vlog the funny, strange, and inspiring moments — say, when your cat demonstrates that it knows how to turn on a light switch, or your son dresses up in his grandma's nightgown, or your daughter launches her first model rocket.

Keep the following tips in mind when you're videoblogging your children:

✔ For your kids, be aware that they do grow up and might not want the "grandma's nightie" video on the Internet for all time. Respect their future — such a video could be painfully embarrassing when the child is a teenager.

✔ Be very selective about where you promote your kids' videoblog — just send the URL out to your family and interested friends.

Being a parent doesn't mean you cease to be interesting in your own right. Vlog your life, including your kids, but don't feel you have to make the kids your vlog's whole focus. Even if it's really your kids' videoblog and not yours, consider developing your own voice in it as well, perhaps talking about choices you make as a parent and your own perspective on your kids' development.

Leaving the script behind

Earlier in this chapter, I talked about writing a line-for-line script. A script is an excellent way to become comfortable in front of the camera, but it's not the only way to create good dialog in a vlog.

Many people find scripts confining. As mentioned earlier, it's hard to get spontaneous emotions from someone who's working from a script, because the words don't come naturally from the actor's heart — they come from a page or teleprompter. Because videoblogs can have both planned and unplanned moments, all mixed together, it's important to honor the spontaneous moments as much as the planned.

You have several options if you decide to discard your script:

- ✔ **Do away with it entirely and just film whatever comes your way.** This approach is useful when you're vlogging an event or occasion, where you can't plan the schedule of the action anyway. People will be conversing naturally, and you are just there to video the moment and put it online later.

- ✔ **Write a script for yourself only.** This approach can be useful when you conduct an interview or want to record a voiceover. Again, other people in the vlog will provide natural dialog, with all its natural beauty and flaws.

- ✔ **Switch to notes, for yourself or others (or both).** Notes, unless they're a full-blown script, give you just a short phrase or sentence to jog your memory. If you were doing an instructional videoblog, you might use notes to guide the lesson. If your interview is planned, you could give the interviewee a chance to jot down some notes about what to say. Or you could keep a couple of note cards in your camera bag for spontaneous interviews, in which you ask strangers about themselves and their lives, and capture the result on video.

Capturing natural (-sounding) dialog

The key to good dialog is relaxed actors and a natural script. *Natural* doesn't necessarily mean *organic* or *real*, though. If you listen carefully to people talking to each other, you will hear a lot of nonsense, a lot of filler words such as "um" and "like," a lot of conversation that fills space but doesn't go anywhere, and a lot of repetition.

Listen to a real conversation from the outside, and you will hear all these little hiccups in the speech of the conversationalists. A five-minute conversation, you will feel, can be captured in 30 seconds of recap.

So, how do you capture natural dialog when real dialog is so hard to listen to? Have the real conversation in advance, and then turn on the video camera. Your actors will have rehearsed the conversation and can trim it down to the bare essentials.

When you do interviews, tell your questions to your interview subject in advance so your subject will have a few seconds or minutes to think about their answers and reply accordingly.

You will find some subjects are more comfortable on camera than others. Some people are just very comfortable on camera, others have more practice talking on camera or on stage, while others have a certain charisma that captures your attention and keeps it.

Filming a reality TV-style vlog

Reality TV has been around as long as game shows, but *Cops*, MTV's *Real World,* and *Survivor* really focused the genre into a more dramatic weekly story.

Most viewers don't realize that reality TV is almost as scripted and contrived as every other TV show out there. The open auditions and nonstop filming make the shows look more spontaneous and organic than they are. But the reality of reality shows is that if the producers want to introduce a conflict, they need only introduce a contest or competition, or place another pressure on their contestants or participants.

In addition, since producers of a reality TV show have thousands of hours of video to sort through, they can pick and choose footage that highlights the story they choose to tell that week, whether that story is the triumph of a country girl over tremendous odds in Hollywood, or a romantic conflict between two unlikely and unwilling roommates.

You can create a reality TV-style videoblog yourself, but you'll need to decide who your participants are, and what format you'll want for your vlog. If you want the *lifestyle* reality vlog — in which you film an unlikely situation (such as a bunch of strangers living in unusual situations) — then you'll need to film a lot of footage in your life. Carrying around a video camera all the time wouldn't be going too far. Setting up several video cameras around your house would be a good idea — just be ready to edit the footage heavily.

Another option is to make a reality vlog that captures the essence of your lifestyle. It's a kind of "day in the life" vlog — either a whole videoblog devoted to that theme, or just an entry in a larger videoblog, if you prefer.

In a reality-style vlog, never try to filter out the "ums" and filler words that you or other people might say. In this kind of vlog, you'll set up the camera and, instead of looking directly at it, you'll look at the other people in your vlog, the people you wish to interact with.

In a reality vlog, keep everything as organic as you can. If you're keeping it real (or close to real), all the advice about scripting, confidence, stage presence, and charisma can safely be ignored. Instead, focus on the *events* that make life interesting, and bring those into your vlog if you can.

Avoiding talking head syndrome

A common problem with new vlogs is the *talking head syndrome.* Turn on any news channel or political talk show, and you will see little else but people's heads while they talk about issues or events. There is no footage of the events they describe, no colorful imagery to go with the heads while they talk.

Okay, sure, when you point the camera at yourself, *you* become the talking head. Sometimes that's all right. After all, your vlog is a reflection of you, and your comments and remarks are a part of your vlog's content. But beware of using too many talking heads in your vlog entries. When someone describes something in your video, see if there's a way you can get footage of the thing they described. After all, a picture is worth a thousand words, right?

When you can get footage of the event that you're talking about in a talking-head clip, consider turning the talking head video into a voiceover. You can do this by extracting the audio from the talking-head clip and placing the audio in the footage clip.

To extract audio in iMovie, follow these steps:

1. **Import both your talking head video and your video of the event, and put the talking head video into the timeline.**

2. **Select the talking head clip and choose Advanced⇨Extract Audio.**

   iMovie extracts the audio, creating a new audio clip in the audio track.

3. **Navigate to the spot in the clip where you want the new video to appear.**

4. **Select the event clip and copy it by pressing ⌘+C.**

5. **Select Advanced⇨Paste Over at Playhead.**

   iMovie will import the video clip on top of the talking head clip without de-synchronizing the talking head clip.

6. **Preview your newly created voiceover by backing up to the start of the clip and clicking the Play button.**

7. **Save your project in iMovie by pressing ⌘+S.**

More editing techniques for iMovie are available in Chapter 10.

Focusing on Good Content

Quality content is the goal of any video producer, whether you're producing video for television, movies, or videoblogs. Good content is defined by what will further the goal of your videoblog in the most efficient or effective way.

Determining the goals of your vlog

I've talked about the purpose of a videoblog. Your vlog's purpose and goals are very similar, though a *goal* should be very identifiable and quantifiable, while a *purpose* might be more generalized.

For instance, if my videoblog's *purpose* is to promote and educate camping and backpacking, then one measurable *goal* of my vlog might be to get five more people interested in and participating in backpacking as a result of my vlog.

If your vlog's purpose is to share your family videos with distant relatives, then a goal of one particular vlog entry might be to get all your relatives to call or e-mail you after they watch it to talk about what they liked about it.

A vlog's goal can help you refine your vlog's message and focus. As you edit your vlog entries, keep your goal in mind and ask yourself — repeatedly — *Will this bit of footage help me reach my goal? Will my audience connect with it?* Similarly, when you get feedback from viewers, you can ask yourself if the feedback comes from someone in your audience, and what it tells you about whether you're achieving your goals.

Limiting your scope to one idea per vlog entry

It's tempting to create a videoblog entry that encompasses multiple ideas. For instance, you might want to make a videoblog about an event — say, a technology convention — in which you take a lot of footage and try to post it to your vlog. You might have lots of video footage showing tech interviews, product highlights, a keynote speech, or even a seminar. Yet if you try to post all those different things, you'll need a streaming server to deliver the hours of video from your videoblog to your subscribers.

Most vloggers, when faced with a lot of video footage, post several shorter vlogs. When you have more than a few minutes of video, try to break it down into one idea per videoblog entry. An idea could be a single interview, one location, one product discussed, one recipe, one kid's antics, one song. It could be a single lesson, a party, or a street fair.

Any videoblog more than five minutes in length may contain more than one idea. Look at your longer vlogs carefully. Can you write down the idea into a single sentence or phrase? If you need more than one phrase ("events at the San Francisco convention center *and* the San Jose Shark Tank"), you should consider editing the video to keep each vlog entry down to just one concept.

Editing to quicken the pace

In addition to narrowing your vlogs into a single idea, you may also need to edit them down for length. A videoblog with a lot of dead time — in which the action isn't moving the story or idea along — is a vlog that needs a bit of editing. Every second — sometimes even fractions of seconds — should be evaluated, each for its contribution to the vlog as a whole.

In some cases, the decision will be easy — cut the video wherever it drags to shorten it. Sometimes, you'll want to cut a part in the middle. Apply a transition (such as a fade) between the edited clips to bring them together seamlessly, or if nobody changes position too much, leave the clips raw and let one clip just run right into the next.

In other vlog entries, you might apply a filter to speed up the video so it appears to go faster (and take less time). You can achieve some great effects by speeding up video. A common way to show the passage of time quickly is to film the changing light or a busy street throughout a day, then speed it up so it only takes a few seconds on the screen.

One way to help speed up your vlog is to think of every second as having a value — and a cost — to the viewer. I use *vlog points* — an arbitrary unit of measurement that roughly means how much content a videoblog has, compared to how long it takes to download. (This emphasis on rewarding your viewers' time gets away from thinking of your vlog in monetary ways, something not all videobloggers are comfortable doing.)

If the cost of an 8MB vlog is 80 vlog points (perhaps 10 per MB), then every second in which nothing happens has a value of only 1 or 2 vlog points, or may even decrease the overall value of the vlog (credits, for instance, while necessary, have a negative value, at least to the viewer's perspective). Every second in which something interesting happens, however, increases the value of the vlog by 5–10 vlog points. When the value of the vlog entry is higher than its cost, it's a good vlog. When the cost is too high, go back to the video editor and keep working on it.

Always preview your vlog before you post, so you can double-check its vlog-point value. It keeps your vlog in tune with your audience.

Part III
Lights, Camera, Vlog!

The 5th Wave   By Rich Tennant

TROUBLE ON THE SET

©RICHTENNANT

All the software in the world won't make this a great film. Only you can, Rusty. Only you and the guts and determination to be the finest Frisbee catching dog in this dirty little town. Now come on Rusty—it's magic time.

We're losing the light, Dad.

In this part . . .

*V*ideoblogging can be a fun — but challenging — undertaking. As you shoot more video, you'll want to learn better techniques for making better movies.

This part covers those techniques, from composition and lighting to sound and editing videos for posting to the Internet.

Chapter 9

Setting Up and Shooting Your Vlog

· ·

· ·

You have come now to the parts of videoblogging that are less about the technology, and more about the art. As a result, you will find in this chapter a lot of advice that you should feel absolutely, 100% free to ignore — a lot of rules that are just itching to be broken (though you might want to try 'em out first).

This chapter talks about deciding what angle and frame to use for a shot, how to move a camera, and how to improve the lighting in your videoblog.

Composing a Shot

Shot composition is one of the sexy phrases that film and art students use to answer the question, *How does it look on camera?* A lot of factors can influence how well-composed a shot is. So here's where I cover the basics of using background, color, and framing in composing shots for video.

Emphasizing or de-emphasizing backgrounds

One of the eternal truths you'll run into when you shoot a lot of video is that human beings are really good at glossing over the backgrounds. For example, have you ever had friends or family members over to your house, and been surprised when they noticed some neglected item in your home (or just some embarrassing dirt or clutter)? And then you realized that you had had that thing there for about six months — and looked at it every day without really noticing it?

People are good at ignoring things that they see too often. Unfortunately, when you open your world to the Internet on video, suddenly you're broadcasting all your dirty laundry (perhaps literally) for the whole world to see.

Sometimes this is a good thing. For instance, if you have a terrific back yard, why not use it as an outdoor studio for your vlog? If it's pretty and you like showing it off, go for it!

But then, some unnoticed details of everyday life might barge in — the pile of unraked leaves, the thistle patch in the back, your old Bronco that you're going to sell when gas prices go down a bit — and you didn't even *see* any of these until you played back the video to edit it. Suddenly, what you thought looked terrific turns out to make you look like the world's worst gardener!

De-emphasizing a background (say, if it's too distracting) is generally tougher than emphasizing the background. If you want to make sure the viewer's attention isn't drawn to what's in the background, you can either control your camera's focus or replace (even remove) the background from your frame.

Showcasing the background

To emphasize a background, just light it up as much as possible. In addition to lighting your subject, stick an additional lamp behind the person, either off camera or on. If you're using a directional lamp, point it at the background.

For outdoors shots, just step back a few paces. If you have an auto-focus on your camera, it will automatically refocus to include the background behind your subject.

When you film outdoors, though, be alert to the sun's location and intensity. Overcast days are excellent for filming, because the clouds even out the sunlight and result in softer shadows. If you have a strong overhead sun, or if the sun is behind your subject, you'll get strong shadows on the face. Bring along a light (even a strong flashlight) and point it at your subject — this is the optimal time to use a camera-mounted light. The light will offset the strong overhead or backlighting and soften the shadows as well.

If you light the background without lighting your foreground subjects, then your subjects will be backlit and will appear more or less as silhouettes, which may be an effect you like. The anonymous informant shot from television is a pretty common technique, and you can use it in your vlogs even if you're not ratting out your crime-boss Uncle Ned.

Blurring out the background by controlling the camera's focus

Depending on your model of video camera, you may be able to control the lens focus enough to blur out the background when you're filming.

You can determine whether your video camera has a manual focus by whether the ring around the camera lens moves when you twist it gently and it changes the image in your viewfinder. If it does, then you have a manual-focus camera. Most people use the autofocus on their cameras most of the time, but if you practice a bit, you can get the manual focus to work in your favor.

If you have a manual focus, first turn off the autofocus feature on your camcorder. Then get as close to your subject as is comfortable, and turn the focus ring until the subject is in focus. Keep turning the ring. With luck, if the background is far enough away, it will start to blur. Start filming when your subject is still in focus but the background is blurry.

If you don't have a manual focus camera, you can still de-emphasize the background by putting as much distance as possible between your foreground and your background. Suppose you have a subject, such as someone you're interviewing. Put the person much closer to the camera than the background, such as a building on the street. Keep the camera close and all the background far away. The camera will focus automatically on the image that dominates the foreground — your subject. Because the background is outside the focal length of the camera, it'll be blurry and de-emphasized — which is fine.

Blocking out the background

The simplest way to de-emphasize a background is to cover it or shoot away from it. You can do this by draping a cloth over the background, by placing a large picture just behind your subject to block out the background, or by turning the camera so that it misses the distractions in the background entirely.

For example, suppose you have a nice sofa where you want to conduct an interview, but the view behind it is your front window — which looks out on your neighbor's garage. If you can't simply close the blinds or curtains, you can prop up a large picture or poster behind the back of the sofa and film close enough to your subject that you don't capture the window behind the person.

If you have a really hard time getting the picture to stay propped, consider investing in a small easel you can attach to the picture and position as needed.

Working with color

Color can be either very important — or not important at all — for your videoblog, depending on how much you care about making your videoblog visually appealing (and that doesn't always mean full color!). For instance, you may not worry about getting the most eye-pleasing shots if the purpose of your videoblog is to give a message or provide some kind of information.

Does that mean color doesn't matter? Of course not! It just means that not every vlog needs to be a Technicolor marvel. Read on for a look at why.

Adjusting color

One of the common issues with videoblogs is that the videos have too much of a yellow or blue cast. Usually, this is because there wasn't enough light when the vlog was filmed, and the camera picked up too much yellow from incandescent lights, or it picked up too much blue from low levels of natural light. Most people who don't do film or photography for a living do not realize how dark the house is most of the time.

The human eye is an amazing instrument. It's better than any manmade lens ever designed — more adaptable, and with much better resolution for all its adaptability than any lens that's been manufactured. Human eyes, combined with our brains, allow us to see in lighting, even for long periods of time, that would be considered too dark by photographic standards.

But this built-in human feature can fool you when you pull out the video camera; amateur videographers and photographers tend to forget that the camera is a lot less adaptable than the human eye is. So you start shooting away, using the LCD as a kind of guide for how it's going to come out. And then, when you look at it later, you're surprised by how terrible the picture looks. It's grainy! It's yellow! It's blue! What happened?

When the picture is grainy, it's because the camera couldn't handle the low lighting; it missed out on some of the data. When it's yellow, it's usually because you're using an incandescent lamp for your light source. The lamp gives a yellow glow to everything you see. When it's too blue, it's because you're using natural light, but the sun has already set — there isn't enough light available to fully saturate all the colors, so you get a kind of blue wash, from the most dominant color in the sky.

So. How do you fix this? Well, first and foremost, have enough lighting when you film! That might not always be practical, of course — a handheld flashlight probably won't be enough, and not everyone can cart around several lamps. Besides — what if you want to keep the footage in spite of the blah colors?

If you've already recorded your video and found that the colors are off because of less-than-ideal lighting, you don't necessarily have to reshoot the video. You can adjust the colors of the video using your video-editing software. iMovie provides a video filter to help you shift the color hue. This adjustment is primarily for shifting the color hue slightly (due to equipment issues), but you can use it to fix the color in a low-light videoblog entry.

To adjust the color in iMovie, follow these steps:

1. **Open iMovie and select the clip you want to edit.**

2. **Click the Editing tab, and then click the Video FX button.**

   In iMovie 5 and lower, this will just be the Effects tab.

3. **From the Video FX menu, select Adjust Colors.**

   The Adjust Colors dialog box appears, as shown in Figure 9-1.

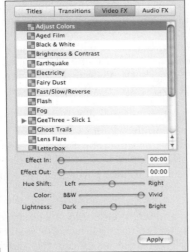

Figure 9-1:
The Adjust
Colors
options.

4. **Select the full range of the clip by using the Effect In and Effect Out sliders.**

5. **Drag the Hue Shift slider to the left or right.**

   Dragging the slider to the left shifts the color to a more green shade (to eliminate the too-blue color cast). Dragging the slider to the right turns it more violet (to eliminate the too-yellow color cast). Avoid drastic color shifts, though; they look unnatural.

6. **Click Apply to add the effect to your video clip.**

When you play or edit the video clip, the color will be adjusted.

Filming in black and white

Remember the good old days of black-and-white movies? Who doesn't remember the corny black-and-white TV advertisements, public service announcements on morality, educational films, and of course the old Westerns?

Monochromatic film has a nostalgic feel to it, like the smell of your grand-mother's shampoo. When you see a black-and-white image, there's a distinct emotional response that, in general, most people find positive. In some cases, like when the black-and-white film is a 1950s-style educational movie, there can even be a lot of humor in it.

One advantage of black-and-white video is that you no longer have to worry about the color appearing too yellow or blue or red. Also, you can really see how much light you needed in a shot if you film it in black and white. When there isn't enough light, the film will be grainy and hard to see.

Another advantage with black-and-white video is that the compressed file sizes can be smaller than a color video, and are therefore faster to download.

Most video cameras allow you to film in black and white, and many of them also have a sepia option as well. However, you can also edit a video into black and white in your video-editing software. In iMovie, you can do this by using the Color Adjustment filter (or Video FX) or the Black and White filter.

If you can't decide between filming in color or monochrome, just film in color and edit it later. The main reason to film in black and white, when you have the option to edit later, is if you yourself, as the creator of the video, need to see the video in black and white while you're filming. Since we're used to watching the world in color, it can be hard to look through a viewfinder and imagine the world in black and white.

If you want to get creative with black-and-white videoblogs, consider doing a whole vlog in black and white. You'll start to notice how color really changes your perception of things. For example, a tree looks completely different when it's in black and white, as compared to its natural shades of brown and green.

Black-and-white video works well for celebrations and special-event videos as well. Consider the effect of a black-and-white video of a wedding, compared to the color version. The color version may be more true to what was actually there, but the black-and-white version lends the affair a more formal feeling.

In addition, monochromatic film tends to de-emphasize backgrounds without a lot of contrast in them. During a family christening event, I took photos out-side the church, on a busy downtown street. I had black-and-white film in the camera instead of color and ended up with some lovely pictures. The cars up and down the street weren't as obvious — or obtrusive — in my black-and-white pictures as they were in the color ones, because they tended to blend into the background.

A creative videographer could even switch between black-and-white footage and full color in the same movie. Try converting (say) your color video of a wedding, baby christening, or similar family event to black and white and see how it comes across to the people who were at the event.

To change a clip to black and white in iMovie, follow these steps:

1. **From iMovie, select the clip you want to edit.**

2. **Click the Editing tab and the Video FX button.**

3. **Click the Black & White effect filter.**

    The Black & White filter options appear, as shown in Figure 9-2.

4. **Select the full range of the video in the sliders.**

5. **Click Apply to apply the filter.**

For the Sepia filter, you also have the option to change the Intensity. This option changes how much sepia tone to wash over the video. The higher the intensity, the more brown the video.

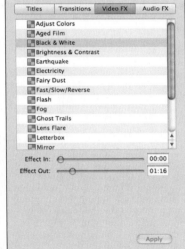

Figure 9-2: Here's where you tweak the Black & White filter.

One nice effect I've achieved in some of my videos is to start out with a black-and-white lead-in, and then switch to the original color footage a few seconds into the film. This little trick gives a classic feel to the movie, but still lets me use color in the main portion of the film.

To switch from a black and white to the color version of a video in iMovie, follow these steps:

1. **From iMovie, select the clip you want to edit and navigate to the spot you want to transition from black and white to color.**

2. **Split the clip at the transition point, as shown in Figure 9-3.**

3. **From the Black & White effect options, set the Effect In slider to 0:00.**

4. **Set the Effect Out to the end of the clip, or any time after the end of the clip.**

   For instance, if the clip is 30 seconds long, set the Effect Out to 00:31:00.

5. **Click Apply.**

When the clip ends, the Black & White effect will automatically fade back to color. If you set the Effect In and Effect Out as 0:00:00 for the monochrome clip, the effect will abruptly switch from black and white to color, without any transition.

Framing a shot

If you're familiar with the old cartoon pose of an artist, holding his or her fingers in a rectangle like a frame, then you're already familiar with one of the basic tools of composing a shot. Really, any frame that you can get your hands on will do, even a rectangle cut out of a piece of cardboard or a blank slide frame.

Figure 9-3:
Split the clip
for the
transition.

The reason it helps to use your fingers or some sort of frame to look through when composing a shot is that human eyes have a field of view of about 140 degrees. A video camera can record roughly half of that — about 72 degrees. So, when you look out at a scene, about half of what you see is left out of your video.

The finger-frame trick lets you quickly cut down your scene into a manageable chunk of visual information. When you look through your frame, you see approximately what the video camera sees.

Unless you plan to hold your camera sideways and rotate your video, hold the frame so it's wider than it is tall.

It's not entirely fair to say that you'll see exactly what your camera sees. To really get an idea of what the camera will see, close one eye and look through your frame. Even though the motion you capture on video helps alleviate it, a video camera only has one lens — it can only take two-dimensional pictures. (If you do make a 3-D video, let me know — and be sure to send me the plastic glasses to watch it!) So remember: Your video will be smaller and flatter than the world you see.

This seems like a no-brainer, so why do I mention it? Because shot composition is all about deciding what to put inside the frame, and how it will appear in your final video.

The rule of thirds

There's an aesthetic rule in photography (okay, one that's broken a lot) called the *rule of thirds.* If you draw lines to create three equal portions of a photograph (both horizontally and vertically), you can use those lines to compose a pleasing photograph. In a balanced photograph, the horizon line should not perfectly bisect the photo. Instead, it should be at a one-third or two-thirds distance from the top of the image. The reason for this is that the eyes are naturally drawn to the center of an image, and the subject of your image will probably be right there — in the center.

If you move the camera slightly, however, you can put the horizon higher or lower — and put your subject in a more balanced image, as shown in Figure 9-4. The horizon line is better put to use as a kind of frame for the subject, drawing the eye toward it. Whether you put the horizon in the top third or the bottom third will also (respectively) emphasize or de-emphasize your subject and the background.

So what does that have to do with videoblogging? After all, a video can move around. It doesn't have to adhere strictly to the rule of thirds. That's true — but if you do stick your camera onto a tripod, look at the background before you walk away. If the background horizon is exactly halfway up the frame, consider tilting the camera slightly to move that line up or down in the image.

Figure 9-4:
Balance the
horizon
using the
rule of
thirds.

But what about indoors? The same principle applies to horizontal lines indoors or even outdoors when they're not the horizon line.

It works for vertical lines as well. In fact, think of any continuous line in your video frame as a potential edge to your frame. Suppose you're filming from behind a tree or architectural column. Consider placing some of the tree inside the camera frame, but just barely visible. It takes space in the video frame, but it also gives the viewer a more voyeuristic sense of the film. You could go even further, and film an entire scene through a window or door frame.

In this aesthetic guideline, a third doesn't have to be precise. You can eyeball it. And of course, not every shot will lend itself to the rule — but keep it in mind as a guideline to aim for.

Keeping hands out of the way

A common hazard in videoblogging, — especially when you want to record a feat of manual dexterity — is that the very hands you try to film get in the way of the shot! This can happen when you set the camera on either side of the subject; many manual-dexterity tasks seem to require two hands.

You can run into this problem in any type of how-to shot, but here are a few other times where hands can get in the way:

✔ Cooking shows

✔ Computer hardware vlogs

✔ Art-making vlogs

✔ Crafting vlogs

✔ Household handyman vlogs

✔ Camping vlogs

If you're filming while someone else is performing the task, you can help ensure that his or her hands don't block the shot if you brief your subject before you start filming. Explain that it's going to feel a little unnatural during the shot, because you need the person to keep a clear line of sight between the focus of the activity and the camera — and to try not to let either hand pass in front of the camera lens.

On very small projects (such as close-up work on computer hardware), this may result in the videoblogger needing to get very close to the subject and film, literally, over somebody's shoulder.

In some cases, the subject will be unwilling to readjust his or her position. That's understandable if the task requires a certain angle (say, to get a wrench on a stubborn bolt), but it's also common with people who aren't enthusiastic about being filmed in the first place. It's also common when someone is just trying to accomplish a task and figures that documenting the task is secondary (at best) to the task itself.

Negotiate this balance of priorities carefully. If you're the only one really interested in recording the experience, and the person performing the task either can't or won't accommodate your camera, then it may be time to find another subject.

You can also change the camera angle. Walk all the way around your subject, if you can, to get the shot, and if possible move the task to a table where you can sit across from the subject to film. In cooking shows, for instance, filming across from the action is just as good as being behind the person doing the task.

Some tasks may be extremely difficult or hazardous to perform without blocking the camera. If the task is simply difficult, try to find another position or angle, and work from there. If it's hazardous to have you there, step back to a safe distance and continue filming. A longer shot in which nobody gets hurt is far preferable to a visit to the Emergency Room.

Don't film a screen! To avoid the unsightly gray bar that slides across a screen when you film a cathode-ray tube (CRT) screen, turn off your camcorder's electronic image stabilization. Or better yet, use a screencasting program like SnapX (`www.snapx.com`) or CamStudio (`www.camstudio.org`) to capture the video and import it directly into your vlog.

Moving Pictures: How to Move a Camera

When you want your video to be steady as a rock, you use a tripod (or, okay, maybe a big rock). But when you can't get the shot you need with a stationary camera, how do you move the camera without getting blurry, shaky video?

Most camcorders nowadays have some kind of built-in image-stabilization feature to help stabilize your video image while you're shooting. These features are almost always automatic — if your camera's moving, they're working. In some cases, image stabilization won't work when you use certain other imaging features on your camcorder — for example, the zoom lens or (if you have it on your video camera) the macro filming lens. In most cameras, image stabilization only goes so far. If you need to run while filming, consider investing in an amateur Steadicam-type equipment, as described in the following section.

There are many ways to stabilize a moving camera. One is to mount the camera on a device that helps keep it from jostling and jogging. Another is to use the camera's built-in software to stabilize the image. Still another approach is to use the camera movement stylistically and deliberately — to make it an artistic choice.

Reducing jostling while moving the camera

A common problem when you walk and record at the same time is a jostling image. It's hard to watch a video in which the image jumps every half second, after all.

The most common reason a movie appears to be jostled is that the human gait is naturally rather bumpy. As people walk, their bodies move vertically as well as horizontally. Because human bodies have adapted to this motion, our brains and eyes adjust for the motion, so we don't find walking or running to be disorienting. When watching such motion on screen, however, you no longer have the physical cues telling you that you're moving, so the image is hard to watch. In particularly sensitive people, it can cause headaches and even motion sickness.

You can reduce the amount the movie jostles by reducing the amount you jostle when you walk. Try to cushion the motion deliberately; bend your knees a little more than normal when you walk with the camera, if you can — or hold the camera low to limit the amount of up and down motion.

You can also reduce jostling by using a device to stabilize the camera. In large production units and television studios, the camera might be stabilized with a wheeled stand called a *dolly*.

In a mobile unit, however, the Steadicam usually attaches the camera to a stand or vest that's been engineered to stabilize a camera of that particular size and weight. A trained operator uses the Steadicam and his or her body to keep the image as smooth as possible. See Figure 9-5.

Professional-grade Steadicams — and operators — can be pricey, though (of course) they offer professional-quality shooting. A typical professional-grade Steadicam can cost thousands of dollars and requires experience, training, practice, and physical endurance to use. Learn more about the professional product at www.steadicam.com.

However, you can build your own amateur Steadicam equivalent for under $20 if you have a few tools and a lot of patience, following the instructions here at the $14 Steadycam Web site: www.steadycam.org. This less-expensive camera stabilizer attaches the camera on a spring-loaded stand with a weight at the bottom. The spring smoothes out all vertical motion; the weight lowers the center of gravity for the camera and keeps it from moving up and down so much.

Figure 9-5:
A
Steadicam.

A similar inexpensive — but lighter — design is the MachoGlide, made by filmmaker Chris Vallone (`www.vtvideos.com/macho.php`), and selling on eBay for $40 to $50, a far cry from the $600 and up needed for a professional stabilizer.

Mounting a camera on your bike or car

Some of the best videoblogs use the most readily available mobile-stabilization devices — a car or bike. Since they're on wheels, cars and bicycles don't have the amount of jerky vertical motion that the human walking gait possesses.

The first and foremost rule of vlogging and driving — or, for that matter, biking — is to always, *always* be safe. If dropping your expensive camcorder on the floor of your car means not getting into a collision with an 18-wheeler, then ditch the camcorder. Fact is, before you set yourself in motion, the best advice is to secure your camera — make it so the act of recording your vlog requires *no more* attention than a conversation with a passenger in the car.

If you're biking, get yourself a tripod mount clamp like the BKA Ultramount (available at `www.bkaphoto.com`) or a C-clamp mount, available online or at professional camera supply stores. These are inexpensive tripod mounts that clamp to your bike's handlebars (or nearly anywhere else). If you want to limit the risk of seasickness in your audience, attach the mount as close to the center of the handlebars as possible, as shown in Figure 9-6, rather than farther out on the handlebar. Doing so also helps keep your handlebars balanced because the weight of the camera is centered.

Figure 9-6: Mount a clamp tripod mount to the center of your handlebars.

For drivers, mount your camera securely somewhere in your car. You can use the same Ultramount as for the bike to attach it to a car door or window, or tie it onto the passenger seat.

Do not put your camcorder unsecured on your car dashboard. In an accident, it will become a flying hazard — possibly lethal if it interferes with the airbag.

To mount the camcorder to your dashboard, use a dashboard bracket to create a basic framework that's secured to the dashboard, and then strap or clamp the camcorder to the bracket. See Figure 9-7. Dashboard brackets for various auto components (like GPS units) can be found in hardware stores as well as online. If you use one, be sure to give the camcorder a firm tug before you start driving. If it moves, resecure the camcorder in the bracket.

Figure 9-7:
Attach your camcorder to the inside of the car.

The All-Important Element of Light

Photo and video and even sight all work on one principle: the collection of light. A photograph is simply a light pattern captured on paper; a video is a sequence of light patterns, captured electronically on a recording medium. Even vision is nothing more than your eye capturing light. All the interpretive work — deciding that a certain pattern of light is a tree, for instance — goes on in your brain.

Basically, when you film something, the direction and strength of the light determines what will be lit in your video. So if your only light source for a video is a table lamp next to your interview subject, then only half your subject will be illuminated.

Lighting with nature

The best light source is the sun. Its light contains the largest range of colors in the spectrum, and it's the most powerful source of light available to the average human being.

However, even the sun can cause problems, when it's harsh sunlight. On a clear day, when the sun is high in the sky (near noon), deep shadows will appear under your subject's eyes. If the sun is low in the sky, turn your subject so he or she has the sun to one side or another, not directly in the eyes and not directly from behind. If the sun is in your subject's eyes, you'll get a squint — which doesn't make very good video. If it's coming from behind, the direct glare from the sun will interfere with your camera.

When filming outdoors on a clear day, look for ways to diffuse the sunlight. Stand under a tree, if you can, or between a couple of buildings. Or wait for a cloud to cover the sun, because the best outdoor lighting condition is a cloudy or overcast day. The clouds diffuse the sun's light without drastically diminishing it; the shadows are softer and nobody needs to squint.

Using your own light

Indoors or at night, you'll need to bring in your own artificial light sources, of course, unless you want to use you camcorder's night-shot (night-vision) or infrared feature. Also, artificial light can help correct for lighting problems, even in the well-lit outdoors.

Lights are usually *directional,* which means they point in a specific direction. There are hundreds of types of lamps you can use for your videos. You can just turn on whatever lights are in the room you're using. You can buy special photography lamps just for your vlog. You can use a lamp from the hardware store that you clamp in place. Or you can use a camera-mounted light. There's even a common photography technique called three-point lighting where you use four lights (three directional lights, plus whatever backlighting is available) to emphasize a subject. Multiple lighting sources soften shadows and make your subjects look more natural.

Any camera-mounted light source that's directly above the lens will cause unnatural shadows on your subject. If you can, find a light that has an extender to move the light away from the camera. Even half a foot of distance makes a difference. You can also use a diffuser to spread the light out more, or gels in front of the light to reduce the light's sharpness or shift its color, or a reflector to direct or amplify a light.

A diffuser is a piece of material which you place between your light source and your subject to soften the shadows cast by the light. The diffuser might be a piece of plastic that attaches to the front of the light, or it could be a piece of thin fabric you place in front of the lamp to cut down the light.

Reflectors direct more light from a lamp towards the subject. You may be familiar with the reflector behind a flashlight bulb — the principle is the same for photography reflectors, though the amount of light involved is usually greater. Figure 9-8 shows a variety of lights, reflectors, and diffusers for photography and video.

Figure 9-8:
Lights, diffusers, and reflectors.

Working around backlighting

The cure to backlighting problems is, of course, more light. Put a light source in front of the subject to solve this one, as shown in Figure 9-9. In fact, backlighting is one of the few cases in which the light from a top-mounted camera light won't look odd. That's because the image already has plenty of light in it, it's just casting shadows in the wrong places. A light shining into those shadows will even out the amount of light overall.

Another option is to turn on a light somewhere off to the side of the subject (also shown in Figure 9-9) — which creates a side-lit subject. The higher contrast with the background gives you much deeper shadows on the unlit side than you'd get without backlighting.

Filming in low-light conditions

The measure of your camcorder will ultimately be how well it works indoors, in the rooms where you most commonly turn on the camcorder, with the lamps you have in those rooms — in other words, in low-light conditions.

Most homes and even many offices have low lighting. It's not usually a problem, because most people's eyes adjust better to low light than a camcorder can. But when you want to record something, you better start looking around for the light sources.

Figure 9-9:
Solving
backlight
with front
lighting and
side lighting.

Start with overhead lights. If you have them, use them. Put the brightest long-lasting bulbs you can find into them to increase the amount of light they put out. Overhead lighting looks more natural because it mimics the light from the sun. White ceilings scatter the light even more, and act as a reflector for the overhead light fixtures.

Next, turn on table and floor lamps if they have shades or are otherwise diffuse. Standard track lighting, for example, is not diffuse — it points and blasts light like a spotlight. A table lamp with a lampshade, however, diffuses the light for softer shadows. Use the table lamps if you don't want your subject to have hard shadows on his or her face.

If you still have lighting problems, consider using any available directional lights . . . indirectly. Point them at a reflective surface (such as a white wall) and bounce the light off the wall to cut the sharpness of the shadows.

Filming at night

Many cameras have a night-vision mode for very low-light situations. In night-vision mode, the camera projects a small (sometimes infrared) light and record the resulting images by that light. Use night-vision mode when you have less light than you would get from two small table lamps set up in an otherwise-dark room. For instance, if you are out at night on a street where you would need headlights, use the night-vision mode there.

Night vision does have some peculiarities, though. In addition to turning the entire image green, the night-vision mode emphasizes highly reflective surfaces. Take, for instance, eyes — which come out looking beady and almost alien in most night-vision shots. It also usually reduces the film speed to gather more light, so it's best reserved for slow-action sequences.

Because of the very specific look of the night-vision mode, viewers tend to perceive this as the voyeur camera, in which the movie is all about snooping on something secret or clandestine, such as a secret rendezvous between spies or a romantic tryst. (I don't have to tell you *not* to go looking for such things in real life without permission, right? Some people get all upset about being watched . . .)

In fact, aside from surveillance videos, night vision is best known from documentaries, like nature shows and military footage; in some cases, it's the only footage available of a particular species of animal. Feel free to reveal the top-secret location of your neighborhood nuisance raccoons, but if you're in the military, I'll assume you have your own set of rules for those videos.

Chapter 10

Editing Your Content

*O*ne of the most exciting parts of videoblogging is taking what you've shot and turning it into something that matches your creative vision. Whenever you shoot a movie, you will find that what you shot does not quite match what you thought you shot, and it needs some refining. If you tend to get a little nervous in front of the camera, you might also find that you had to do more than one take of a scene. That's okay — that's what editing is for.

The instructions and examples in this chapter are for editing video with iMovie on a Macintosh computer. However, many of the same features in iMovie are available in Windows Movie Maker. If you have access to a more professional-grade program such as Final Cut Pro or Adobe Premiere, but don't know how to use it for editing, you should probably pick up *Final Cut Pro HD For Dummies* by Helmut Kobler or *Adobe Premiere Pro For Dummies* by Keith Underdahl, because both programs are more complex than this book could ever hope to cover.

Editing with Your Camera

The first way to edit your film is to simply rewind the tape in your camera and record over any footage you don't want to keep. Of course, this method has a drawback in that you could record over and lose a really wonderful moment that you captured earlier. But rewinding and recording over unwanted footage can save a lot of tape in the long run. In some cases, you might run low on tape and have the absolute best moment of the day sprung on you unexpectedly. It may be a sacrifice, but if the choice is between saving five minutes of a meandering warm-up, and five minutes of absolutely amazing and unexpected video, then tape over the boring stuff.

If you do a lot of rewinding and recording over your digital video tapes, keep the following tips in mind:

- ✔ One common problem with video cameras happens when dirt or lint gets into the tape heads — the moving parts that read the magnetic tape. Investing in an inexpensive tape head cleaner and using it often will help keep the quality of your movies up to par. How often? Well, if you shoot outside the house a lot, try cleaning after every outdoors shoot.

- ✔ Over time, recording over and over on the same tape can result in a few small glitches showing up in your video. Occasionally, your tapes may get out of synch with the timestamp on your camcorder. If this happens, rewind the tape, put the lens cap on, and put it in a dark, quiet room while it records from start to finish without stopping. This will reset the time-stamp data on the tape as well.

- ✔ Even digital tape is still a magnetic medium, which does wear out. If you find the quality of your videos degrading over time, or if you start to get *artifacts* in your videos — say, for instance, frames of older video or just audio or visual glitches — it might be time to retire that particular cassette.

Of course, if you use a non-tape camcorder to record your video as files, whether onto a DVD or a media card, you don't have to worry about tapes tangling or wearing out.

Importing Video into iMovie

Before you can edit your movies, you have to import the video into a video-editing program. *Importing* means to copy the video from your recording medium into your computer.

You can import video into iMovie in two basic ways: by importing the video directly from the camera, or by importing the video from a file stored on your hard drive. Details coming right up . . .

Importing clips from a camera

After you shoot your video, you will need to get the video from the camera onto your computer. (If you don't already have the hardware you need to connect your computer to your camcorder, check out Chapter 3 for instructions, and then come back here.)

Got your hardware in hand? Great! Now, let's get you set up with the software.

To import a video clip from the camera into iMovie, follow these steps:

1. **Launch iMovie and create a new movie, as shown in Figure 10-1.**

   The default title is "My Great Movie," but you can be more creative than that. Rename the new movie by entering a new name in the field and clicking the Create button.

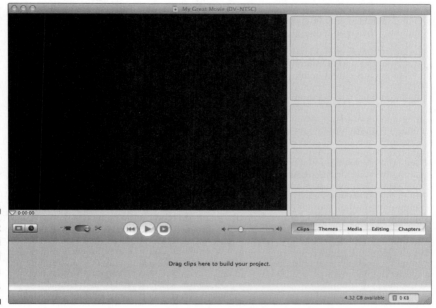

Figure 10-1:
Launch iMovie and create a new project.

2. **Connect your video camera, turn it on, and make sure it's in playback or VCR mode.**

3. **Click the camera icon in the lower-left side of the screen.**

   You see a blue screen with a big Import button in the middle of it.

   Make sure the tape in your camera is rewound all the way.

4. **Click the Import button to start playing the camera and importing the movie.**

   If your camcorder or tape is not digital, you may need to press Play on your camcorder after you click the Import button in iMovie.

5. **After the video is on your computer, click the Stop button or the Import button to stop the camera and connection.**

6. **Disconnect your camera or turn it off.**

Importing from a file

Often, you might need to transfer a video file from your hard drive into your iMovie project. For example, if you use a digital camera to record your video, your videos are stored on a media card, rather than on a tape. This is common with some of the ultra-small camcorders and cellphone cameras as well. Additionally, some video cameras store the video on a DVD or CD-ROM, rather than a tape — in these cases, the video may be stored as a file that you can copy from the disc to your hard drive, or you may need specialized software (included with your camcorder) to retrieve the video.

Fortunately, importing a video file into iMovie is a fairly simple exercise, if the video file is compatible with iMovie's file formats. To import a video file, follow these steps:

1. **Open iMovie and create a new movie project, or open your existing one.**

2. **Select File⇨Import from the menu bar.**

3. **Navigate to the file on your hard drive using the Mac Finder, as shown in Figure 10-2.**

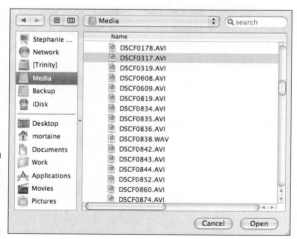

Figure 10-2:
Find the
file on your
hard drive.

In versions of iMovie before version 5, iMovie projects were stored in a normal folder, named after the iMovie project. For example, My Great Movie would be a folder called My Great Movie on your hard drive. Inside, there is the project file, a QuickTime movie file (My Great Movie.mov), and a folder called Media, which contains the unedited versions of your video clips.

iMovie 5 and above (also now called iMovie HD) stores movie projects a little differently than previous versions of iMovie did. The project folder is a special type of folder called a package. As a result, double-clicking a project folder created by iMovie HD will just launch iMovie and open that project.

To open media clips from an iMovie HD project, navigate to the project, and right-click (or Ctrl+click) it with your mouse. Select Show Package Contents to open the contents of that project in a new Finder window.

4. **Double-click the file.**

It will begin to import, which may take some time. When iMovie has finished importing the video file, it will appear as a clip in the clip library, as shown in Figure 10-3.

Figure 10-3:
The imported file in the clip library.

You also might find yourself wanting to re-use a video or clip you previously used in iMovie, such as a video you already shot, or your intro credits or ID tag. You can import these clips via the File menu in iMovie (as described in the preceding steps), or you can drag and drop them into iMovie from the Mac Finder.

You can also drag and drop video clips between two open iMovie projects.

Editing Your Video by Trimming the Excess

Ask a bunch of videoblog watchers what they like in a videoblog, and one of the things you'll hear a lot is "it's short." Why short? Have people really lost all ability to concentrate for more than eight minutes at a time?

Attention spans notwithstanding, there is one advantage to posting short videoblogs, and it has little to do with length. In a short videoblog, every possible second of the video is filled with something valuable and meaningful. To achieve that goal, you absolutely have to edit the video down to the minimum amount of space that still lets you express yourself. The following sections describe how to use iMovie to pare your raw video footage down to a lean, mean — and short — videoblog entry.

As with any creative project, when you're editing your videos in iMovie, it's a good idea to save often. Because iMovie prompts you for a project name when you first start a project, you don't need to give one the first time you save your project. You can quickly save to the same project name using the Mac keyboard shortcut ⌘+S, or select File➪Save. Choose File➪Save As if you want to save the project under a different project name.

Killing your darlings

Many writers are credited with the phrase referring to editing as "killing your darlings," a process of sacrificing the things that you personally love in a work, in favor of a better overall work of literature or storytelling. This is true in writing, it's true in filmmaking, and it's even true in videoblogging.

When you edit your raw footage, start out by simply trimming out the parts that didn't work at all. Remove the clumsy or awkward moments, or when you sound really flustered, and all the shaky, bad camera work that you get when you decide in the middle of filming to put the camcorder on your tripod after all.

To trim video clips in iMovie, follow these steps:

1. **Highlight the video clip in the iMovie clip viewer or timeline.**

2. **Click the Play icon to preview the clip.**

3. **Wherever the action starts, press the spacebar to pause the video playback.**

4. **Select Edit⇨Split Video Clip at Playhead.**

   iMovie will cut the video into two parts at that point in the clip.

5. **Drag and drop the part of the clip that you don't want to keep (in this case, the first part) into the Clip Library or over to the Trash.**

6. **Repeat for the end of each clip.**

7. **Save the movie project by pressing ⌘+S.**

iMovie saves everything in the Trash until you empty it, even if you save the movie project and empty the computer's Trash icon. This means a lot of hard drive space may be used up with iMovie project trash files. When you finish with a video project, empty the trash.

Even after you edit your video as described in the preceding steps, and you think you have perfected your videoblog, you may still find that it's 12 minutes long. What do you do then?

That is when you have to kill your darlings. First, watch your videoblog all the way through. What does it say? What message or story are you telling here? Imagine someone is sitting next to you, perhaps a really belligerent teenager or sarcastic friend, and at the end of each scene, this helpful person says to you "so what?" And after watching the entire videoblog, they still say "so what?"

Now look carefully at each clip, each scene in your vlog. Does it add to your story? Can you tell the story without it? If you can take it out and the story will still make sense, then cut it. Do that with every clip in your story until you have the absolute bare-bones of the story you want to tell. If it's less than a minute long by then, you can add your very favorite clips back in. Otherwise leave it.

Then go find an objective person (or if you can't find one and have a thick skin, ask a belligerent teen or sarcastic friend) and ask him or her to watch your videoblog and tell you if it's too long. Sometimes, a good objective friend is your best critic, because they'll tell you when you've already beaten a point into the ground, just when you thought you were getting started.

Length matters

It bears repeating: The length of a videoblog affects how many people will watch it. For one thing, the longer videoblogs take longer to download, and not everyone is willing to wait. (And then there's attention span, but that's another matter.)

Even though there are many video RSS readers that can download videos in the background, when users aren't sitting at their computers, the fact remains that some people prefer to watch videos on a Web-based RSS aggregator. Or, for that matter, they may be using laptops that inconveniently go into Sleep mode on them when the aggregator is supposed to be downloading videoblogs.

But some people seek out the long-format videoblog — and prefer to watch a longer vlog, if the content is good. Longer-format videoblogs might cover multiple topics in each entry, turning the vlog posts into more of an episodic TV show than a personal video diary or report.

The longer videoblogs currently on the Internet are formatted for television shows. In some cases, they're re-broadcasts of TV station shows, or they're the Internet version of shows that are also shown on local stations.

Adding Photos and Stills to Your Movie

I've mentioned before that you don't actually need a camcorder in order to do a videoblog, though it helps. And that's true. You can make your videoblog sing with any visual content — the pictures don't have to move to be meaningful. You can create a narrated (or just music video style) slideshow of still photos, or you can add still photos to your video to change things up a bit.

Adding a photo in iMovie

Adding a photo in iMovie is similar to importing any movie clip to iMovie. You can drag and drop the photo file into your clip library from the Finder, or from another iMovie project. If the photo is stored in your iPhoto library, you can also open it from iPhoto.

To import a photo from iPhoto into iMovie, follow these steps:

1. **From iMovie, click the Media tab to open your available media types, including music from iTunes and photos from iPhoto.**

2. **Click the Photos button to view your photo library.**

3. **Click a photo from your iPhoto library to highlight it.**

4. **Click the Show Photo Settings button to display the options for the photo to import.**

   The Photo Settings dialog box appears, as shown in Figure 10-4. The two main options are as follows:

- **Zoom:** Use the Zoom slider to determine how much to zoom in or out on the photo.

- **Speed:** Use the Speed slider to determine how long to show the photo. Move the slider towards the rabbit for a shorter duration, or the turtle for a longer duration.

iMovie uses a combination of frames and seconds to show time. In an iMovie time signature, from left to right are hours, minutes, seconds, and frames: hh:mm:ss:ff, with 24 frames per second, the standard for film (not digital) movies.

5. **Click the Apply button to import the photo into your video at the end of the timeline.**

   When that's done, you can then drag it to the clip library if you like.

If you decide to change the duration of a still photo that doesn't have the Ken Burns Effect applied, just double-click the photo's clip in the clip viewer and enter a new duration.

Using photo effects

Ken Burns is a name you'll see a lot in this section. He's a famous filmmaker and documentarian known for a particular type of work in which the camera zooms slowly in on a subject or image. He uses this effect in his documentaries, and it lends a certain intimate feel as well as some dynamic action to otherwise-still photos in a video. iMovie comes with the Ken Burns Effect built into the interface. All other effects on a photo need to be done in iPhoto, or by applying the Video FX to an imported photo clip.

To apply the Ken Burns Effect, follow these steps:

1. **From the iMovie project, select Media and choose a photo to import from iPhoto.**

   The Photo Settings dialog box will display with the photo preview.

2. **Check the Ken Burns Effect check box in the Photo Settings dialog box, as shown in Figure 10-5.**

Figure 10-5:
The Photo
Settings
dialog box.

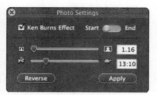

3. **Flip the Start/End switch to Start and slide the zoom magnification slider to the zoom level at which you'd like to start the clip.**

   If you start with the zoom set at smaller than 1.00, you get a black border around the image because it will be smaller than the movie frame. This is also the case if the photo is cropped to a different scale from the movie frame (for example, if the photo is in portrait layout).

4. **Toggle the Start/End switch to End and select the degree of zoom magnification you want to be in effect at the end.**

   By default, the Ken Burns Effect zooms in on a photo. Optionally, you can click the Reverse button in the Photo Settings dialog box to zoom out from the image, rather than in.

5. **Select a speed to set the duration of the entire clip by sliding the speed slider.**

If you set the Start and End magnifications to have a very large difference, and you don't increase the duration with the Speed slider, then the Zoom effect will seem too fast. You may have to do some experimenting with these settings to get a good balance.

Since these are still images, don't leave them up for more than a few seconds. Even Ken Burns can't make a stalled slideshow fascinating. If you use the Ken Burns Effect on more than one photo in your movie, use the same settings for each photo so your video will have a more consistent feel.

Because the Ken Burns Effect turns your photo into a small video clip, making adjustments after the photo has imported into your project is harder to do than on a still photo. For instance, you cannot simply adjust the duration of the effect by double-clicking the image.

However, you can make adjustments using the Photo Settings dialog box. With the Photos tab still open, select the clip that has the Ken Burns effect applied, and then click the Show Photo Setting button. The Photo Settings dialog box appears, where you can adjust the effect or even remove it. Click the Update button in the Photo Settings dialog box when you're done.

Transitioning between Clips

When your movie goes from one clip to another, you have the option to let it jump to the new clip, or give it a transition. When the video doesn't change much between one clip and the next, it's sometimes best to just let it jump — which is called a *cut* because it's a sudden, sharp transition over to the new shot or clip without any smoothing.

However, you can add transitions to smooth out the switch between one shot and the next. This is useful when the shots differ visually a great deal, when the clips look jarring when you cut over, or when you're significantly changing the subject matter and want to present the break visually.

Most transitions have one or two options: Speed and Direction are the most common. The Speed option determines how long the transition will be.

The transition must be shorter than either of the clips it's between — if the transition is longer, you will not be able to apply it.

Although most transitions must be placed between two clips, some transitions are *terminal* — they can serve as endpoints, placed before the first clip at the beginning of the movie, or after the last clip at the end of the movie. An example of a terminal transition is Fade Out, which lets you transition the last clip in a movie to a black screen.

To apply a transition in iMovie, follow these steps:

1. **Click the Editing button below the clip library, and then select Transitions.**

2. **In the clip viewer or timeline view, select the two clips you wish to place the transition between.**

3. **Highlight the transition you want to use.**

   The panel will display any options available for the transition.

4. **Select any options, such as the duration of the transition.**

5. **Click Add to add the transition between the clips, as shown in Figure 10-6.**

Figure 10-6:
Add a
transition.

Sound in transitions

In most transitions, the sound goes with the video. As one clip disappears, the sound disappears with it. However, there are a few issues with sound in transitions. First, if you've extracted the sound for a clip or series of clips, iMovie mutes the original sound by default. Then, when you apply a transition, the transition may suddenly turn the sound back up to 100%. You can adjust how this works in the timeline viewer.

Another common issue is when the sound gets out of sync with the video, after extracting the sound from a clip. There's more information in Chapter 11 for preventing and resolving this issue, but the short version to solve this problem is to make sure you lock the audio clips to the play head whenever you extract audio.

Another reported issue is that the transitions sometimes cause audio artifacts, such as static, distortion, and even audio from other clips to crop up in a transition. This appears to be a bug that Apple has been unable to resolve, because it is very inconsistent regarding which versions of iMovie and computers it affects. Sometimes iMovie will work fine on a particular machine, and then an upgrade to the next version introduces this bug — and a later update may or may not resolve it. The only known workaround is to extract the audio from the clips, but even this is inconsistent. Apple continues to work on the problem, no doubt.

iMovie comes with the following standard transitions:

- ✔ **Billow:** Brings the new clip in as bubbles.

- ✔ **Circle Closing/Opening:** The first clip disappears into a closing circle or opening circle, replaced by the second clip.

- ✔ **Cross Dissolve:** The two clips overlay each other, with the first clip becoming more and more transparent until it's gone. (This is one of my favorite transitions.)

- ✔ **Disintegrate:** The first clip seems to burn away, leaving behind the second clip.

- ✔ **Fade In/Out:** The clip fades into or out of a black background. This is a terminal transition.

- ✔ **Overlap:** Nearly identical to Cross Dissolve, but iMovie 6 seems to handle it a little better than Cross Dissolve.

- ✔ **Push:** Clip 2 pushes Clip 1 out of the way. You can choose in which direction the push comes from: left, right, top, or bottom.

- ✔ **Radial:** A line sweeps around the video from the center, like a clock hand, replacing Clip 1 with Clip 2.

- ✔ **Ripple:** Clip 1 is replaced by Clip 2 with a wave.

- ✔ **Scale Down:** Clip 1 reduces in size until it disappears, leaving Clip 2 in its place.

- ✔ **Warp Out:** Similar to the Circle Opening transition, but Clip 1 appears to warp as it is pushed out by Clip 2.

- ✔ **Wash In/Out:** Similar to Fade In/Out, but the video transitions to or from a white frame. This is a terminal transition.

As with Video FX, Sound FX, and Titles, you can purchase plug-ins that will give you additional transitions to use in iMovie.

Applying Special Effects

You can use special video effects in your movies to alter the way your movie appears. For instance, Chapter 9 shows how to change a movie to black and white or sepia tone using special video effects — but why stop there?

Some of the special effects allow you to change the way the video image appears, such as switching to black and white, or shifting the color balance, or even sharpening the video a little — especially useful if you have blurry film. Other effects are more obvious, like mirroring an image, or adding pixie dust trails of animated sparkles to your video.

All special effects in iMovie appear in the Video FX tab. The basic steps you perform to use a video special effect are as follows:

1. **Add your clip to the clip viewer.**
2. **Open the Video FX tab and select the effect you'd like to use.**
3. **Choose the options you prefer for that effect.**
4. **Click the Apply button.**

The Video FX tab offers many special effects and options you can use to enhance your movie. When you select an effect, its options will appear in the tab, as shown in Figure 10-7.

Figure 10-7:
The special-effects options.

Among the common options for video effects are Effect In and Effect Out. These options determine when an effect starts or ends, relative to the length of a clip. For example, if your clip is 24 seconds long, you can set the Effect In option anywhere between 00:00 and 24:00 seconds, and the Effect Out option to anywhere after the time you specified for the Effect In option.

To apply the effect to the whole clip — but have a smooth transition back to normal video — set the Effect Out to the end of the clip. If you set both Effect In and Effect Out to 00:00, the effect will be applied to the whole clip — but with no transition from the effect to normal video.

The following list describes the effects and the options available in iMovie's default installation. (Note that these may differ slightly in various versions of iMovie — and, of course, third-party effects have their own options and features.)

- ✔ **Adjust colors:** Use the Hue Shift option to shift colors from purple (left) to green (right). The Color option decreases the amount of color in the video. The Lightness option makes a video lighter overall.

- ✔ **Aged Film:** Use the Exposure option to lighten or darken the video. The Jitter option makes the film look poorly aligned. The Scratches option adds a scratched film look that suggests an old, much-used print.

- ✔ **Black & White:** Use the Black & White option to convert the film to a grayscale video.

- ✔ **Brightness and contrast:** Use the Brightness option to increase the light in the video (but note that if you apply too much of the effect, it makes the video look washed out). Use the Contrast option to emphasize color and shadow contrasts.

- ✔ **Crystallize:** Size determines how large the crystals are in your pointillist video.

- ✔ **Earthquake:** The Sideways setting determines how much horizontal shake to add to your video. Vertical, on the other hand, sets how much up-and-down shake to add to the video.

- ✔ **Edge Work:** Radius determines how far out from an edge to detect. This effect converts a video into a black-and-white (not grayscale) representation that is very abstract.

- ✔ **Edges:** Intensity determines how much emphasis to give to the edges. This is another abstract effect.

- ✔ **Electricity:** Radius sets the direction that the electrical current appears to come from. You can also click the video preview to set the apparent destination of the electrical current.

- ✔ **Fairy Dust:** Direction determines whether the sparkles originate on the left side of the movie or the right. Trail determines the length of the trail of sparkles behind the dust. You can also click the video preview to direct the fairy dust to cross a certain point in the video; by default, it will cross the center, going from the bottom to the top.

- ✔ **Fast/Slow/Reverse:** Use the Speed setting to speed up or slow down a video. The Reverse Direction check box makes the video play in reverse.

- ✔ **Flash:** Count sets how many flashes to include in the clip. Brightness determines how bright the flash should be. Speed sets how quickly the flash fades in and out.

- **Fog:** Amount determines how much the video should be obscured. Wind sets the direction in which the fog appears to drift across the screen. Color sets the shade of gray applied to the fog.

  Set the Color option to Black to make the effect look like smoke instead of fog.

- **Ghost Trails:** Trail determines how long the motion trail should be. Steps to set the size of the trail. Opaque sets how much you can see through those trails.

- **Glass Distortion:** The Scale setting determines how large the distortions are.

- **Lens Flare:** Sweep sets the direction in which the lens flare crosses the video. Intensity determines the strength of the light causing the flare. You can also click the video itself to center the flare automatically.

- **Letterbox:** Specify an amount of Shift to move the video up or down in the letterbox area. Setting Size determines how much of the video is masked off by the letterbox.

- **Mirror:** Vertical settings determine where to mirror from top to bottom. Horizontal settings specify how much to mirror from left to right.

- **N-Square:** Here you determine how many squares to duplicate in the video.

- **Rain:** Here you set how much rain to include. You can also determine how much the rain will shift and bend in gusts of virtual weather.

- **Sepia:** This is an intensity setting that determines how much color to remove.

- **Sharpen:** Here you set how much to sharpen the video. Note that a highly sharpened video can look artificial.

- **Soft Focus:** Softness and Amount determine how soft the overall video effect should be.

When you select a Video FX, a preview of that effect will automatically start, which can slow your computer down. Click the X icon on the preview window to stop the preview.

Installing new effects plug-ins in iMovie

Many companies other than Apple have created plug-ins that offer special effects, titles, and transitions plug-ins for you to use with iMovie. Some of these are free, but most are for-pay programs.

✔ **Gee Three Slick iMovie Plugins:** Here you'll find hundreds of plug-ins covering a wide range of transitions and effects; most cost $35 for a package of several, or you can buy bundles of packages. Available at `www.geethree.com/slick/index.html`.

✔ **Dan Slagle's iMovie FAQ:** A site with links to various plug-ins and information on how to use them, at `www.danslagle.com/mac/iMovie/index.shtml`.

✔ **BKMS plugins:** Collections of transitions and effects, ranging from $10 to $35 for collections of plug-ins. Available at `http://plugins.bkms.com`.

✔ **PluginsWorld directory of iMovie plug-ins:** A directory of plug-ins from many manufacturers in a wide range of options and price ranges. Online at `http://imovie.pluginsworld.com`.

Remember: When you download plug-ins to install, first run them through a virus checker before you install them. Fewer viruses are written for Macintosh computers than for Windows computers, but an easy way to target a Mac user is to disguise a virus inside a Mac-only plug-in program.

Plug-ins usually include an installer program that you start by double-clicking, or they include installation instructions (likely in a readme file). If the plug-in you want to install does not include an installer program or installation instructions, open your Home folder in the Macintosh Finder and navigate to the Library⇨iMovie⇨Plugins folder. Drag and drop the plug-in into the appropriate subfolder (some plug-ins are for Effects, and others are for Transitions). The plug-in then becomes available in iMovie.

Chapter 11

Adding a Soundtrack

· ·

· ·

*O*ne of the toughest parts of videoblogging is getting the sound quality good enough that everything is perfectly audible and identifiable. For some reason, the "A" part of "A/V" doesn't always work too well for videobloggers, and it's sometimes hard to know why. After all, your camcorder has a microphone, right? Shouldn't that be enough?

Sometimes it is. Sometimes your camera will pick up perfect audio, every person speaking to the camera will be completely audible, and somehow you'll have avoided any ambient noise in the room.

This chapter covers how to get better audio from your video camera, and how to edit sound in your video after you download it to your computer.

Recording Superior Audio on Your Camera

At least as often as not, the audio from your camera will be less than perfect. It might have a lot of background or ambient noise from crowds nearby, street noise, or even TV or radios on in the background. Or the sound could be too quiet, or have a muddy quality to it.

The first line in troubleshooting poor audio quality in your videoblog is to look at your camcorder. Your camera determines how good your video and audio quality can get — and past a certain point, no amount of processing and software will fix a bad image or bad sound.

Positioning the camera for audio

Most video cameras have the built-in microphone mounted on the front or side of the camera. The microphone might be labeled, or you might be able to identify it as a small hole or grille where the sound enters the camera.

Sound travels in waves. As each wave hits a sound-receiving instrument (such as an ear or a microphone), it's picked up as noise, with more-frequent waves sounding higher in pitch than less-frequent waves. (See Figure 11-1.) Anything standing in the way of a sound wave blocks the sound from reaching the receiving instrument.

Since the lens is on the front of the camera, front-mounted microphones are always pointed towards the source of the sound. Some cameras have the microphone mounted on the side of the camera (as shown in Figure 11-2), but these need to have a better pickup in order to get the same quality of sound as a microphone mounted on the front.

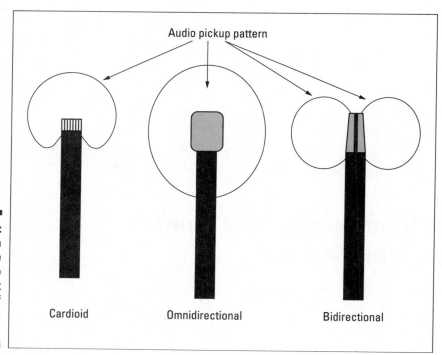

Figure 11-1:
How a sound wave is picked up by different types of micro-phones.

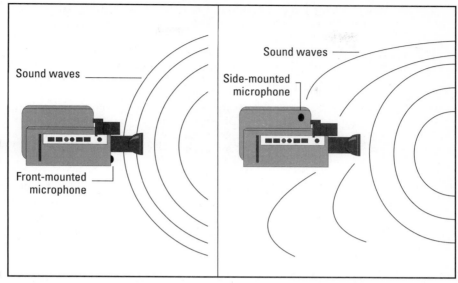

Figure 11-2:
Front- and side-mounted microphones and sound waves.

How you hold and move the camera can greatly improve the sound quality you get from your video. If you hold it level at (or near) the same height as the head of the person speaking, the microphone will be in a direct path from the speaker's mouth, ensuring that his or her voice is recorded clearly.

If you move the camera around a lot, you run the risk of increased wind noise, accidentally hitting it (which makes a terrible scraping noise on the video as well), and possible sound distortion if you turn the camera away from the source of the sound. Keep the camera steady, and you'll have a steady soundtrack.

Reducing ambient noise

Human beings hear with the help of a shaped dish (the ear) that funnels sound waves into the ear canal. When there is a lot of noise in an area, the brain filters out the ambient noise to a certain degree so that you can hear what you're focused on. Facial cues, body language, and lip-reading all help humans hear and understand conversation. Truly, ears are amazing.

Mechanical sound receivers, also known as (you guessed it) microphones, do not have all the wonderful things that human ears have. They do not, usually, have a dish to funnel sound to the receiver. Although a microphone can have a filter to reduce ambient noise, it usually needs more than one type:

✔ A grille over the pick-up cuts down on the wind and reduces noise from accidentally bumping into the microphone

✔ A windsock to cut down wind noise

✔ Noise-canceling electronics to reduce other ambient noise, such as talking or music

✔ Noise-canceling software used to process the audio after you download it onto your computer

Most camcorders' built-in microphones have a grille and may or may not have some noise-canceling features. When you go into a noisy environment, you may find it is easier to film without paying special attention to the noise around you, and just edit the video later to add a soundtrack or voiceover.

Using external recording equipment

The last way to improve the audio in your video camera is to not use the build-in audio at all. Instead, you use external audio — either a microphone plugged into your camera, or perhaps an external audio recorder that's entirely separate from your camera.

I talk about buying an external microphone for your video camera in Chapter 3, and the guidelines given there apply here: You don't need an expensive microphone; you just need one that's better than the built-in microphone in your camera. The price break on plug-in microphones seems to be about $50: you can get a decent microphone for under $50, a slightly more convenient one that mounts on top of your camcorder for under $100, and then you're looking at over $1000 for a high-end mic.

Another option is to get an external, dedicated tape recorder and microphone and use those. With this setup, you're no longer limited to the audio processing ability of your video camera. For instance, you could get a stereo recorder and two microphones to record a videoblog in true stereo.

If you separate audio and video this way, you'll have to synchronize them after you import them into your computer. You can do this the hard way or the easy way. The hard way is to import your video and painstakingly try to match up, frame by frame, the speaking mouths of your subjects and the words in your recorded soundtrack.

Or you can make it easy on yourself. You've seen the clapstick and slate that the director snaps together and says "Take one — action!" The clapstick actually serves an important purpose. In film, the sound is not recorded on the same medium as the film — it's recorded separately. The clapstick provides an audible and visual cue to the editors to indicate where to sync the sound and video. When the clapstick snaps closed, that frame is where the SNAP on the audio track goes.

And you can use a clapstick in your videoblogs! Get yourself two wooden, non-beveled rulers and a sideways hinge at the hardware store. Screw the sideways hinge to both rulers so they can slap together. See Figure 11-3 for an example of a homemade clapstick.

Figure 11-3:
Make yourself a clapstick, or use a commercially available clapstick slate, when recording audio separately from the video.

Typically, the clapstick is attached to the top of a slate, which is a white board or card that includes information about the particular shot and take. For instance, the slate might include the scene name, the time in the tape, the take number, and the production and which camera faced this particular clapstick. On large, multi-camera productions, you might use the clapstick more than once, since not all cameras will be able to record the clapstick clearly and you might have a harder time later syncing it up.

In iMovie, you can sync the audio and video together using a clapstick or any sharp noise caused by an action caught on the film.

1. **In iMovie, import your audio and video clips (see the rest of this chapter for information on importing audio to iMovie).**

2. **Switch to the Timeline Viewer and drag the audio to the Timeline.**

3. **At this point, you may need to turn on the waveform view by selecting View⊃Show Audio Waveforms in the menu, as shown in Figure 11-4.**

   The waveform view enables you to see a representation of the sound. Look for a spike in the waveform — that's likely when your clapstick snap occurred.

4. **Navigate the Timeline view to as close to the clapstick snap as possible in the video.**

5. **Split the audio clip on the frame where the clap appears.**

6. **Drag the audio clip to match the video — you want the snap in the sound clip to be lined up with the frame showing the closed clapstick in the video clip.**

   By default, iMovie attempts to snap the beginnings of the clips to each other, but you can turn this feature on and off in the Preferences dialog box. Choose iMovie⊃Preferences from the menu bar, and in the Preferences dialog box that appears (see Figure 11-5), select or deselect the Snap to Items check box.

Figure 11-4: Turn on the waveform to view the sound.

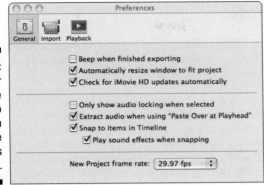

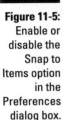

Figure 11-5:
Enable or
disable the
Snap to
Items option
in the
Preferences
dialog box.

7. **If necessary, move the audio frame by frame by clicking it and pressing the right and left arrow keys.**

8. **When you have the audio and video synched together, select Advanced⇨Lock Audio Clip at Playhead (or press ⌘+L) to pin the audio to the video.**

   You'll still be able to drag the audio clip in the Timeline, but if you move the video clip around, the audio will move with it.

Adding a Soundtrack Later

There are many cases where you'll want to edit the audio on your videoblog after you're done shooting. For instance, if you want to add in a song, or make a whole music video out of your videoblog, you can do that by editing the video and then putting the music into a soundtrack.

There are several ways to add audio to a videoblog after you've shot it:

✔ Import audio from your hard drive, an audio recorder, or another movie clip

✔ Record a voiceover on your computer

✔ Import music from iTunes

✔ Add sound effects from a standard sound-effect library

Importing audio

I mention a few times in this book that you need to have a digitizer if your video camera doesn't have a FireWire or other digital connection. The same principles of analog and digital media apply to audio.

If you record your audio on a tape, you have to get the audio off of the tape and onto your hard drive. That means you need some way to convert it to a digital file. Probably the easiest way, if all you have is a tape deck, is to connect it to your computer with an audio cable (to the Audio In or microphone jack on your computer) and use an audio-recording program to capture the sound. That program might be something as simple as the Sound Recorder program in Windows, AudioIn (a freeware recording program for the Mac), or a more fully-featured program, such as GarageBand or professional-grade programs like Adobe Audition and Soundtrack Pro (Apple's audio application for Final Cut Studio).

I talk about importing a song or audio file from GarageBand or iTunes in the later section "Adding music to your videoblog." When you create or edit your audio in one of these other applications, you can usually export it to a common audio format (such as `.wav`, `.mp3`, or even a QuickTime `.mov` file) or import any of these formats into iMovie or Windows Movie Maker.

To import an audio file from your hard drive in iMovie, follow these steps:

1. **From iMovie, open the movie project and navigate to the frame where you'd like to import the audio.**

   There is no audio-clip library as there is for video clips, so iMovie imports your audio directly to the soundtrack.

2. **Select File⇨Import.**

   The Import dialog box appears, prompting you for the file to import.

3. **Navigate to the audio file in the Open dialog box and double-click it.**

   If the audio or video file type isn't supported, it appears in gray.

   The audio file is imported and appears in one of the soundtracks in the Timeline Viewer. From there you can drag it into place on the Timeline.

Recording a voiceover

One of my favorite ways to fix bad audio on a recording, especially if the problem stems from too much ambient noise, is to record over the video with my own voice, often narrating (or in many cases commenting on) what's happening in the clip.

If you are the kind of person who has a running commentary going through your mind when you go through your everyday life, and that commentary is humorous, sarcastic, or otherwise apt to make people chuckle if you said it out loud, your videoblog is an excellent opportunity to do exactly that.

Plus, if you're an aspiring filmmaker, it's good practice for when you get to make the director's commentary for your blockbuster hit's DVD release.

Some of the creative ways to use a voiceover:

✔ To narrate an event as it unfolds on-screen.

✔ To add an internal monologue to your videoblog.

✔ To provide your "director's notes" commentary to the vlog.

✔ To give voices to animated characters.

✔ To dub a translation over a foreign-language video. It's customary to allow the original speaker to have a few words in the original language before beginning the voiceover translation.

✔ To correct a poorly-recorded audio. Use sparingly, because it's difficult to sync up with your video self's lips.

✔ To edit what someone actually said into what you _wish_ the person had said. For instance, a voiceover of yourself saying "Of course" over a video of your dad saying you can't borrow the car could be quite amusing. Again, use sparingly — and only in fun.

For most newer Macintosh computers, you'll need a USB microphone or USB adapter to perform any voiceover work.

To record a voiceover in iMovie, follow these steps:

1. **Plug your microphone into your computer and start iMovie.**

2. **Open the movie project and navigate the Timeline to where you want the voiceover to start.**

3. **Click the Media tab and select Audio from the buttons at the top of the panel, as shown in Figure 11-6.**

   At the bottom of the Audio sources are the controls for recording your own audio.

4. **Position the microphone, prepare yourself to talk, and click the red Record button.**

5. **When you're done, click the red Record button a second time to stop recording.**

   iMovie will take a minute or so to process the audio and add it to the Timeline.

Figure 11-6:
Select the
Audio media
panel.

In Windows Movie Maker, the feature to add a voiceover is called Narrate Timeline. Plug your microphone into your computer and choose Tools➪ Narrate Timeline from the Windows Movie Maker menu bar.

Adding music to your videoblog

You can add music to your videoblog directly from iTunes or GarageBand. In addition to simply importing a file from your hard drive, iMovie also has a connection to the other iLife products, such as iTunes and GarageBand.

To add music from your iTunes library in iMovie, follow these steps:

1. **With your iMovie project open, navigate to the place in your Timeline where you want the song to start.**

2. **Select the Media tab and click Audio.**

3. **Choose iTunes and Library in the source panel (refer to Figure 11-6).**

4. **Click the song you want to import to highlight it.**

5. **Either click the Place at Playhead button, or drag it onto the Timeline.**

iMovie will take a minute or so to import the song file and will place it on one of the soundtrack channels.

In iTunes 4.0 and up, digital-rights-management software prevents you from importing songs purchased in the iTunes Music Store into iMovie projects. To work around this, burn the song to a CD then re-import it to iTunes. However, remember that *securing the license to use the song in your videoblog is still necessary, even if you paid 99 cents for it on the iTunes Music Store.*

To import an audio file from GarageBand, use the same Media/Audio source, but select GarageBand from the source panel instead of iTunes, as shown in Figure 11-7.

Figure 11-7:
Use the
Garage-
Band
source.

Save any audio files you create in GarageBand with an iLife preview. You'll be prompted to do so when you create a GarageBand file.

Editing the Soundtrack

Editing a sound clip in your movie is a fairly basic task that you might want to do to correct sound issues and blend clips into each other. However, editing a sound clip is among the *last* things to do before packaging your movie into a handy file and posting it to the Internet. Editing might also be the *first* thing you want to do to a sound clip after you record it, but in the last run through your video is more likely to reveal sound issues than blatant video problems.

Editing a sound clip

You have a couple of ways to edit an individual sound clip in iMovie. You can change the volume, including adding fade-ins, fade-outs, and otherwise changing the sound levels at any point in the clip. You can cut the clip, move it around in the Timeline, and lock it into place in relation to the video.

When you import an audio clip to iMovie, it shows up in the Timeline Viewer as a long block of content in one of the two audio channels. These audio channels do not in any way correspond to the right and left stereo channels, by the way — iMovie is not sophisticated enough to provide multichannel stereo or surround-sound options.

However, these audio channels do allow you to mute or unmute an audio track for the whole duration of the video (helpful if you want to have a single video with two audio tracks that you export into two versions of your movie). For instance, you might do this for a translated videoblog, in which you have the original audio track and one or more translation channels.

To mute or unmute an audio track, simply check the check box next to the track in the Timeline Viewer, as shown in Figure 11-8.

Figure 11-8: Check the check box at the far right to mute the audio track.

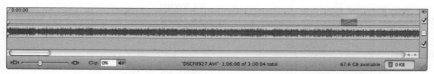

The Timeline Viewer is also where you choose to edit an audio clip's volume. To change the volume for a whole clip, follow these steps:

1. **In iMovie, click the sound clip to highlight it.**

   If you're using a version prior to iMovie 6, click the Edit Volume check box, or select View➪Show Clip Volume Levels to see the volume of the clip. In iMovie 6 and later versions, select View➪Show Clip Volume Levels to see the volume.

2. **Enter a volume in the Volume text box.**

   This value can be between 0 and 150%. If you need to increase the volume on a clip that recorded too quiet, this is a quick way to do so.

In addition to changing the volume for the whole clip, you can gradually increase or decrease the volume at different points in the clip's Timeline. To add a gradual fade, click the point where you want to raise or lower the volume and drag the volume level up or down. The volume will increase or decrease from that point forward, and the change will be marked with a small dot, as shown in Figure 11-9.

If you drag the point forward along the Timeline, the change will be more gradual.

Figure 11-9:
Various
styles of
audio fades.

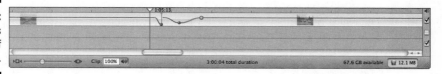

You can create a *cross-fade* (where one audio track fades in as the other audio track fades out) in iMovie with a little audio editing. To create the audio cross-fade, simply reduce one audio clip's volume level and increase that of another at the same point in the Timeline.

To move an audio clip, just click and drag it around in the Timeline. You can move audio clips forward and backward along the Timeline, move them from one audio channel to the other, or drag them onto the Trash Can when you want to delete them.

To split an audio clip, click to highlight it, and then navigate to the point in the clip where you want to make the split. Select Edit⇨Split Audio Clip at Playhead to cut the clip in two.

Earlier in this chapter, I explain how to lock an audio file to a video clip. You can lock any audio clip when it's in the soundtrack for your iMovie project.

Adding sound-effect clips

iMovie comes with some basic sound effects supplied by Skywalker Studios, as well as from a standard sound library from Apple. These sound effects are like audible clip art. They let you include short sound clips that you might not otherwise have available, such as a racecar zooming by or a jet airplane taking off. But because the sound-effect clips are included in iMovie, they're far from unique — and many people will instantly recognize the sound effect and know where it came from.

To use a sound-effect clip in iMovie, follow these steps:

1. **Open the iMovie project and navigate to the place in the Timeline where you want the sound effect to play.**

2. **Click the Media tab and select the Audio button to open the audio library.**

3. **Click either Standard Sound Effects or Skywalker Sound Effects to open these sources.**

4. **Click a sound effect to select it.**

   You can preview it by clicking the Play button.

5. **Click the Place at Playhead button to insert the sound-effect clip.**

Using iMovie's Audio FX

An addition to iMovie 06 is a feature only available to users of Macintosh OS 10.4 and above: the Audio FX features. With the Audio FX functions, you can perform basic audio-editing functions on your soundtrack, without having to run the sound through an external software program to process and re-mix it.

If you have iMovie 6 but a lower version of Mac OS X, you will not be able to use the Audio FX feature.

To use the Audio FX in iMovie, follow these steps:

1. **With your iMovie project open, click the Editing tab and click the Audio FX button at the top.**

2. **Click the audio or video clip that you want to edit.**

3. **Select the Audio FX you want to apply from the list.**

4. **Select any options you want to use and click Preview to test them out.**

5. **When you have the effect you want, with the right options, click Apply to change the audio on that clip.**

The Audio FX that come with iMovie are

✔ **Graphic EQ:** An all-purpose graphic equalizer that enables you to tinker with all sound levels (including those of treble, bass, and midrange) on the audio.

✔ **Reverb:** Changes the tone of the audio to enhance an echo. For example, this effect can make the audio sound like it's in a cathedral, night club, or outdoor plaza.

✔ **Delay:** Adds a slight delay to the end of the sound. You can adjust the amount of delay.

✔ **Pitch Changer:** Lets you take the pitch higher or lower (from chipmunk to monster).

✔ **Highpass:** Cuts lower frequencies out of the sound, to allow the higher pitches through. This is useful if you need to cancel out a background drone, so long as your subjects don't speak in the same general pitch range.

✔ **Lowpass:** Cuts higher frequencies out of the sound. Useful to cancel out whine, hiss, or high-pitched whistle.

✔ **Bandpass:** Allows you to set the frequencies to pass through either a wide or narrow band, and set where the center resonance for the band should be.

✔ **Noise Reducer:** Reduces ambient noise, such as from nearby crowds, traffic, industrial machines, or even babbling brooks.

Each effect has different options for changing the quality of the sound. However, in most cases, you won't want to crank any of these effects all the way up, down, or sideways. Human ears, being the wonderful instruments they are, are very sensitive to subtle changes in a sound, and anything extreme will sound distorted and "off." Keep it natural, don't try to eliminate every audio flaw you can detect, and your videoblogs will have a superior sound.

Chapter 12

Saving Videos for the Internet

*F*iles, formats, videos, codecs . . . it's enough to drive you crazy if you let it! There are a dizzying number of patented and proprietary formats for compressing video files and exchanging them with programs. To make matters worse, a file format and a codec, while being completely different things, may have *the exact same name*.

The most important thing you need to know about file formats, compression settings, and codecs is to try not to change them once you've decided on one. The more you change, the more your viewers at home will have to download new codecs or software, just to watch your vlogs. When you figure out something that works for you, stick with it for as long as you can. Your viewers will silently thank you, and you'll be glad not to have to troubleshoot compression issues.

Understanding Video-File Formats

One of the bewildering things about videoblogging is that there are so many video-file formats available, yet a video file might play in one version of QuickTime, but not in another version.

The reason video-file formats are so complicated boils down to the fact that a digital video contains a lot of information — more than you probably need for a small videoblog post. One uncompressed digital video format is .avi, which can be more than *six times larger* than a comparable MPEG-4 video compressed for an iPod.

When you post a video to the Internet, you should compress it using special software called *encoding* software. When you export a video from QuickTime, iMovie, or Windows Movie Maker, you do exactly that — compress the video file into a format and file size suitable to the Internet, a DVD, or whatever other device you wish to use to share the video. This is why, when you use the Export, Share, or Save Movie commands in these programs, you have more than a dozen options for specifying how you want to save the video.

The main video-file formats you'll encounter online are

- ✔ **.avi:** Often uncompressed video (can also be compressed, but is usually larger in file size than other file formats).
- ✔ **.mov:** Compressed video for QuickTime.
- ✔ **.mpeg:** MPEG1, MPEG2, MPEG4 are the main formats. These formats can compress for VHS, DVD, or online quality.
- ✔ **.rl:** Real streaming video format for compressed and streaming video.
- ✔ **.wmv or .wmf:** Windows Media Player format.

Explanation of some video-file formats is at `www.petesvideo.com/vidDVformats.htm`.

Proprietary and open-source video

Most compressed video, to one extent or another, is proprietary, because the code that compresses a large video file into a smaller file uses algorithms and programming logic that companies usually patent and then license for money.

However, that shouldn't stop you from creating video with these formats. With rare exceptions, the proprietary nature of the video merely limits which operating system your audience must use to watch your videos. Even proprietary video *codecs* (coder-decoders) are usually free for players; the cost is in is in the compression tools, and it's usually footed by the company creating the compression software.

One of the video formats that is well suited for videoblogging, MPEG-4, is an industry standard put out by the Moving Picture Experts Group. MPEG-4 is heavily developed and well supported by Apple for QuickTime (which is available for both Macintosh and Windows).

Reaching across the platforms

One of the crucial questions you have to decide when you start videoblogging is whether you want to create videoblogs for Windows users, Mac users, Linux/Unix users, or all users, regardless of what platform they're using.

Videoblogging for Linux users

For videobloggers using some flavor of Linux as their preferred operating system, the options are a bit more limited than for Windows and Mac users. Fortunately, nearly everything on Linux is free — so at least you're not spending a lot of dough on a closed system.

Several RSS readers for Linux support media enclosures, and PenguinTV (http://penguintv.sourceforge.net) even plays them inside the reader. Others, like Liferea (http://liferea.sourceforge.net), require a video player program to play a video. MPlayer (www.mplayerhq.hu) is one of the more popular ones, with support for most common file types and compression codecs. Much of the video software available from the

open-source community is based on the ffmpeg project; more information is available at http://ffmpeg.sourceforge.net/index.php.

Finally, LiVES (http://lives.sourceforge.net) is a Linux video-editing program that also exports to some common video types (including MPEG-4, but not .wmv). As a bonus, it's available for Windows and Mac, too.

Linux users will do best with a video camera that records to a file stored on a media card or hard drive, unless you want to get a compatible FireWire card and driver. Check the Linux IEEE1394 project for more information and compatibility lists (www.linux1394.org).

In an ideal world, it would be easy to create a video file that could be viewed on all computers everywhere, with no loss of quality when played on different devices. In the real world, however, this just isn't practical due to competition and compatibility issues: it's also not technologically possible. For example, a video that plays on a cellphone is necessarily smaller and of lower quality than an ideal video for a high-definition TV.

For example, in early 2006, Microsoft stopped supporting Windows Media Player for Macintosh — which means that any .wmv videoblog excludes Macintosh users unless they use third-party programs, such as Flip4Mac (www.flip4mac.com), to convert Windows Media files to QuickTime files. However, don't get too mad at Microsoft. Apple hasn't played very fair, either, coming out with codecs for the Macintosh version of QuickTime long before they're available for the Windows version, and not making the video-capable iPod compatible with Windows Media files.

If you want your videos to be sure to play on both Mac and Windows machines, you'll have to use a compression-free format, such as an uncompressed .avi file. .avi files are the trick to transferring files between Mac and Windows computers, in case you need to do so in your cross-platform video studio.

Creating vlogs in multiple file formats

One way to work around platform-incompatibility problems is to create multiple videoblog feeds for different platforms. Many videobloggers create multiple video files to support feeds for two or more players, such as Windows Media Player, QuickTime, iPod, PocketPCs, or PlayStation Portable devices.

To create a multiple-format videoblog, you'll need some way to convert your video to both Windows Media Files *and* QuickTime-compatible files.

One way to do this is to use two computers — one a Mac and one a Windows machine, and convert the video on both computers, as follows:

1. **Edit the movie as normal and save it to either a MPEG-4 or WMV file.**

2. **From your video-editing program, export the video to an `.avi` file, using no compression settings.**

   This is the file you will use to transfer from one computer to the other.

3. **Transfer the `.avi` file to your other computer.**

   You can do this using a USB drive or over a computer network (for example, through e-mail).

4. **In the other computer's video-editing program, import that `.avi` file and save it as a WMV or MPEG-4 file.**

5. **Upload both files to your Web-hosting provider.**

For this method, you need two separate videoblogs with two RSS feeds. After you upload the two files to your Web host, you make the post to your blogs.

Another option is to upload your video to a videoblogging service that automatically converts it into different video file formats for your viewers — such as vlogcentral (a.k.a. vblogcentral).

Follow these steps to use vlogcentral to store, upload, and convert your video files:

1. **Go to `www.vblogcentral.com` and create an account.**

   Note that you need to have your own blog account before you sign up with vlogcentral.

2. **Click the <u>Upload Video</u> link, and then download and install the Vlogcentral Vlog client tool, shown in Figure 12-1.**

   Note that you may need to install QuickTime 7.0 or Java 5.0 before you can install the Vlog client tool.

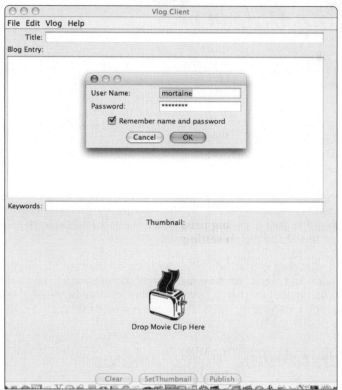

Figure 12-1:
The
vlogcentral
Vlog Client
uploader.

3. **In the vlogcentral Vlog Client window, select Vlog⇨Vlog Settings, and then enter the server and login information for your videoblog.**

4. **Write your blog entry as usual, and then drag and drop your video into the Vlog Client tool.**

   On your videoblog, your files will be posted with a <u>Click to Play</u> link — when your viewers click it, they can select their preferred video format. Note that you do not need to upload a highly compressed video, because vlogcentral will produce appropriately compressed video for you automatically.

Currently, vlogcentral doesn't generate separate feeds for each file type it converts to, so you may need to have subscribers visit your site directly if they want the cross-platform version of your vlog.

Compressing Videos

A digital video file can take a huge amount of space on your hard drive (or on a DVD) if it's uncompressed, or if it's compressed for a digital video format at a full-screen size and resolution.

However, except when playing a video on a projected screen (such as in a movie theater), all that high-quality, high-resolution video is wasted on most modern video devices. With the exception of HDTV, television screens aren't designed for the kind of high-resolution digital video you can create on your computer.

Also, computer screens are much closer to the people viewing them than are television sets and movie screens. So the video can be a much smaller size, even as small as just a few hundred pixels wide, and still be clear enough for the viewer to see the necessary details.

What this all means is that, while hardcore cinephiles are disappointed by the image quality and size of Internet video, the current visual standards are such that you can create and post a small digital video that other people won't mind watching when it shows up on a computer screen or projected on a TV.

Understanding video codecs

I've mentioned that digital video is compressed and encoded using custom and proprietary algorithms. These algorithms are packaged as codecs (coder-decoders) — packages you can download and install in your computer so you can decode and play encoded video files.

For example, the compression codec recommended for iPod video is H.264, which is an encoding algorithm created by Apple for QuickTime applications. When Apple released this encoding format, the Windows version of QuickTime didn't have full support for H.264, so videos created with this format couldn't be viewed on Windows computers. Apple released a new version of QuickTime a few months later, but in the meantime, H.264 was too proprietary to be useful. It's useful now, but be aware that folks on older computers — Windows or Macintosh — will have trouble getting your H.264 files to play.

There are many codecs for digital video. Some are available for both Windows Media Player and QuickTime, while others are specific to one platform. You can find out more about and download some of the more common codecs at

> ✔ **DivX (www.divx.com):** Both a file format and a codec, DivX is one of the most commonly available compression formats.
>
> ✔ **XviD (www.xvid.org):** An open-source codec for multiple platforms that is mainly used in MPEG-4 files.

✔ **3ivx (www.3ivx.com):** A codec used for MPEG-4.

✔ **Sorenson Media (www.sorensonmedia.com):** Built into QuickTime 3 and above, the Sorenson Media codec is intended for high-quality Internet playback.

✔ **RealVideo (www.real.com):** A codec used for RealMedia streaming video.

As you become familiar with the programs, you'll want to download and install more codecs for your software. You can do this by visiting Microsoft's and Apple's Web sites (www.microsoft.com and www.apple.com, respectively) and downloading the codecs, or by visiting the individual codec-makers' sites to download each one.

Compressing video for a vlog

Because I talk a lot about compression and file types in this chapter, this section includes some quick recipes for exporting a video to a size and format that you can easily use in your videoblog.

For this exercise, I use a 30-second video I made as an example. It's an indoor shot, with fairly standard lighting and an audio voiceover.

Exporting an MPEG-4 file on a Mac

To save a video to MPEG-4 from iMovie, follow these steps:

1. **From iMovie, select Share⇨QuickTime.**

   The Share dialog box appears, as shown in Figure 12-2.

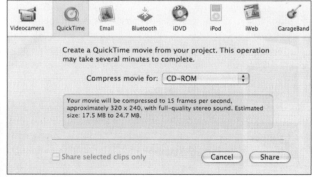

Figure 12-2: The Share dialog box.

2. Select Expert Settings from the drop-down list and click Next.

You're prompted to select a location for the movie and settings, as shown in Figure 12-3.

3. Select Movie to MPEG-4 from the Export drop-down list, and then click the Options button to determine the options for how the video will be compressed.

The MPEG-4 Export Settings dialog box appears, as shown in Figure 12-4.

4. Select the video options as follows (see Figure 12-4):

In the File Format drop-down list, select MP4. Select H.264 in the Video Format drop-down list. Enter **256** in the Data Rate text box, enter **320** in the W text box, **240** in the H text box, and **30** in the Frames text box (for 30 frames per second).

5. Click the Audio tab to set up the audio options, as shown in Figure 12-5.

In the Audio Format drop-down list, select AAC-LC (Music); in the Data Rate drop-down list, select 128 kbps; in the Channels drop-down list, select Stereo (even if your movie is not stereo); in the Output Sample Rate drop-down list, select 48.00 kHz; and in the Encoding Quality drop-down list, select Better.

Figure 12-3:
Select a compression method and location for the movie.

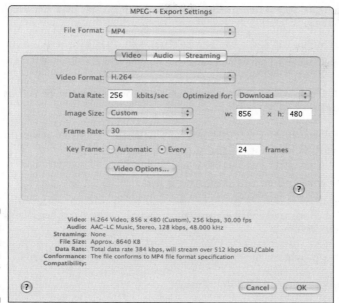

Figure 12-4:
Set the
Video
options for
your movie.

MPEG-4 Export Settings

File Format: MP4

Video | Audio | Streaming

Video Format: H.264
Data Rate: 256 kbits/sec   Optimized for: Download
Image Size: Custom   w: 856 x h: 480
Frame Rate: 30
Key Frame: ○ Automatic ⊙ Every   24   frames
Video Options...

Video: H.264 Video, 856 x 480 (Custom), 256 kbps, 30.00 fps
Audio: AAC-LC Music, Stereo, 128 kbps, 48.000 kHz
Streaming: None
File Size: Approx. 8640 KB
Data Rate: Total data rate 384 kbps, will stream over 512 kbps DSL/Cable
Conformance: The file conforms to MP4 file format specification
Compatibility:

Cancel   OK

Figure 12-5:
Set the
Audio
options for
your movie.

MPEG-4 Export Settings

File Format: MP4

Video | Audio | Streaming

Audio Format: AAC-LC (Music)
Data Rate: 128 kbps
Channels: Stereo
Output Sample Rate: 48.000 kHz
Encoding Quality: Better

Video: H.264 Video, 856 x 480 (Custom), 256 kbps, 30.00 fps
Audio: AAC-LC Music, Stereo, 128 kbps, 48.000 kHz
Streaming: None
File Size: Approx. 8640 KB
Data Rate: Total data rate 384 kbps, will stream over 512 kbps DSL/Cable
Conformance: The file conforms to MP4 file format specification
Compatibility:

Cancel   OK

6. **Check the summary at the bottom of the dialog box for the finished file size.**

   If the file size is too large (more than, say, 15MB for a five minute video), reduce the data rate for the video or the frame rate down to as low as 24 frames per second.

7. **Click OK to close the dialog box, and then click the Save button to export and save the video.**

At the time of writing this book, merely exporting to MPEG-4 would not result in iPod-ready videos without some tweaking.

Exporting an iPod-ready video on a Mac

The Video iPod's release in 2005 and Apple's support for videoblogs in iTunes means that iPod-ready videos are (dare I say it?) the Next Big Thing for Internet video.

To export a movie as an iPod-ready video file, follow these steps:

1. **From iMovie, select File➪Export.**

2. **In the Share dialog box that appears, click the iPod icon.**

3. **Click the Share button to export the video.**

You can also export the video using QuickTime Pro, or convert it in iTunes, or run a QuickTime movie through iSquint (www.isquint.com). QuickTime Pro isn't free software, but it does let you do more than watch videos. If iMovie weren't so easy to use, QuickTime would be a good replacement editor.

If you export with QuickTime or iMovie, you won't have much control over the file size. If you run it through iSquint, however, you can adjust how much to compress the file, and whether you want it to comply with the H.264 codec.

Creating fast-start QuickTime videos

QuickTime has a feature in its file formats that allows you to create fast-starting QuickTime videos. This means that users can start watching a video before it finishes downloading — an attractive option for most audiences, since it means they don't have to wait. As a bonus, it doesn't cost you anything in file size or quality to create a fast-starting video. However, when you use a hyperlink to include the video in your vlog post, the linked file may not be able to use the fast-start feature.

To use Fast Start in QuickTime, export your video to QuickTime and, in the Export Settings dialog box (which is different from the Export Settings for other file types described elsewhere in this chapter), select the Prepare for Internet Streaming check box, and make sure to select Fast Start from the drop-down list.

Exporting for the Web in Windows Movie Maker

To save your video as a .wmv file for the Web, follow these steps:

1. **In Windows Movie Maker, select File⇨Save Movie File.**

   The Save Movie wizard appears, as shown in Figure 12-6, prompting you to select a location to save your video file.

Figure 12-6:
The Save
Movie
wizard.

2. **Select the My computer option and click Next.**

   Even though there's an option to save to the Web, you won't be able to choose that option and still have the movie saved on your hard drive.

3. **Enter a name for your video file and choose a folder to save your movie by clicking the Browse button and navigating to the folder. When you're done, click Next to continue.**

4. **Select the Other Settings radio button, and then choose Video for Broadband (340 Kbps) from the drop-down list, as shown in Figure 12-7.**

   This setting keeps the display size to the common Internet-ready size of 320 x 240 pixels, while also keeping the file size and image quality comparable to an iPod-ready video or MPEG-4. Note the file size at the bottom of the dialog box.

5. **Click Next to start the compression and export the file.**

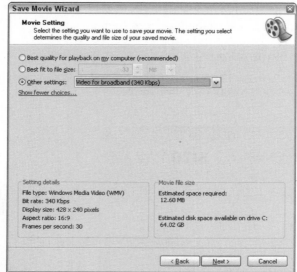

Figure 12-7:
Select Video
for
Broadband.

When the file is done, Windows Movie Maker will ask whether you want to play the video. It's a good idea to play it, just to make sure it compressed nicely.

Exporting for PocketPC

PocketPCs are Windows-based personal digital assistants (PDAs) that have a number of useful applications, including a small version of Windows Media Player.

Of course, PocketPCs don't have hard drives the way iPods do, so they have very limited storage space and video capability. As a result, when you compress your movie for a PocketPC, the quality of the movie will be somewhat lower than you might otherwise use, but it will still create a very playable video for your vlog.

Follow these steps to export a video file for a PocketPC using Windows Movie Maker:

1. **In Windows Movie Maker, select File⇨Save Movie File; in the Save Movie wizard that appears, select My Computer, and then click Next.**

2. **Enter a name and choose a location for the file; click Next.**

3. **Select the Other Settings radio button, and then choose Video for PocketPC (Full screen 218 Kbps) from the drop-down list.**

4. **Note the file size.**

   The file is smaller because the PocketPC format uses about half the number of frames per second (15) as when you compress a video to play on your PC (30). The slower frames-per-second rate is why the video doesn't look as crisp when you play it.

5. **Click Next to start converting the video.**

Changing the video size from widescreen

You'll notice in all the examples given so far, the video size I use is 320 pixels wide and 240 pixels high. This is a 4:3 *aspect ratio* (length-to-width ratio) common for video; it's the size of a standard computer screen or television screen. However, some camcorders enable you to you shoot a video in widescreen format, which has an aspect ratio of 16:9. (Note that although many high-definition TV displays are widescreen, high-definition does *not* define the screen's aspect ratio.)

You can set the screen aspect ratio in Windows Movie Maker by choosing Tools⇨Options and

changing the Video Properties setting in the Advanced tab in the Options dialog box. Although the PocketPC export option will still confine your video to a 4:3 aspect ratio, other export options will not.

To export a movie in a 16:9 aspect ratio in iMovie, export the video as normal (such as to MPEG-4 file format), and then in the Export Setting dialog box, select Custom from the Image Size drop-down list. (Hint: A comparable display size is 428 wide by 240 high.) See the accompanying figure.

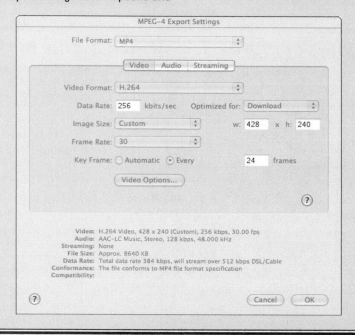

Streaming large videos in a videoblog

One of the challenges with Internet video is the size of the video files and how to download them efficiently. You can use an RSS feed to let your audience download videos while they do other tasks, or they can download and watch them in real time with streaming video. In fact, streaming technology has been around for many years, providing Internet radio and TV stations with a means to deliver longer and larger media files that play as they download.

The following list describes some of the advantages of using streaming technology for your vlog:

✏ Web protocols don't handle very large files (especially those over 100MB) very easily; streamed media is less likely to fail if it's interrupted.

✏ The user's computer may not have enough memory or storage space to download such large files to its internal cache before storing to the hard drive. A streamed file isn't stored after it plays, so the file doesn't take up hard drive space.

✏ Web users don't like waiting for anything. Streaming media can play while it's downloading.

✏ Streaming servers handle live media easily. For broadcasting events or live meetings, streaming media is the way to go.

✏ For large files or long movies, users can skip ahead without waiting for the whole movie to download.

✏ Streaming makes it harder for all but the most determined users to make (unauthorized) copies of your content.

You can discover more about adding streamed videos to your videoblog at the *Videoblogging For Dummies* Web site (www.mortaine. com/vlogdummies).

Using compression utilities and tools

In some cases, the software that seems like it should be perfect to convert and compress a video, turns out not to be so. For example, when you want precise control over a video, Windows Movie Maker isn't the best choice, because it has a set list of pre-set compression formats, and you can't choose the options individually. Similarly, iMovie would seem to be the best choice for making video for an iPod, but until Apple corrects their iPod file requirements, you can't deviate from the pre-set profile. If you want to convert a video to be iPod-ready, but you also want to decrease some part of the quality in favor of a smaller file size . . . well . . . you can't.

If iMovie or Windows Movie Maker seem too confining for your video-file exporting needs, you may prefer to use one the following programs to convert and compress your video files:

- ✔ **QuickTime Pro:** For $29, you can unlock QuickTime's editing features and open the door to saving movie files in many formats and compression settings. This basically turns QuickTime from a video *player* into a video *editor*. Available for Windows and Mac at www.quicktime.com.

- ✔ **iSquint:** A free drag-and-drop utility that quickly converts a video into an iPod-ready file, with options for how much quality to sacrifice for file size, and whether to use the H.264 codec or stick with MPEG-4. Available for Mac only at www.isquint.org.

- ✔ **Sorenson Squeeze:** This program offers advanced video-compression tools from an industry leader and codec developer. Available for Windows and Mac at www.sorensonmedia.com.

- ✔ **DivX:** Converts videos to the DivX compression codec. Available for Windows and Mac at www.divx.com.

- ✔ **PSP Video 9:** Converts videos to play on the PlayStation Portable. Available for Windows only at www.pspvideo9.com.

- ✔ **Videora Converter:** A conversion program to change a Windows Media File into an iPod-ready MPEG-4. Available for Windows only at www.videora.com.

Part IV
Going Public

"Well, that's typical. Ever since my parents started watching my videoblog, my mother keeps commenting that I need to add a function to brush the hair off my forehead."

In this part . . .

Of course, videoblogging is only fun if someone gets to see what you've created, right? Well, maybe not (if you're more into technical details than self-expression), but if you want an audience for your work, you may need to go out and get one.

This part talks about finding Web services for your videoblog and promoting it. It also discusses collaboration and permissions, and how to keep an eye on your visitor traffic.

Chapter 13

Making a Home for Your Vlog

In This Chapter
▶ Storing your video on the Web
▶ Posting to your videoblog
▶ Setting up subscriptions

*T*he whole idea behind videoblogging is not merely to post video to the Internet, but to make a space for your video creations and give your voice a chance to shine. In Chapter 4, I briefly talked about posting your videos to a Web-hosting service and getting them into your vlog. In this chapter, you find out more about video hosting services, different types of blogs, and how to set up a subscription for your blog.

Hosting Your Video Files

If you want to make your videos available on the Internet, you need to store the video files on a Web server provided by a Web-hosting service. The following sections discuss finding a Web-hosting service to store your video files and make them available on the Internet.

Web servers are computers set up to store Web pages and any files associated with those pages and deliver them to visitors' Web browsers, via the Internet. They do this by using a protocol called HTTP (HyperText Transfer Protocol). Web pages can contain many types of content, from regular text to images, audio files, and (of course) videos.

The server on which you store your videos is called a *hosting service,* and there are many types of hosts. Some hosting services offer basic storage space, with no bells and whistles, while others may provide a Web-based or e-mail-based uploading option, and may have page templates for you to post your video directly. Some hosting services are free, but offer less storage space and other options than hosting services that require you to pay a monthly fee.

Finding free hosting services

They say the best things in life are free, and that's certainly true. Everything seems a little better when it's free, and when you're starting a new hobby, sometimes free is the only way to afford it.

Search the Web and you will find hundreds of free hosting services. However, these sites almost always come with a price. If they don't put ads on your pages, they block remote loading of your graphics and video files — or they may not allow video at all. Many free services try to claim ownership of your content, restrict usage, or limit what you can post video about.

As with the RSS aggregators discussed in Chapter 2, the best hosting services for videobloggers have typically been sites created by other videobloggers. So sites such as http://blip.tv, http://vlogcentral.com, and http://ourmedia.org tend to have a better sense of what videobloggers need.

Since videoblogging is a new technology, many available videoblogging services are still free because the revenue models haven't been determined yet. Watch for early-adopter and beta programs to get in on the ground floor.

When you're looking for a free hosting service, read the FAQ and Terms of Service carefully. You might want to create an account and try out the services with a test video, just to make sure it works for you.

They also say that there's no such thing as a free lunch — which is true, to an extent. Hosting services are rarely 100% free. Usually, the hosting company will use your content as a way to build revenue for themselves. For instance, visitors to their site are considered a revenue source, if they can show advertisements to those visitors. So, in exchange for your free service, you may have to display an ad on your site, or the hosting company may require visitors to come to their home page (so they can display those ads) *instead* of viewing your files (say, your images and videos) directly or in your own Web page.

Although it's understandable that these companies need to make money in order to stay around, this situation also gives you a difficult choice to make. At what point is the hosting company taking more than they offer? If they have a ton of limitations, they need to be really great in all other respects to justify your using them.

A site that offers unlimited hosting without such strings, like the Internet Archive (www.archive.org), may have a very difficult user interface that makes it hard to use.

Reject any hosting service (free or not) that

- ✔ **Grabs for your rights.** Some sites try to claim exclusive rights to your content, commercial rights, or the right to redistribute your content in forms other than the one you upload it in.

- ✔ **Prevents your type of content.** If your videoblog is commercial, make sure that your free host will permit commercial content — many free hosts do not. If your videoblog contains material that's explicit or adult in nature, you'll have to search carefully for sites that permit that type of material.

- ✔ **Is too hard to use.** If you can't figure out how to upload a video and find a link to include in your blog, you won't be happy with the service anyway.

- ✔ **Requires ads in your content.** You might be willing to live with this, but personally, I prefer not to. If you do accept ads, they should be discreet text ads, or non-obnoxious banner ads at the top of your page, not interruptions in your page's content.

- ✔ **Requires pop-up ads (including pop-under ads that hide behind the current Web browser window).** Everyone hates pop-ups. Why this form of advertising is still around, I don't even know, but some hosts still use it.

- ✔ **Sells or gives your e-mail address to spammers.** Seriously big no-no. Most sign-up forms have a check box (which is automatically checked) that says it's okay for you to receive "offers from partners," *which means spam.* Some sites sell your address to spammers, or make it easy for spammers to find you by publicly listing it. A good test for this problem is to create a free e-mail address at some place like Yahoo! or Gmail, just to use for signing up, and then wait two weeks to see if any spam comes into those accounts.

- ✔ **Does not permit hot-linking or direct linking.** You can't create a hyperlink directly to your video file without direct linking. Typically if a site prevents direct links, it means you won't be able to send your video in an RSS syndication feed, discussed later in this chapter.

- ✔ **Does not permit remote loading.** Even though this primarily pertains to still images, if you embed your video in your blog entry, it won't show up if your hosting provider blocks remote loading.

These requirements apply to paid hosting services as well, though you will find that most for-pay services do not attempt to put advertising on your site or block linking and remote loading.

You'll notice that in the list I've included here, I don't mention *unlimited* bandwidth options. That's because if visitors are the currency of free hosting services, bandwidth is the big *expense*. Some reputable Web hosts offer unlimited bandwidth, as they try to scale their services up. However, past experience with Web-page hosts has shown that offering unlimited bandwidth eventually results in overloaded servers and poor performance for everyone. This may not be the case for any individual service, especially services that have just started up. But evaluate such services carefully and find out what kind of growth plan they have in place, if possible.

The Videoblogging Testing Ground at `www.beginningwithi.com/vlog/test.html` is an excellent resource for comparing and evaluating hosting services and other videoblogging services.

Using the hosting service you already have

Do you already have a Web site or Web hosting? Chances are, you do and don't even realize it. When you sign up for Internet access from your ISP (Internet service provider), you usually get a small amount of Web space included with your monthly fee. The Web space might not be much — maybe not even as much as you would need for a full video — or it could be several gigabytes of storage that you can use for your videoblog.

Check your ISP and find out whether you have Web space and how much space is available. Find out how much bandwidth you have per month, and whether they permit remote loading (some ISPs don't, even if they're running a for-pay service). If you already have a Web page, check your storage space and bandwidth to see whether there's enough to store your videos there.

And how much Web space do you need? Well, it will depend on how popular your videoblog is, how often you post videoblogs, and how big your videos are. For my videoblog, which has about 90 – 100 regular viewers, plus anyone who stumbles by, I get about 3,000 visitors a month, and use 15–16GB of bandwidth each month. Some months when I post more often, the bandwidth usage spikes up to almost 30GB per month. I also use 420MB of storage space, but have over 8 months' videos stored on that one server.

You can calculate your hosting needs by planning ahead. Figure out how many videos you will make in a month, and how long your videos will be. Then decide how often you will remove a video from your Web server (that is, archive it).

The following list gives you some guidelines to use when you're calculating your hosting needs:

✔ **Space needed for storing your videos:** The approximate size (in MB) of a video is three times the length of the video in minutes.

✔ **Number of downloads:** Calculate the number of downloads you expect to have per month by adding the number of subscribers and random visitors. Personally, I multiply the subscribers times five to get a safe estimate, but if you promote your blog videos on other Web sites, your number of downloads will be even higher.

✔ **Approximate bandwidth cost of the video:** You can estimate the amount of bandwidth you'll use per month by taking the size of your videos (in MB) and multiplying by the number of downloads you expect in that month.

For example, I have a video that is 2 minutes in length. It's about 6MB in size. I have 100 subscribers, but on average, about 300 people download any given video. To be safe, I estimate that the video will be downloaded 500 times. The bandwidth cost of this video works out to

```
6 × 500 = 3,000
```

In other words, I can expect this one video to require 3,000MB (3GB) of bandwidth. If I post five of these videos in a month, that's 15GB of bandwidth that I'll need to pay for from my Web-hosting service, and 30MB of storage. As your vlog gets more popular, your bandwidth needs will increase. Talk to your Web-service company about how to scale your service up if you need to increase your available bandwidth.

Any time you get media attention or when you kick up your promotions, you can expect a rise in the number of hits to your Web server. Keep your ear to the ground about possible media attention (sometimes reporters do not contact you to talk about your videoblog before they write a story) and monitor your server logs carefully for a couple days afterwards.

After a few months, consider archiving your old videos offline. That keeps them from being downloaded by search engines or automatically snagged by RSS aggregators. It won't make a big difference in terms of your monthly bandwidth, since most of your videos will be downloaded within the first two weeks after you post them. However, a video that can't be found doesn't cost bandwidth — and that's a good way to cut those costs if you find yourself running into trouble.

Paying for hosting service

Naturally, one option is to pay for a hosting service. In addition to the considerations and requirements already mentioned in the previous section, you'll want to find a reliable service at a reasonable price. One way to do that is to ask people you know who have Web sites about the service and reliability of their hosting services, and the response time from customer support.

You can also search online for affordable Web-hosting services. Budget web.com (www.budgetweb.com) is a directory of for-pay Web-hosting services that charge under $50 per month. I use this service for searching for Web-hosting companies, when I don't want to use my own Web server.

Here's an example of what a budgetweb.com listing includes:

- ✔ **The name of the service and IPP or VAR:** IPPs (Internet Presence Providers) own the actual hardware. VARs (Value Added Resellers) just resell space on the hardware. In general, IPPs will have more direct access for troubleshooting problems.

- ✔ **Contact information:** This should include URL, mailing address, e-mail address, and phone number.

- ✔ **Rates:** These should include monthly fees and setup fees.

- ✔ **Included storage space:** Note, as well, the cost for extra storage.

- ✔ **Bandwidth costs:** Keep in mind that additional bandwidth costs extra, and find out how much.

- ✔ **Minimum contract length:** Know the shortest contract you can sign up for.

- ✔ **How long they've been in business:** This is crucial to choosing a Web host or ISP. Web services tend to grow pretty well for a year or two — then, as soon as they get popular, they grow faster than the business can keep up with. The quality of customer service goes downhill. Find a host that's been around for at least 3 or 4 years.

- ✔ **Server connection speed, operating system, and features available:** These include CGI scripts, commercial use, non-profit discounts, access reports, secure servers, database, and support for Microsoft FrontPage (or other authoring-support environments).

- ✔ **Any notes or comments from the service provider that may be useful.**

Make sure any hosting service you find allows you to put an .htaccess file on the server if necessary, either through telnet access or from an administrator. This is also called a *password-protected directory file* — and you'll need it to make your RSS feed work in FeedBurner if you have difficulties.

In most cases, the Web-hosting services you find through Budgetweb or elsewhere will use FTP for posting files. Some may offer a secure, Web-based file-upload script that you can use to post your files. The "Uploading your files" section, later in this chapter, has instructions for using FTP and Web-based file uploaders to post your files to your Web server.

All-in-one hosting and vlogging

You will find, as you start searching for places to store your video files, that there are some sites that offer all-in-one solutions for videobloggers to store video files as well as provide their videoblogs, if they want them. These services can either be a really good thing, or not, depending on your goals.

First, let me say that, at the time of writing this book, these services were (by and large) free. They're free because they're new. So far, most of the people who run the sites haven't figured out yet how to charge for them appropriately, or what to do about bandwidth issues.

When you look at all-in-one videoblogging services, pay particular attention to the Terms of Service and how the service plans to use your content, and how they intend for you to use it. Just as with the free hosting services, it's wise to do a little research. Make sure your spam filters don't suddenly and mysteriously clog up two weeks after you subscribe to a service.

Check the Terms of Service to make sure the hosting service allows your kind of content. See if they provide an RSS feed for your videoblog, or if it's an option you can add later. They should provide a direct link to your video file and any individual blog entry.

Some of the video hosting services offer an RSS feed option. If you're not big on writing, and you just want to have a place where people can watch your videos, this may work for you. Places like Veoh (`http://veoh.com`), Dailymotion (`www.dailymotion.com`), and MySpace.com (`www.myspace.com`) offer this option.

Even though it's impossible to go into all the all-in-one services, here are some of the big ones: blip.tv (`http://blip.tv`), Ourmedia (`http://ourmedia.org`), Hipcast (`www.hipcast.com`),and TypePad (`www.typepad.com`).

In some cases, media-storage space might be included with your blog service. Usually this is true with paid blogs only, though some free services, such as blip.tv (`http://blip.tv`), offer storage as part of the blog space. TypePad (`www.typepad.com`), for instance, provides media storage for users who pay for the service, and even provides an e-mail gateway to upload files to the server.

Syndicating Your Videoblog

As I mention in Chapters 2 and 4, one of the key elements to videoblogs is the syndication — that is, the RSS or Atom feed. The *feed* is a URL that gets updated when you update your videoblog, with information on the content of your blog.

These types of feeds use XML (eXtensible Markup Language) to structure the content included in them, so while you can view a feed URL in a Web browser, it looks like a bunch of text and tags unless your browser is RSS-capable (as is Safari RSS).

One of the questions you may have is what the difference is between RSS and Atom, and if one is better for videoblogging. RSS stands for Really Simple Syndication, and Atom is a standards-oriented alternative to RSS. With either type of feed, you may be able to include enclosures, which means including a separate media file (such as an image, an audio file, or a video) along with your blog post.

Whether or not a feed can include enclosures depends on the feed's configuration, but it is one of the defining features of a videoblog is to have a feed with enclosures that visitors can subscribe to. As you set up your RSS feed, avoid services or software that do not support media enclosures.

Setting up your RSS feed

One of the easiest ways to set up an RSS feed is to use one of the RSS or Atom feed generators available online, and one of the easiest services is also free. FeedBurner is used by thousands of bloggers, podcasters, and videobloggers to deliver an RSS feed of blogs and Web sites. For most personal — and new — videobloggers, FeedBurner will meet your needs for a long time.

If you use one of the dedicated videoblogging hosting services discussed in this chapter, you may already have a feed available to you. For instance, blip.tv includes RSS and Atom feeds with single-click subscription buttons from your blip.tv site.

To create a FeedBurner feed, follow these steps:

1. **Visit www.feedburner.com and type your blog's URL into the main form, as shown in Figure 13-1. Check the I Am a Podcaster check box and click Next.**

2. **Enter a username, password, and e-mail address to create a new account on FeedBurner.**

   You will be prompted to continue setting up your feed. At the very least, click Next to continue to set up your iTunes tags for the enclosure-ready part of your feed.

3. **Select the options and include descriptions for your iTunes listing.**

   Be sure to select all rich-media content, if you might include still images or audio files instead of video files as enclosures in any individual vlog post.

4. **Click the Clickthroughs option in the stats tracker if you want to see how many times your videos are actually downloaded.**

TECHNICAL STUFF

Troubleshooting a common FeedBurner issue

Perhaps the most common issue FeedBurner users encounter is when they upload a file to their Web-hosting service, and include it as an enclosure, but FeedBurner doesn't seem to enclose the file. This is because the Web server needs to know that the file you stored there is a video file, not a text file. The file types are all defined by their MIME types in the Web server software.

By default, most Web servers are configured to report any unknown file type as a text file. But FeedBurner won't include text files in enclosures. What to do?

If you have access to the Web-hosting server through telnet and are on an Apache Web server, you can upload a file named .htaccess to your home directory that will tell the Web server how to handle your video

MIME types. Include the following lines in the .htaccess text file:

```
AddType video/x-ms-wmv .wmv
AddType video/mpeg .mp4
AddType video/quicktime .mov
```

You can add or remove MIME types if you wish. A list of MIME types is at www.w3schools.com/media/media_mimeref.asp.

If you can't upload the .htaccess file or you aren't on an Apache server (or you just have no idea what to do), contact the system administrator for your Web-hosting service, or whoever maintains the server where you have stored your videos. Ask them to add support for these MIME types. If they can't or won't help you, look for other Web-hosting services, since this is something of a deal-breaker in getting your videos out to your subscribers.

Figure 13-1: Quickly create a feed in FeedBurner.

When you're done, FeedBurner prompts you to publicize your feed through various services, such as ping services (to automatically tell aggregators that your vlog was updated). In addition, you'll find some tools for troubleshooting. Note that your feed won't pick up more than one enclosure per post, so if you want to have multiple files in a post, you'll have to pick one to enclose and post it as the first link in your vlog post.

Creating your own RSS feed

The RSS feed is just a file stored on your Web server that tells RSS readers where to find the latest posts; it is tagged with XML tags that RSS readers can decode. In some cases, you can hand-code your RSS feed using software that goes on your desktop, like FeedForAll (`www.feedforall.com`), shown in Figure 13-2.

If you manage your own Web server, you can put a hand-built RSS feed file on your server, or install an RSS or Atom feed automation script to pull content from your blog automatically. RSS scripts are available in nearly every programming architecture, including PHP, Perl, and .NET, and if you also manage your own blogging server, you may find the blog software has feed automation built in (or easily available).

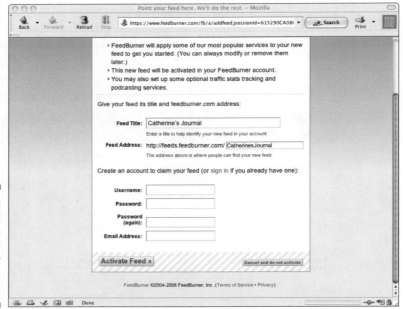

Figure 13-2: FeedForAll lets you create and update your RSS feed file.

Here's a sampling of the available feed programs and services:

- **U2U SharePoint:** http://blog.u2u.info/DottextWeb/patrick/archive/2005/02/17/1129.aspx
- **PHP:** www.phpclasses.org/browse/package/2957.html
- **2RSS:** www.2rss.com/software.php
- **Code Project RSS Feed creator:** www.codeproject.com/csharp/rssfeedcreator.asp
- **MyRSSCreator:** www.myrsscreator.com
- **Feedforall:** www.feedforall.com
- **ListGarden:** www.softwaregarden.com/products/listgarden/index.html

For a really in-depth look at Web syndication of all kinds of content, check out *Syndicating Web Sites with RSS Feeds For Dummies* by Ellen Finkelstein (Wiley).

Using other types of syndication

Another option for syndication that doesn't use RSS is to use scripting languages (such as JavaScript) to include your content on someone else's Web site. Naturally, this only works if the other person participates in the syndication.

JavaScript has been used for years to syndicate content from various sources into Web sites. A tutorial on creating a JavaScript-based syndication is available at www.barelyfitz.com/projects/jssyndicate.

Adding metadata to a feed

In RSS, you can include a lot of data that isn't content, but is instead *about* your content. For instance, when you sign up for a FeedBurner feed, you have the option to include about a dozen iTunes-specific *metadata tags* that describe the file (such as creator, date, copyright, and so forth). These tags are only for iTunes, but you can use them to send information about a specific videoblog post, such as its copyright or creative commons license information, summaries, or information about the whole videoblog.

You can get a complete list of the tags that are specific to the iTunes Music Store at www.apple.com/itunes/podcasts/techspecs.html.

Enclosing files in your feed

Aha! Finally you get to the actual process of including the files in your feed! Most blog interfaces do not have a space that says "add your video file here." So how do you include the video, once you have a home for it on the Web?

First, make sure you have the URL of your video file, wherever you stored it on the Web. You absolutely need that URL if you want to enclose your video as a file.

When you post to your blog, you will have to use HTML. Many blogging programs offer a rich text editor where you just click buttons to add hyperlinks and formatting. That won't do for enclosures, so you'll have to wrestle with a tiny bit of HTML. Now, in your blogging software, type the following hyperlink:

```
<a href="http://www.example.com/Video/MyVideo.mov"
   rel="enclosure">Click here!</a>
```

That's it. Replace *http://www.example.com/Video/MyVideo.mov* with the complete URL for your own video, of course, but all you really need is a link to the video with `rel="enclosure"` inside the hyperlink tag. Notice that the URL and enclosure are both inside quotes, and that there's a closing `</a>` tag at the end of the link.

At this point, your RSS feed sends the video file to your subscribed viewers when their RSS reader programs check your site. In the next section, I talk more about how to get the video to play in your blog and still get sent to your subscribers.

RSS feeds can only pick up one enclosure per post, and many feeds pick up the first media file found. Always use the enclosure attribute for the first link to a media file on your page.

Posting to Your Blog

Once you have selected a Web-hosting service to store your video files, you can upload your files to the server and post them to your blog. This is the key step that takes you from making video to publishing and distributing it. As I mentioned in Chapter 4, you'll upload your files to your Web-hosting server, and then post to your blog with a link to include your video.

Uploading your files

Once you have your video file ready to go, you have to get it from your computer onto your Web server. You do this by uploading it to your Web server. That's because there is no practical way to keep the files on your desktop computer and make them available on the Web, so trust me on this: *You will need to store your video files on your Web server.*

There are many ways to get the files from your computer into your Web server. If your server is in your garage, you can use the SneakerNet. That's where you put the files on a diskette (remember those?) or CD-ROM, and wear your sneakers while you walk over to the server to copy the files onto it.

A more common method to upload your videos, however, is to use the Internet in one of the following ways:

- ✔ **Web page:** Your Web service might offer a Web page where you can upload your files.
- ✔ **E-mail:** Your Web service might even provide an e-mail address where you can send the file and have it stored automatically.
- ✔ **Client program:** You might use a separate software program on your computer, called a client program, to upload your file.
- ✔ **FTP:** You might upload files by using FTP (File Transfer Protocol). FTP is a very stable technology for transferring files over the Internet; it's been around longer than the World Wide Web has.

Uploading using a Web interface

The most common method for uploading a file to free Web-hosting services is to use a Web interface, and it's not uncommon even for paid or dedicated Web hosts to offer it. With this method, your Web hosting provider has installed a script on your Web site that includes a form to upload a file to your server. Figure 13-3 shows an example of a Web interface for uploading files to a hosting service.

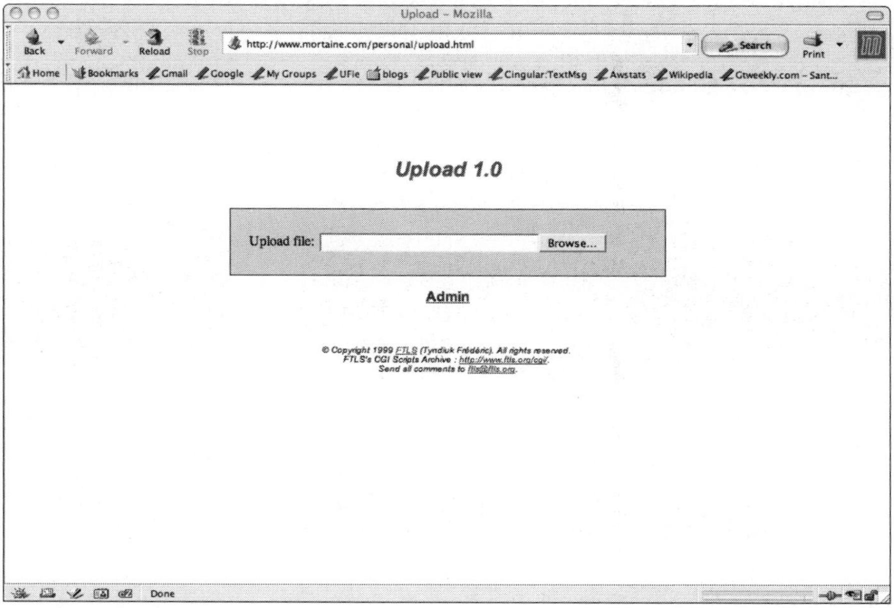

Figure 13-3:
A Web-based upload page.

Each hosting service uses its own unique Web-based upload page, so the names of buttons and fields may vary from host to host. The following steps provide the basic actions required to upload a file using a Web-based upload page:

1. **Fill in any fields about the file, such as the name of the video, your licensing requirements, or the genre.**

2. **Click the Browse button.**

3. **From the File dialog box, locate the file you want to upload.**

4. **Highlight the desired file and click OK to add it to the page.**

    The path to the file will appear in the file fields next to the Browse button.

5. **When you are done filling in the whole form, click the Submit button to send your video file to the server.**

Uploading via e-mail

E-mailing a file to the hosting service is the easiest way to upload a file, but also the one you're least likely to encounter, and the one with the most restrictions. You're most likely to find a post-by-e-mail setup for your blog, and if your blog accepts video attachments, you may be able to post them through the e-mail gateway as well. For example, TypePad offers this service, as do a few others.

In this method, your Web-hosting provider gives you an e-mail address to send your files to, and you send an e-mail to that address, with the video as a file attachment.

As part of this method, the e-mail address you post to is usually pretty obscure, containing a secret code that spammers can't guess. Keep that e-mail address to yourself. If you post that address anywhere on the Internet, you'll start seeing spam for online pharmacies and "great business opportunities" showing up in your blog.

E-mailing your vlog posts as your upload method is pretty easy, but the main limitation for this method is that you'll be restricted in the file size of your videos. It's very hard to send large files by e-mail; anything more than 10MB, and the e-mail server will probably reject the file, even if it doesn't take forever to accept it.

Uploading through a desktop client

Some Web hosting providers, particularly those dedicated to video, have created their own client programs you can use in uploading your videos to these providers. The main reason these services offer such a client is because Web and e-mail can both be slow about transmitting large amounts of data. In addition, using the Web or e-mail for uploading large files means that you can't use your Web browser or e-mail client while it's busy uploading your file.

The standalone client, on the other hand, installs on your own computer. Thus it may be platform-dependent, running only on a Mac or a Windows computer (or having separate installation programs for each).

Figure 13-4 shows the standalone client for Vlogcentral, a video-hosting service that provides Web space to videobloggers. When you use this tool to post a video, the program uploads the video to Vlogcentral, then posts directly to your blog with the video and any comments you've added in the program. It's small, easy to use, and relatively fast compared to other uploading methods.

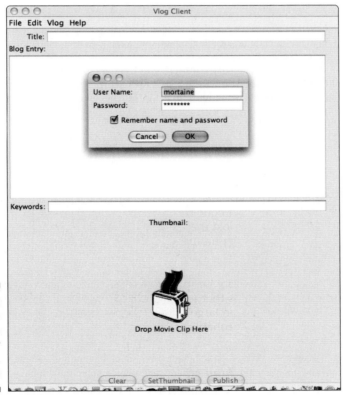

Figure 13-4:
The standalone client for Vlogcentral. com

Uploading via FTP

One of the oldest, most reliable technologies for transferring files over a network — FTP — is still around after decades of use. It's small and works on every platform, everywhere, as shown in Figure 13-5.

Figure 13-5:
An FTP
transfer.

Unfortunately, FTP is not terribly easy to use, unless you use a separate FTP client program (such as CuteFTP, shown in Figure 13-6), or you're comfortable with command-line programs, such as those favored by UNIX users.

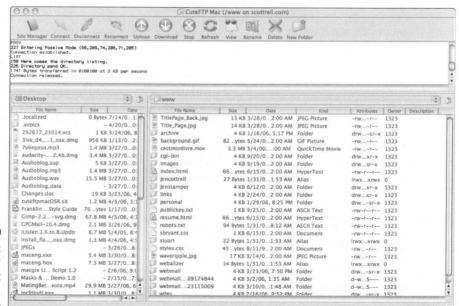

Figure 13-6:
An FTP
client
program.

For security reasons, there's now a new protocol called sFTP, for Secure FTP. The commands are the same as for FTP, but it works over an encrypted connection.

Whether you access FTP with the command-line program or a client with a graphical user interface, the basic commands are the same. A client with a graphical interface just converts your on-screen clicks and drags into the commands listed in Table 13-1.

Table 13-1	FTP Commands
Command	*Description*
open *example.com*	Connect to the server.
binary	Switch to transferring binary files (such as images, music, and video).
ascii	Switch to transferring text files (such as .txt and .html files).
lcd *path/to/local/file*	Change the current directory on your hard drive to the directory specified in the path.
cd *path/to/web/directory*	Change directories on the server to the Web directory.
put *filename*.mp4	Upload the file (filename.mp4) to the server.
get *filename*.mp4	Download the file from your server.
close	Logout of the FTP server.

In an FTP program with a graphical user interface, you may have side-by-side panels to drag files from one system onto the other, but the underlying communication is no more than put *filename.file* and cd *directory/name*.

To use the command-line interface for FTP, just open a console window. In Windows, you can do this by launching the MS-DOS window, or by selecting Run from the Start menu. The Run dialog box appears, as shown in Figure 13-7.

Figure 13-7: The Run dialog box.

Run

Type the name of a program, folder, document, or Internet resource, and Windows will open it for you.

Open: ftp mortaine.com

OK   Cancel   Browse...

When the Run dialog box appears, type

```
ftp www.exampleserver.com
```

where `www.exampleserver.com` is the URL for your Web server or hosting company (the hosting company may have provided this information for you in their customer support pages).

In Mac OS X, the console is called Terminal, and you can launch it from the Utilities folder in your Applications folder. Launch it and type `ftp www.exampleserver.com`, as in the Windows example.

Typing `ftp www.exampleserver.com` from the command line before you have an active FTP session is the same as launching FTP and then typing `open www.exampleserver.com`.

Once you open an FTP connection to your Web server, you will need to provide your username and password. This authenticates you and grants you permission to upload files. FTP can also be used anonymously to download files from anonymous FTP servers. In such cases, the login name is usually `anonymous` and the password is your e-mail address.

Once in, you need to navigate to the directories where your video file is stored on your hard drive, and where you want to put it on the Web server. In Table 13-1, `path/to/local/file` indicates the local path. On Windows machines, this usually starts with `C:\` and uses a backslash (\) to separate directories, as in the following example:

```
C:\Users\Me\My Documents\Videos
```

On Mac OS X, it's `/Volumes/` followed by the hard drive's name:

```
/Volumes/Media/Videos/
```

When you send the `put` command with the filename, FTP will upload the file to the server.

Change the file-transfer type to `binary` before uploading video files! Some FTP clients do this for you automatically.

Writing your vlog entry text and markup

Once your video file has been uploaded to a Web server, you can make a blog entry that includes the video as part of the entry. To write the blog entry, just write a post that describes your video, or talks about creating it, or just makes a little joke. Then you use a bit of HTML code, either to include a link to the video or to embed the video directly into the blog entry.

If you're looking for a quick way to generate the code for your page, and don't want to hassle with all that HTML stuff, visit Free Video Codes (`http://freevideocoding.com`) and fill out the form to generate the code. You'll need to know what type of file it is — and its URL on your Web server — but you'll be able to quickly create the code to make a link to your video or embed it in your blog, as you desire.

Including a link to the video

People differ on whether they want to include a link to their video, or just include the video itself. Many people prefer to have the video appear in their Web page directly, so visitors can just click it and go. Others want to spare their visitors the bandwidth stress of downloading a video that they may or may not want to watch.

In either case, you can attach your video file to your blog entry as an enclosure for your RSS feed, whether you use a link or an embedded video (or even use both). To link to an embedded video and have it included with your RSS feed, use the following code:

```
<a href="http://www.exampleserver.com/video.mp4"
   rel="enclosure">Click here for the video!</a>
```

Note that the URL you put in place of *http://www.exampleserver.com/ video.mp4* should be the direct URL to your video file. Make sure you include the `rel="enclosure"` part in the hyperlink, to include the file in your RSS feed.

You can also include an image from the video to use as the link to the video. (See Chapter 6 for details on saving a frame of a video as an image.) In this case, you'll need to save a frame as a JPEG image, upload it to your Web server, and then include it in addition to or instead of the `Click here` text in the example just given. The code for that would look like this:

```
<a href="http://www.exampleserver.com/video.mp4"
   rel="enclosure"><img src= "http://www.exampleserver.
   com/video.jpg" />Click here for the video!</a>
```

All HTML tags have to be *closed* in order to comply with XHTML and XML (like your RSS feed). *Closing tags* are the same as the initial tag, but with a slash in front of them: For example, `</a>` is the closing tag for a hyperlink, and `</b>` is the closing tag for bolding text. For a very few tags, usually for single-instance items like images, you close the tag by putting the slash at the end of the single tag, for example: `<img src="http://www. exampleservercom/video.jpg" />`. To discover more about HTML and

XHTML, check out `www.w3schools.com/tags` or any good HTML or XHTML book, such as *Creating Web Pages For Dummies* by Bud E. Smith and Arthur Bebak or *XHTML For Dummies* by Ed Tittel et al. (Wiley).

If you want to embed a video that does not load until the user clicks to play it, visit the vPiP (video Play in Place) generator at `http://cirne.com/blog/lucid_media/?p=8`. The author of that tutorial, Enric Teller, also has a plug-in for the Wordpress blogging platform based on the same tutorial, available at `http://utilities.cinegage.com/videos-playing-in-place`.

Posting an embedded video

An *embedded video* works similarly to an image: It displays directly in the Web page, as shown in Figure 13-8. Not all Web browsers support embedded videos correctly, so if you use this method, be aware that you may alienate potential viewers, and always include a link for people who want to download the video file directly instead of trying to watch it in their browsers.

To post an embedded video, you use either the `<embed>` or `<object>` tags. These two tags work more or less the same, but the `<object>` tag complies with the XHTML standard and is supposed to be used for any embeddable media — be it video, images, or audio.

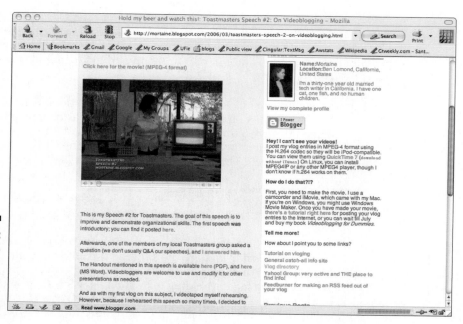

Figure 13-8: A video embedded into the page.

Unfortunately, Safari, the default Web browser for Mac OS X, does not support the <object> tag prior to version 2.0, which is only available to users of Mac OS X 10.4 and later. Even more unfortunately, due to a patent conflict, recently updated versions of Internet Explorer 6.0 for Windows won't display *any* embedded files until the user clicks to confirm an annoying pop-up box. You can post your video as an embedded object and annoy a bunch of your videoblog visitors, you can post the video as a link only, or you can use Java-Script to embed the object, as described in the next section on posting with JavaScript.

So you have the choice between supporting the standard <object> tag (leaving your Safari/OS X 10.3 visitors out in the cold), supporting all but a few browsers by using the <embed> tag, and not annoying your Internet Explorer users by working around their Web browser's newly-imposed limitations. Or you can try to serve them all by using JavaScript to detect the browser and deliver the right tag, or by including *two* tags — one an <embed> and the other an <object> tag.

If you use the <embed> tag, also use a <noembed> tag with a plain hyperlink to your video file, so browsers that don't support <embed> can still see it. In the <object> tag, you can just include the HTML for the link between the <object> and </object> tags:

```
<noembed><a href="http://www.exampleserver.com/video.mp4"
    rel="enclosure">Click here for the video!</a></noembed>
```

How much of a difference does this make? Well, despite claims to the contrary, I found that Web browsers that claim not to support <embed>, even Internet Explorer, actually did display an embedded QuickTime movie just fine — whereas the <object> tag in Safari definitely resulted in a blank space where the video should be. But the dialog box in Internet Explorer can't be denied.

As for how to use these tags, they work more or less the same:

```
<object src="http://www.exampleserver.com/video.mp4"
    rel="enclosure" height="260" width="320"
    autostart="false"></object>
```

This code tells the Web browser the height and width to provide for the video file. In this case, the video is normally 320 pixels wide by 240 pixels high (the standard scale for iPod-ready videos). However, you'll note that I added 20 pixels to the height. That's for player controls such as the Play/Pause button.

The rel="enclosure" attribute should be familiar by now; it tells the RSS feed, in case you didn't have a link earlier in the post, that this file is the one to enclose. If you define the `autostart` attribute as `false`, then your video will load on the Web page, but will not start playing until the visitor clicks the Play button. This is important so users don't accidentally stumble on your site and start playing a video they didn't want to play in the first place. It's also handy if you have more than one videoblog post on a blog page, so they won't all start playing at once. If you use a clickable link, you don't have to set the `autostart` to `false`. Presumably visitors will click the link themselves after they've already chosen to download and play your video.

Finally, you can include the `<embed>` tag inside the `<object>` tag:

```
<object src="http://www.exampleserver.com/video.mp4"
    rel="enclosure" height="260" width="320"
    autostart="false">
<embed src="http://www.exampleserver.com/video.mp4"
    rel="enclosure" height="260" width="320"
    autostart="false">
<noembed><a href="http://www.exampleserver.com/video.mp4"
    rel="enclosure">Click here for the video!</a></noembed>
</embed>
</object>
```

This approach displays the embedded video as an `<object>` for browsers that support it, or as an `<embed>` for those that don't. (It's also the approach I use in the next section, "Posting with JavaScript.")

Some video-hosting services do not permit remote loading of your video, so embedding video from those services will not work. The file will not appear on-screen, even if you can visit it directly by going to its URL.

Posting with JavaScript

Let me first say that using JavaScript to post your video is a workaround to sidestep a change made by Microsoft to Internet Explorer 6. The summary of the situation is this: In April 2006, as a result of a patent conflict, Microsoft changed the way Internet Explorer 6 handles embedded objects, that is, anything using an `<embed>` or `<object>` tag. As users updated their Web browsers, they found that they would get an annoying pop-up box prompting them to let an ActiveX object run, as shown in Figure 13-9).

Figure 13-9:
The ActiveX
prompt in
Internet
Explorer.

There is currently no way for users to disable the prompt on their own computers — the only way to get around it is for them to stop using Internet Explorer 6. To work around this obstacle and still have your video appear embedded in your blog, you must use JavaScript to load it into your blog page. To do this, you will need to have some place to store your JavaScript file, or you can use the one I have posted to the book's Web site. Unlike most JavaScript applications, this one requires you to have the JavaScript outside the Web page in order to get around the dialog box. You then insert a small bit of code into your blog post that calls the JavaScript file and tells it to use your own movie file.

This approach does not work in Blogger, because as of this writing, Blogger does not allow you to run a script from your blog post. However, there are other approaches that do work in Blogger, which are mentioned at the end of this section.

Start with the external JavaScript file. It's a fairly simple script that writes the `<object>` or `<embed>` tags into the page when it runs. The lines with `//` at the start are comments about what each line does. You can leave them out of your own JavaScript code if you wish.

```
// create a function to write the object and embed tags:
function embed_vlog(vlog_url,vlog_width,vlog_height) {

// writes the object tag.
document.write('<object src="' + vlog_url + '" width="' +
    vlog_width + '" height="' + vlog_height + '"
    autostart="false">'

// and the embed tag, for older browsers.
+ '<embed src="' + vlog_url + '" width="' + vlog_width +
    '" height="' + vlog_height + '"
    autostart="false"></embed>'

// and the noembed tag, for really non-compliant browsers.
+ '<noembed><a href="' + vlog_url + '">Click to play the
    video!</a></noembed>');

// closes the object tag.
+ '</object>');

//ends the function
}
```

Save this code in a text file and name it `embed.js`. In your blog post or in your blog template, use the following line of code to call this JavaScript:

```
<script src="embed.js"></script>
```

The line of code just mentioned must only appear once on your blog page — and it should appear first, before any of the videos show up. If more than one video appears on your blog at a time, put it into your template, preferably in the <head> section of your blog page template.

Now, in the blog post itself, wherever you want the video to show up, you include this code to send the video file information to the JavaScript and embed the video:

```
<script language="JavaScript">
    embed_vlog('URL','320','260')
</script>
```

The embed_vlog part in this code calls on the embed.js file you created and referred to earlier. Replace the URL with your own videoblog file's URL. 320 is the width of the video in pixels, and 260 is its height (which adds 20 pixels extra for the video player controls). Using this script and instructions and a post template, you can post your videos without taking much more time than writing the blog text.

Having trouble typing everything into your Web site? Don't worry — you can download the embed.js and example templates at the *Videoblogging For Dummies* Web site at www.mortaine.com/vlogdummies and copy and paste them into your blog.

There are cases where this workaround just won't work, such as when users don't have JavaScript enabled on their Web browsers. For these cases, always include a plain-text link in your vlog post, outside of the JavaScript-generated code.

Microsoft has fixed the way embedded objects are handled in Internet Explorer 7, but until IE 7 has been released and adopted by nearly everyone, this is the way to go.

There are other solutions to this issue, some more elegant and standards-compliant than mine, and some that are friendlier to non-JavaScript blog services. In particular, Enric Teller's vPIP (video Play in Place) (http://utilities.cinegage.com/videos-playing-in-place) is a great tool for creating a one-click interface to changing from a JPEG to the movie. And David Meade's Video Player Test JavaScript converts any media file referred to in a Web page into an embedded player (www.davidmeade.com/resources/media_test.php).

Posting with alternative formats and options

Another option is to use JavaScript to offer your visitors multiple choices of file format and viewing options. For instance, you can use JavaScript to let users select from some available video file formats, such as QuickTime .mov, MPEG-4, or Windows Media File.

If you use a JavaScript to let users select a file format, you will need to convert every video into each file format you make available — and upload all those versions to your Web server. This is where some video-hosting services like blip.tv and Vlogcentral.com come in handy — they'll convert your videos for you and generate the form to let users select a preferred file format, as shown in Figure 13-10. If you have multiple sizes of your video, or different encoding options, you can use a similar JavaScript for users to select the larger size or smaller size, or the different encoding options.

A couple of all-in-one solutions — particularly VlogCentral.com — generate the code for multiple media formats so you don't have to (and, in the case of VlogCentral, they convert and compress the video from your high-quality file as well).

Figure 13-10:
A JavaScript can generate a form to select the file format you'd like to use.

There are many browser-detection JavaScript tutorials available that you can use to detect what kind of plug-ins a user has available — and either display that file or provide a form with options to choose from, perhaps even saving the users' preferences in a cookie so they won't have to fill in the form when they visit your vlog again. Some of these tutorials are

- ✔ The JavaScript Kit Plugin Detector at `www.javascriptkit.com/script/script2/plugindetect.shtml`
- ✔ Page Resource's JavaScript browser detection script at `www.pageresource.com/jscript/jbrowse.htm`
- ✔ The JavaScript Browser Sniffer at `www.webreference.com/tools/browser/javascript.html`
- ✔ JavaScript City at `www.javascriptcity.com/scripts/detect1.htm`

Additionally, any search for *JavaScript browser detection* or *browser plug-in detection JavaScript* in your favorite search engine will yield a heaping helping of JavaScript tutorials to help you figure this out.

Using Peer-to-Peer Services to Share Your Vlogs

The popularity of technology used on the Internet seems to wax and wane in cycles. Technology that was old finds a new space somewhere else. Streaming media, once a hot technology for the Internet, becomes a delivery medium for online radio and television. What used to be called *streaming* is now simply *webcasting*. Similarly, peer-to-peer file sharing has been around since 1981, when the Internet was still the exclusive domain of government and educational institutions. Even RSS is a new technology for an old concept: subscribing to a source of content and reading it in a software program and format of your choosing. Internet users have been reading Usenet news posts this way for decades. The difference is in the details: while Usenet is authored by anyone with a computer, an RSS feed is authored by a single authenticated source.

These technologies may not be new, but the ways they combine with new technologies and fads are. For example, although peer-to-peer systems used to be a way to transfer files from one computer to another, these days they're used to share files across a distributed network, and they have built-in mechanisms for searching for — and managing — content.

There are certain sticky legal issues with these peer-to-peer networks, which have cast a lot of shadow on these services. This is unfortunate, because videoblogging might just be the most legitimate use for peer-to-peer media networks — ever. After all, videobloggers post their own content, for free, to the Internet. Peer-to-peer networks allow users to distribute content easily, for free, over the Internet. Just because a large number of individuals have posted copyrighted songs and movies does not automatically make the entire technology illegitimate.

Peer-to-peer services use standalone applications for downloading and sharing media — BitTorrent and Napster are the most commonly known peer-to-peer network services. In this chapter, I talk about BitTorrent, but many of the concepts also apply to publishing with Napster, Gnutella, and other peer-to-peer services.

With BitTorrent, shown in Figure 13-11, you download files at the same time that you upload them, a kind of bandwidth-sharing circle that means nobody downloads for free. To install BitTorrent, go to `www.bittorrent.com` and download the installation program for your operating system and run it.

Figure 13-11: BitTorrent downloads and uploads simultaneously.

The main advantage to using BitTorrent is if you have a very large file, sharing it on BitTorrent can cut down your bandwidth costs. When you publish a single `.torrent` file, the file is shared from one computer to the next, distributing the bandwidth cost around the world, like a high-tech and more reliable game of Telephone.

Downloading a Torrent

The key to a BitTorrent download is the `.torrent` file. After you install the BitTorrent client, search the BitTorrent site for a media file you'd like to download. As an example, I've posted a `.torrent` file called `VideobloggingForDummies` to my Web server.

Follow these steps to download the `VideobloggingForDummies.torrent` file:

1. **Search for the at the BitTorrent site (or get it from `www.mortaine.com/blogs/vlogdummies.torrent`).**

   (If you search for the file on BitTorrent, make sure you get the version from `www.mortaine.com`!)

2. **Download just the `.torrent` file to your desktop.**

   This text file tells the BitTorrent program where to find the videos in that Torrent.

3. **Open the Torrent in BitTorrent and watch the video.**

   You'll notice that the program shows the download and upload bandwidth used so far, as well as an estimated time for completing the download.

4. **When the file finishes downloading, click Show to view the file on your hard drive, and double-click it to open it.**

This is an `.avi` file, which means it's large, at a higher quality level than a more compressed file format, and you can edit it if you want.

Uploading a Torrent

Remember that the main reason to publish a Torrent is to make it easier to download large files. So don't use this technology to publish vlog entries of only a few minutes or under 50MB.

The full instructions for publishing with BitTorrent are available from the BitTorrent official Web site: `www.bittorrent.com/guide.html`. The basic steps are as follows:

1. **Create the video file and store it on your hard drive.**

2. **Install a BitTorrent tracker on your Web site (or get permission to use someone else's).**

   One tracker program you can install on your blog is BlogTorrent: `www.blogtorrent.com`.

3. **Generate a `.torrent` file and upload it to your Web server.**

   Your Web server will need to have the MIME-type for `torrent` set to `application/x-bittorrent` in order for this to work. Otherwise, when people download the file, it downloads as plain text.

4. **Download the .torrent file from your Web server, but specify your download directory as the directory in which you stored the full video file.**

5. **Post a link to the .torrent file to your Web site or blog.**

Once people start downloading your file, more people will be able to download it — and the bandwidth cost will be shared across many computers, not just your Web server.

Syndicating a Torrent with RSS

The main two things you need to know about including a .torrent file in an RSS feed are that your Web server needs to have the MIME-type for the .torrent file set correctly, and your viewers must have BitTorrent installed before they can download the file and upload it to the next peer.

From there, including the Torrent file is not much different from including a video as an enclosure. You can either include it as a <link>, or use the rel="enclosure" attribute in your hyperlink to send it along with your RSS feed.

Chapter 14

Getting the Word Out

In This Chapter

▶ Getting your videoblog listed in directories

▶ Attracting the media

▶ Promoting your videoblog creatively

▶ Becoming active in the videoblogging community

Making a videoblog is great, and many people stop there and keep their vlogs as a personal medium, just for a small circle of friends. If you're content to let momentum spread your vlog for you, that's great; don't do a lot of promotion, just make sure you know your intended audience is aware of it.

But if you got into videoblogging to share your vision with the *whole* world, or you really do think you'd like a little bit of fame, then you'll need to promote your vlog and make sure people know who you are and what you're doing. This chapter shows you how to get the word out about your vlog.

Getting Exposure on the Web and in the Media

Promoting your work can be a daunting prospect. After all, there are all those search engines to submit to! And . . . well, wait. Isn't that all of it?

It's not. Search engines are only one small part of promoting your videoblog, and search engine results can be bought. There's also advertising, vlog-specific directories, the iTunes Music Store, and all the avenues of the mainstream press and media. Don't be discouraged, though. You can control how much exposure you want from most of these, and for the ones you can't control, such as the mainstream media and word of mouth, the value of those visitors, who are usually more interested and have already been sold on your vlog (even if you're not selling anything) is priceless.

Listing your videoblog in directories

There are two main ways to increase your videoblog's visibility. You can create a great videoblog site and wait passively for the hordes to come beating down your door — or you can put some effort into promoting your videoblog and getting the word out.

Although promoting your vlog requires greater continuing effort, you can have a lot of fun with your public image, communicating with the public, and finding just the right blend of personal and professionalism in your outward, Internet-enabled self.

Also, promoting your vlog gives you a greater connection with your audience. As you get feedback from your vlog entries, you get a sense of who you're attracting to your site. As you spend more time or money on promoting and marketing your videoblog, you also find out which marketing techniques work best for drawing in the audience you want.

The following directories are good places to list your videoblog. I've put information on listing with the bigger names in Internet media — iTunes, Yahoo! Video, and Google Video — in the following subsections.

- **Mefeedia (www.mefeedia.com):** A listing and aggregator service for videoblogs. Lets you add your feed and subscribe to vlogs from the Web page.

- **Vlogdir (www.vlogdir.com):** The original videoblogger's directory. Lets you add a feed and categorize it based on content.

- **Vlogmap (www.vlogmap.com):** A geographically-based vlogging directory. Add yourself by Zip code or GPS coordinates, and see who's vlogging nearby.

- **FireANT (http://fireant.tv):** The directory that links into the FireANT vlog-reader program.

- **PodcastAlley (www.podcastalley.com):** A more general-purpose directory for podcasters, with monthly ratings competitions and a Video Podcast category.

- **The Pod Lounge (www.thepodlounge.com.au):** Another podcast-oriented directory, this one based in Australia.

Additionally, if you have a videoblog that's targeted to a specific theme or audience, look for directories that relate to that specific subject matter. For instance, if you're interested in Siamese fighting fish, the California Betta Society's videoblog should be listed, along with directories of fishkeeping and resources on betta fish. (Though they may not tell you who's the betta fish.)

Getting listed in iTunes

Probably the number-one question the iTunes Music Store gets from podcasters is, "How do I get listed?" Apple is a bit pickier than most directories, and they do review podcasts and videoblogs as they go into the system. Even if you do everything right, you might end up waiting several days before your vlog shows up in the store. Just remember that users can still subscribe to your videoblog directly from iTunes — they just can't search for your videoblog in the iTunes Music Store until it's listed.

To have your vlog appear in the iTunes Music Store, you'll need an RSS feed with enclosures, a podcast image that will display as a placeholder for your videoblog in the store, and an RSS feed with the iTunes-specific tags for the iTunes categories. You'll also need to have iTunes installed on your system.

Your videoblog must use MPEG-4 or QuickTime movie (.mov) file formats to be listed in the iTunes Music Store.

If you use FeedBurner or a similar service to generate your feed, you may have the option to automatically include the iTunes tags, as shown in Figure 14-1.

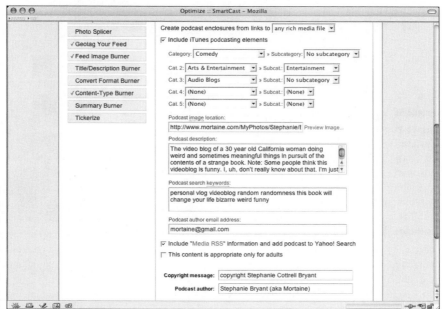

Figure 14-1:
Add the iTunes-specific tags to your feed in FeedBurner.

If you don't have this option, you'll need to add the tags to your feed. Configure your RSS feed to include the iTunes feed to include the author and category tags, the image, owner, and whether or not it's explicit.

You can find the technical details for iTunes, including all the iTunes RSS tags, at www.apple.com/itunes/podcasts/techspecs.html.

After you've added to tags to your feed, follow these steps to add your videoblog to iTunes:

1. **Launch iTunes.**

   Note that you must be using iTunes 4.2 or higher.

2. **Launch the iTunes Music Store by selecting it in the Source panel, as shown in Figure 14-2.**

Figure 14-2:
Select the
Music Store
to open
iTunes
Music
Store.

3. **Click the <u>Podcasts</u> link to open the Podcasts directory.**

4. **Click the <u>Submit a Podcast</u> link.**

5. **Enter the URL for your RSS feed to add it to the directory.**

6. **Click Continue to add your videoblog.**

If the videoblog doesn't have iPod-compatible files, such as `.mov`, `.mp4`, or `.m4v`, iTunes will reject the feed outright. The feed will be added to iTunes, but may take several days to appear in the Music Store.

If you have trouble with your listing later, find the videoblog listing in the iTunes Music Store or in your Podcasts list and click the <u>Report a Concern</u> link at the bottom of your screen, as shown in Figure 14-3. In the comment field, type **is mine**, and then report your concern or issue.

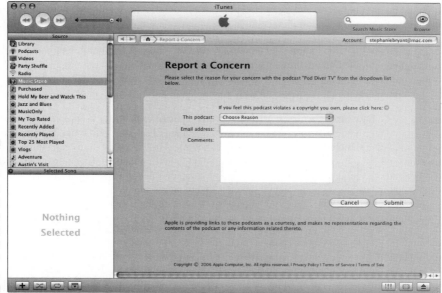

Figure 14-3:
Click the Report a Concern link to give feedback to Apple on your videoblog.

Listing with Yahoo! and Google video services

Yahoo! and Google recently added video features to their search engines, and videoblogs can now be found in both directories.

For Google Video, you have to use the Video Uploader tool offered at the Google Web site in order to have your videos appear in their directory, and they don't support feeds. They also hand-approve each video before it goes live — a time-consuming process that makes it difficult for videobloggers to get their feet in the door. Additionally, Google's mainly Web-based interface using Flash flies in the face of what videobloggers generally perceive as the best videoblog viewing environment — one in which the audience controls what browsers or viewers they use, and when and where they use 'em.

If you're willing to upload each videoblog entry twice (once to your videoblog and once to Google) — or if you're a major media producer who can get in through Google's separate approval process for what the videobloggers like to call "the big money guys" — then it may be worthwhile to upload video to Google. Or, by the time this book makes it to press, Google may have figured it out and jumped on the RSS-enclosure bandwagon, and started including RSS feeds in their Google Video service.

As for Yahoo! Video, the process is much easier, because they know the value of Media-enabled RSS feeds. Follow these steps to list your videoblog on Yahoo! Video:

1. **Go to Yahoo! and click the <u>How to Suggest a Site</u> link at the bottom of the page.**

   It's a tiny link that's very hard to see, but it's there.

2. **In the Yahoo! Search Submission list of options, click the <u>Submit Your Media Content for Free</u> link.**

   A form appears where you enter the required info about your videoblog, as shown in Figure 14-4.

3. **Enter the feed URL for your videoblog, your e-mail address, and your videoblog's Web site URL in the form and click the Submit Your Feed button.**

   In a few days, your video will show up when users search for it in Yahoo! Video.

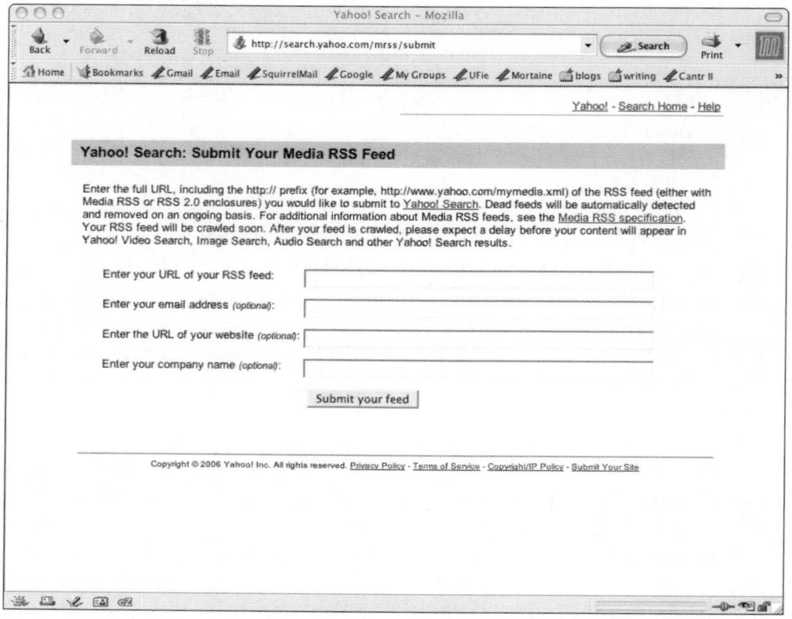

Figure 14-4:
Submit your videoblog's RSS feed.

Placing online advertisements

One of the quick ways to generate hits to your videoblog is to place online advertisements. There are many ways to do this, of course, some more intrusive than others. For instance, you can contact an individual Web site owner about placing an advertisement on their site. Or you can use an online advertising company to help promote your vlog.

In general, vloggers have avoided all but a few advertisements because they cost money that could be better spent on new camcorders and microphones. If your videoblog is non-commercial, you might want to stay out of the ads unless you're independently wealthy. If your vlog is commercial, however, you probably will need to promote it through ads and search engine placements. Google (www.google.com)

offers keyword buys, where you can make your videoblog show up at the top of the search results for a keyword, provided you're willing to pay for it. You can also place an ad in the unobtrusive Google text ads. Both of these are controllable advertising expenses that reap good results.

Later in this chapter, I talk about becoming part of the videoblogging community. If you find a videoblog you like and think their viewers would like your vlog, talk to the vlogger about appearing in their vlog, either as a paid sponsor of an individual vlog post, or just as a friend, if your vlog is non-commercial. Depending on your vlog's content, you might just get some positive results!

Getting your name in the press

Of course, your 15 minutes of fame don't really begin until you have real, honest-to-goodness press coverage in the mainstream media. That means newspaper, radio, and television.

But wait! Isn't the point of videoblogging to get *away* from television? Sure, but TV isn't going away — and it's one of the most effective communication forms out there. Why not set up an oasis in the vast wasteland?

If your videoblog is unique in some way, with a local angle or a specific format that you think is distinctive, contact your local press and give them the scoop on videoblogging. Most newspapers have a technology section, and many television news programs also feature a blogs section in their technology columns.

The first and most important thing you can do to get yourself featured in the press is to write and submit a terrific press release and send it to specific people at the publication. This means research, writing, and follow-up. If you're not a virtuoso at any of those, of course, you can just skip the press coverage and focus on your online promotional options.

A *press release* is basically an article you write about your own project and then submit to the editors of newspapers and magazines, radio station managers, and television show producers. It's okay to write a single press release and send it out to several outlets, but only send your releases to press outlets you have already researched. Media outlets get thousands of press releases each day — if yours doesn't have something compelling in it, they won't read past the first line.

The standard press-release format looks like this:

FOR IMMEDIATE RELEASE:

CONTACT:
Your name
Phone Number
E-mail address
Website URL

LOCAL VIDEOBLOGGER GETS TO THE HEART OF DOWNTOWN CONFLICT

Your city, State, Date — Local videoblogger Stephanie Bryant brings the downtown conflict to a worldwide audience by interviewing street performers, local merchants, and the young crowds seen hanging out in the downtown area, in her videoblog "Eye on Santa Cruz" this week.

The rest of the release reads like a news article; make sure you mention the URL of your videoblog, as well as any angle that will make it interesting to an editor of a newspaper. Be sure to include the 5 Ws (and an extra H) that a reader might ask:

- ✔ **Who** is doing this? Who's involved?

- ✔ **What** is it?

- ✔ **Where** did this happen? Where do you film interviews?

- ✔ **When** did this happen? When do posts go up?

- ✔ **Why** do you do this? Why should I watch?

- ✔ **How** do you do it? This last "W" may not be feasible to answer, but maybe you can answer a question such as, "How do I learn more?"

Becoming a featured site or podcast

Another way to gain publicity for your videoblog is for it to become a featured site, podcast, or videoblog in one of the popular directories. Obviously, this method isn't a reliable (or necessarily repeatable) way to gain exposure for your vlog. However, it can mean many new viewers in the short term — and may result in more subscriptions in the long term.

The first step to becoming featured in any directory is to submit your videoblog to it, using the site's submission formats or rules.

For most of the directories, you can get to the top in a few key ways:

- ✔ **Have excellent, consistent content in your videoblog.** This is the best way to become a featured videoblog anywhere.

- ✔ **Keep your videoblog to a standard format.** If you want to be featured in iTunes, that means MPEG-4, QuickTime movie, or specifically iPod-ready.

- ✔ **Make sure your videos are high-quality files.** Don't skimp on compression, but keep the quality of your videoblog's visual appearance high. Invest in good lighting and sound equipment.

- ✔ **Be funny.** It may not be in your format, but if it is, be funny. People love to watch funny movies from the Internet.

Once you have at least four videos posted to your vlog, and you have a good feel for what you're doing, contact the administrators for the directories and tell them about your videoblog.

When you send a directory editor or administrator an introduction, it's like writing a press release, but more personalized. Only write to one administrator at a time — don't spam. If you want to send to 500 sites and directory listings, check them over carefully first; they don't like spam any more than you do! Address the administrator by name, if you know it, or just generally and in a friendly manner. "Hello!" works pretty well as a catch-all opener.

Be direct and to the point. Remember that the person you're e-mailing may receive hundreds of messages a day, all from people who want to talk about themselves. Be specific, and keep it short. Include the name of your videoblog, its theme, the URL for both the videoblog and its feed, and your name and e-mail address. Here's an example:

```
To: editor@podcastdirectory.org
From: me@myemail.com
Subject: New video podcast/videoblog

Hi, there! I'm writing to tell you about my new videoblog,
"Betta Bettas." It's a video newsletter for betta fish
owners and breeders, produced by my local betta club.
The vlog is at http://cbsbettas.blip.tv, and
Its RSS feed is http://feeds.feedburner.com/cbsbettas.

Please check them both out and consider my videoblog for
Podcast Directory's Featured Podcast of the Week.

Sincerely,
Stephanie Bryant
me@myemail.com
```

The chances are, your e-mail will go into cyberspace and you may never receive a response. But if you get into their directory early, or you just have a really awesome videoblog that the editors think their audience will enjoy, or you just happen to be lucky, you may be surprised by a sudden increase in traffic to your vlog.

Indulging in shameless self-promotion

The last way to promote your videoblog — and the one you have the most control over — is online self-promotion. Every time you send an e-mail message, post to a forum, or even comment in someone else's to a blog, you have an opportunity to get the word out about your videoblog.

First, you should include your videoblog in your e-mail signature line. Your e-mail signature line (also called a .sig file) is a block of text that you configure your e-mail program to include in your outgoing e-mail messages. Most e-mail programs offer some kind of signature line option in the preferences or options for the program. Here's an example of my .sig file that mentions my videoblogs:

```
--
Stephanie Bryant
myemail@example.com
Blogs, videoblogs, and audioblogs at
http://www.mortaine.com/blogs
```

The thing to remember about your signature file is that it has to be short and narrow. Four lines is the longest you should go, and you should keep the width to no more than 70 characters — an old standard screen width still used in UNIX programs.

Once you have your e-mail .sig file composed, any e-mail-based online discussion groups, such as Yahoo! Groups (which you can subscribe to in your e-mail as well as online) can include your .sig file to promote your vlog to other people interested in the same things you're into.

Of course, walking around with a video camera glued to your eye is a rather conspicuous activity. Not only are you likely to get footage of people staring at you sometimes, you'll also get a lot of folks coming up and asking you what you're doing. If they're friendly, tell them about videoblogging and your vlog, and explain what you hope to accomplish in the vlog you're making today. Don't be dismissive if they've never even heard of a blog, or they've heard of it but don't really know what it is. We've all been there; this entire *For Dummies* series exists for folks who are very intelligent and just don't know much about one particular subject . . . yet.

When you meet people at non-vlogging events or club meetings, go ahead and tell them about your vlog, too. One of the #1 reasons why people watch other peoples' videoblogs is because of a direct, personal connection they've made with that person. Of course, if people ask you about videoblogging, one of the cool things you can do is pull out a handy business card, flyer, or brochure — and hand it to them. As you tell them about your videoblog, point out the URL for your vlog, and tell them where they can learn more about vlogging in general, if they seem interested.

It's very chic to videoblog, of course, but it's even chic-er to do so wearing a nifty T-shirt that promotes vlogging and, if possible, your own videoblog. You can buy these online at `http://node101.org` as well as several other vlogging sites (including mine), to wear as a sign of affiliation and honor. After all, who hasn't had a stranger come up to ask about their T-shirt's slogan or logo? If you're wearing a shirt that says "I'm Vlogging This" and carrying a camera, it's like you're a walking, talking ad for the videoblogging movement.

If you want to make your own T-shirt with your own design and videoblog URL, use CafePress (`www.cafepress.com`) or another custom T-shirt shop. However you go about it, shamelessly self-promoting your videoblog is a good thing. Just be aware of the line between self-promotion and spam — and don't cross it!

Joining the Vlogging Community

One of the very best ways you can promote your videoblog is to find other videobloggers. After all, here are people who are interested in your videoblog — and they haven't even seen it yet! A lot of vloggers will subscribe to new videoblogs just to get to know a new person.

The videoblogging community hangs out in a Yahoo! group at `http://groups.yahoo.com/group/videoblogging`. It's a high-traffic group with a lot of members, which means the forum gets almost 100 posts on any given day. As with other Yahoo! groups, you can subscribe to receive all messages as individual e-mails, as a daily digest of all the messages for the day, or only delivered to you via the Web if you prefer not to receive that many messages by e-mail.

With so many members, of course, it's easy for the discussion to stray into unrelated topics, but new videobloggers are always welcome in the group, to announce their new videoblog as well as to ask questions about videoblogging. Although people are welcome to share really cool vlogs they've made, generally it's *not* a great idea to post an announcement every time you make a new videoblog post. I know it's tempting — you want instant feedback on your videos, and you want everyone to watch. But be patient — many people won't download your video for a couple of days after you post it, but many of them will stop by to comment on your vlog posts.

Getting to know other vloggers

Of course, with such a huge group of videobloggers, you know that opportunities to get acquainted will come along! In addition to watching other videobloggers' posts and giving them comments, you can get to know your local vloggers by going to meet-ups and seminars, if they're held locally.

Vloggercon (www.vloggercon.com), which has been held twice as of publishing this book, is an annual convention for videobloggers of all levels of expertise. It's a great way to go and meet a bunch of other videobloggers and get to know them personally. It's been held in New York City and in San Francisco, and the date for the event varies as well.

In addition to the annual Vloggercon, though, 2005 also saw Vloggercue, a one-day event held in various locations across the U.S., in which videobloggers held summertime barbecues and invited other videobloggers to come participate. The Vloggercues were also broadcast by videoconferencing software, so folks who were not present could enjoy the fun. You can check out the Vloggercues at these sites:

```
http://vloggercue.blogspot.com
http://vlogmidwest.blogspot.com
http://vloggercuewest.blogspot.com
```

Generating goodwill

Goodwill refers to a general attitude that other people have towards you, and which you foster in others, in which other people want good things to happen for you. One way to build goodwill is to do good things for others — what goes around really does come around, you know.

It can start out with a simple task, such as testing something out for someone on the videoblogging Yahoo! group. You test it, find it doesn't work, and think, "Gee, why didn't that work?" The next thing you know, you're troubleshooting that problem until you figure it out — the AHA! moment where you say, "So *that's* what's wrong!" You make a mental note, report it to the original requestor, and voilà! You've helped solve someone's problem.

Or maybe someone's new to videoblogging. And hey, you haven't been in it long, either — but you've read this book and you've made a few posts. And sure enough, wouldn't you know it, the same problem you had when you got started, some other person had. Just when they post saying, "I'm going to give up!" you swing by to say, "Hey, I'm new, too, but this is what I did to solve it."

Sharing information in a supportive way is one of the easiest ways to build goodwill in a group as dedicated to learning new things as the videobloggers. And you can take it a step farther, too. You can help people more formally, by participating in online events or local ones. For instance, many videobloggers organize various informative seminars and workshops called "Meet the Vloggers" (`http://meetthevloggers.blogspot.com`), which you can help out with locally. There's also a distributed learning project called Node101 (`www.node101.org`) to set up educational groups to teach videoblogging to anyone who wants to learn. In some cases, Node101 sets up actual studios with space, while others, such as the Road Node, put the educational resources and inspiration into a van and headed out on a road trip in Fall 2005 to spread the word.

You don't have to volunteer two months out of your life to promoting videoblogging, but offering some of your own time to other videobloggers — even in the form of just providing some video clips for a collaboration — can really help forge friendships with other vloggers.

Cross-linking

As part of being in the videoblogging community, you can provide cross-links between your videoblog and others' videoblogs, as shown in Figure 14-5. You might want to link to videoblogs that are similar to yours in subject matter, tone (if you have a comedy vlog, for instance), or geography. Cross-linking serves not only to provide cross-pollination between your audience and that of another videoblog, but also as a way to make important contacts with other vloggers and form relationships.

Figure 14-5: Cross-linking to other vlogs helps you create relationships with other vloggers.

Chapter 15

Getting Help from Others

• •

• •

*I*n moviemaking, it's accepted that no man is an island (using "man" generically here). All major movie productions involve many people, sometimes hundreds, even if the actual on-screen cast is small. From the set designers to the costumers, to all the special-effects programmers, film editors, cameramen and equipment handlers, assistants, stunt professionals, and so on, the list of people who contribute to a movie can scroll across a screen seemingly endlessly.

Videoblogs tend to be less elaborate productions, with much more modest cast and crew credits, but your videoblog may still use the talents and expertise of many other people. This chapter is all about enlisting help and collaborating with others when you vlog.

A lot of the advice in this chapter is a mix of common sense, advice from the Fair Use best practices, and a layman's understanding of law. I am not a lawyer. I know a lot of lawyers, which is why I know better than to pretend that I am one. One thing I've learned from lawyers is that whether or not something is legal depends on more factors than I could possibly fit into a single book — that's why they have law libraries! Any advice given in this book on what is or isn't legal should not be taken as the absolute word on what you may or may not do legally in your town, city, state, nation, or planet. In other words, if you have doubts about what you can film, call your *own* lawyer, a *real* lawyer, and get his or her advice.

Filming on Location

A *location shoot* happens any time you leave your studio (or house, apartment . . . or studio apartment) to go out and film somewhere that isn't your normal place. When you go to a public event and film it, that's a location shoot. When you wander around downtown filming random people, that's a location shoot.

When you film on-site, check with whoever owns the site and make sure it's all right to film there. If not, you might have to adjust your filming plans. In general, publicly owned places can be filmed — *but you need permission first* before you can film in merely publicly-accessible ones, such as stores and coffeeshops. Some locations have a sign specifically prohibiting filming on that site.

If you don't get permission to film a site, you can still film it, just from a public place, such as a park across the street.

Here are some other considerations for filming on location:

- **Site policies:** Especially in convention halls, local A/V unions may have an exclusive deal with a location, or filming may be limited to registered press. Call ahead and find out if you can obtain permission to film at such events.
- **Employees of the site:** Make sure they don't mind being taped!
- **Ambient sound:** If it's a public place, you will probably want a microphone.
- **Lighting issues:** A lot of indoor venues have poor lighting.
- **Traffic:** Foot or car traffic means you may have a perfect shot ruined by a passer-by wandering across the camera's field of vision.

Shooting special locations in the U.S.

The United States has become increasingly vigilant about terrorism since 2001, so filming on location has become more of a challenge. No longer can you sidle up to the unoccupied side of a bridge and pull out your camera for some amazing and unique shots. At least, not without having some friendly person in a uniform come by to have a chat with you about your activities.

One Seattle photography student, Ian Spiers, found himself in exactly that predicament when he tried to photograph the Ballard Locks for a photography assignment. For the story, see `www.notinourname.net/detentions/ photo-seattle-14jul04.htm`.

When you head out to film on site, go with friends and try to blend in with the tourists. Of course, being arrested for your art will probably boost your traffic, but I wouldn't recommend it.

Filming on location can be fun and exciting, especially if it's somewhere you haven't been before, or if you travel to a place for the express purpose of shooting video and memorializing the event.

Videoblog LoFi St. Louis (`www.lofistl.com`) is a local-interest show dedicated to bands in St. Louis, Missouri. Bill Streeter, the host of LoFi St. Louis, offered a few tips for other local-interest shows, especially if filming local bands at night:

- Buy two or three cheap clamping flood lamps from the hardware store and bring them with you. Put one on either side of the stage, directed towards the stage for maximum lighting.

- Get verbal permission to film individuals.

- Most independent bands want publicity and are happy to be filmed. Still, it's important to respect the band's wishes, as well as those of the site owner.

- Smaller cameras are best when working in crowds and there's a need to be relatively inconspicuous.

- Use a monopod when shooting in crowds. It stabilizes the camera, but doesn't take up the 8 feet of floor space that a large tripod would.

- Take along a white foamcore board to use as a reflector when shooting in bright, sunny days.

- Use a top-mounted camera lamp in hard light to fill in dark shadows on your subject's eyes.

Videoblogging Other People

I've talked quite a bit about videoblogging other people, particularly working with actors and interview subjects who already want to be involved in your videoblog. But what about ordinary people?

Well, some ordinary people will just jump at the chance to be in an Internet video — while others might be more hesitant.

As I mentioned in Chapter 7, fear of public speaking is the number one phobia in America. More people are afraid of public speaking than of death (even though bodily injury caused by going on camera or on stage is extremely rare, and usually the result of clumsiness).

As I've mentioned time and time again, you'll need to get the OK from your subject before you roll film (or at least before you post it to your vlog). Some people are adamantly opposed to being filmed. In particular, artists seem to be more reclusive than most other creative professionals, and this may simply be protectiveness of their work, or perhaps outright shyness. For some people (not just artists), bad experiences with traditional media in the past may keep them from being enthusiastic, or legal issues can come into play. Whatever the reason, if you can't convince them to let you film, keep the camera off.

A note about filming children and minors: You not only need the child's permission to film, *but also their parent or guardian's permission.* You never know when a child might give you permission without realizing that his or her parents are involved in a custody battle that could be jeopardized by the child appearing in an Internet video. Kindness and caution are the order of the day.

Some folks are outright gung-ho, of course, and will not only say yes, but may actually ask if they can be in your video, sometimes without even knowing what it's about!

Most people you try to film will be somewhere in the middle. They might be willing, but need more information about what you want to do with the video. They need just a smidgeon of convincing.

- ✔ Start with the absolute basics: "I'm recording video of this event/party/ meeting for the Internet."

- ✔ Explain how you plan to use it: "I'll be editing and posting it to my videoblog later — a videoblog is an online journal where I post the videos I shoot. Don't worry — I edit out any embarrassing stuff!"

- ✔ Let them follow-up: "Here's a card with my e-mail address and the URL for my videoblog, so you can learn more."

- ✔ If they're still resistant, offer to give them a preview of the film before you post it.

In the United States, you should only offer the preview when you're filming a non-newsworthy activity. For instance, if you capture a video of a police action in a public place (or a private place where you were legitimately invited to be), you have every right as a citizen to continue filming, and to use the footage without running it past the police. You will need to blur out suspects' faces, because suspects are innocent until proven guilty in a court of law, and your tape may be subpoenaed as evidence *for either side* in any resulting case. (Be sure to make a copy before handing over any tapes.) Other countries' laws differ, so check with your local government for information on filming police or public servants' activities.

For more on filming in public, see Chapter 7.

Collaborating with Others and Making Derivative Works

Frequently, in the videoblogging community, you'll come across a request or two for video contributions to a project. These artistic-collaboration efforts are, for many, the heart and soul of the videoblogging experience. A remix vlog — or *mashup* — is a video that takes other people's clips and mixes them together, usually with an artistic (often musical) goal, such as setting various video clips of vloggers to a hip-hop track. The idea comes out of the DJ mix movement, but it's taken on a whole new meaning when the videos being mashed are found in vlogs from around the world.

Collaborating with other vloggers

A *collaboration* is a group video project in which several videobloggers contribute clips or material. The material might be from a videoblogger's existing work, or it might be something they create especially for the project.

To contribute to a collaborative project, you'll first want to find out about which ones are going on. The videoblogging Yahoo! group is the best way to keep abreast of all kinds of videoblogging topics, including collaboration project announcements. You might also learn about collaborations through MySpace (www.myspace.com) or other social networking sites, or through contacts on Flickr (www.flickr.com) and other media-sharing sites.

Here's an example of the kind of announcement you might see on the Yahoo! videoblogging group e-mail list:

```
To: videoblogging@yahoogroups.com
From: Stephanie Bryant
Subject: Birthday collaboration project!
My mom's birthday is this weekend, and I messed up
and didn't send her a gift in time. I'm hoping that all
you wonderful vloggers can send or post a short video
of yourself singing Happy Birthday or saying
"Happy Birthday, Bonnie!" so I won't be in the doghouse
for the next year.
I prefer a Mac-ready format, like .mov, but I can convert
almost anything if needed.
E-mail me the URL, or the file, by July 26th, so I can
edit them by her birthday (the 29th).

Thanks!
--Stephanie
```

Videobloggers who have a little extra time — or who consider you a friend — would then make their own short video clips and post or send 'em to you with their birthday messages. It's up to you to do something with them, such as edit the clips together and post them to your own vlog. You can get some wonderfully creative things from other vloggers, who will interpret your invitation however they see fit.

Collaborations don't have to be limited to birthday messages, of course. Some recent collaborations include these:

- ✔ **Green Thing:** Receive something green in the mail and vlog yourself interacting with it.
- ✔ **We Are The Media:** Vloggers claim the media (also used as a promotional tool for videoblogging events).
- ✔ **Halloween:** Post a special Halloween clip.
- ✔ **Carp Caviar:** Create an advertisement for Carp Caviar.
- ✔ **EvilVlog:** An ongoing collaborative vlogging satire site.
- ✔ **MS Yes:** A fundraiser to combat Multiple Sclerosis
- ✔ **Beer Note:** A musical collaboration of blowing into a bottle to create a musical note.

Want to participate in a collaboration of your own? Visit the *Videoblogging For Dummies* Web site at www.mortaine.com/vlogdummies for ongoing collaboration projects through 2007!

When inviting people to collaborate on a videoblogging project, make sure you answer the following questions in your announcement:

- ✔ What is the concept behind the collaboration? Is it for a specific purpose? What do you want in the clips?
- ✔ What artistic limitations are there? For instance, do the clips all need to conform to what you'd see in a typical PG-13 movie?
- ✔ When do you need to have the clips?
- ✔ How long or short should the clip be?
- ✔ What type of file do you need?
- ✔ How should people get them to you?
- ✔ What kind of license do you require from submitted clips? For instance, if you're going to use the clips commercially, you must disclose that.

And of course, if you want to participate in a collaboration, don't be afraid to e-mail with some follow-up questions if the person posting the request wasn't clear enough about what kinds of video they want.

Remixing video

A *remix vlog* is a videoblog post that includes videos found online from other videobloggers, and from stock footage archives such as the Prelinger Movie Archive (at www.archive.org/details/prelinger).

Remixing isn't hard, but it can be time-consuming. To remix a video, follow these basic steps:

1. **Search for video clips and download them onto your computer.**

   You may use clips that other videobloggers have sent you, or use Creative Commons released or public domain clips from sources such as the Internet Archive. When checking the Creative Commons license for your right to use it, make sure it says derives-ok — and follow the other guidelines for using it in commercial work (if your vlog is commercial), and how to attribute the creators.

2. **Import the clips into your video-editing program.**

   Importing multiple clips at one time into iMovie is covered later in this section.

3. **Edit the clips if necessary — you most likely want to trim the clip to just use part of it.**

   See Chapter 10 for the steps to edit clips.

4. **Paste the edited clips together until you have a movie you like.**

For example, let's assume I want to make a video of people saying "Hello" or "Hi." It should be pretty easy to find, right? Many personal videos have the person at one time or another greeting the audience.

The first thing I would do is check for videos that are already online that have someone saying, "Hi!" I might go back through some of the videoblogs I watch and see if anyone I know has posted a video in which they say "Hi," even if they then go on to talk about completely irrelevant stuff. As I go through the videos, when I find one I want to use, I download it, place it in a designated folder, and make sure to note where I got it. Sometimes vlog posts aren't labeled with the vlogger's URL or identity, and I want to give credit for using them.

Once I have those videos, I'll visit the Prelinger Archive and other movie archives on the Internet Archive (www.archive.org). This is a source of royalty-free or public-domain videos, usually older films and educational or government films, but there are also a lot of nature videos there. If you like the kitschy appeal of the 1950s morality propaganda, you will love the Prelinger Archive. As I grab those, I'll put them into the same folder, and note, if I can, their source.

Even when something has passed into the public domain, it is respectful to give credit to its creators. Shakespeare's works are in the public domain, but it's bad form to quote him without giving credit.

If the video files include both Mac-friendly `.mov` or `.mp4` files and Windows-capable `.wmv` files, you'll need to convert them to either Mac- or Windows-friendly formats before importing them. You can use QuickTime Pro to convert most video file types into a `.mov` or `.avi` file, or iSquint (`www.isquint.org`) to convert and resize most video files to `.mp4` or `.mov`.

Once I've got the videos in a file format I can use, I import them all at once into iMovie by following these steps:

1. **Open iMovie and create a new movie project.**

2. **Open the Finder and navigate to the folder where I have all the movies stored.**

3. **Select the movies and drag them onto the clips area of the iMovie project window.**

4. **Wait.**

This method is a little less frustrating than importing each movie file individually (described in Chapter 10), although it takes just as long.

After I've imported the files, I'll navigate to the "Hi" or "Hello" bit in each video clip and trim to before and after it, until the clip is trimmed to just the few seconds I want to use.

I'll then drag and drop each clip into the iMovie Timeline to place them in the order I want them to appear in the movie. I'll add my opening credit, closing outro, and a title with all the credits I want to include in this vlog entry. I'll play the completed movie to make sure it looks good, and then post it as usual to my vlog.

Knowing When You Need Permission to Use Others' Works

You'll notice, in the previous example, that my sources for the clips were all videobloggers distributing their work under a particular Creative Commons license (`derives-ok`), and the public-domain archives. That's because I know my use here doesn't fall under the satire and parody clause for fair use of a media work — and I wouldn't feel comfortable, with so many freely usable videos out there, to step over the line into using a video clip from a commercially produced TV show or movie.

The MPAA (Motion Picture Association of America) and the RIAA (Recording Industry Association of America) would like you to believe that just putting a file on your computer violates copyright law, but they are not the authorities on this subject. (Even though they're the ones with all the scary lawyers.)

The Center for Social Media, a documentary filmmaker's organization, hosts the Documentary Filmmakers' Statement of Best Practices in Fair Use. This document, which was authored by several filmmakers and teams, provides everyman guidelines for using media in remixes and in commentary documentary creations. You can find this document at www.centerforsocialmedia.org/fairuse.htm.

The premise of the Best Practices — and the cornerstone of fair use — is that some uses of copyrighted media are permitted without licensing from the original copyright owner. In general, the idea is that the usage needs to be in good faith, not exploiting the original work in order to profit from it, and not diminishing the original work.

Any work that does not fall into the category of fair use must be licensed. That means you must obtain written permission from the copyrighted work's owner before you can use that work in your video. In some cases, that might be more difficult than it's worth to you; in others, you might be better advised to find a different clip to use.

Some of the most common violations of copyright are videos with unlicensed musical soundtracks. Music permissions can be complicated; they're negotiated differently for a motion picture than for a simple radio show. The RIAA has also become more and more rabid about suing customers for using their products in ways they can't make money from.

If you use works licensed under the creative commons license (www.creativecommons.org), and use those works within the strictures stated in them (such as using nc only in Non-Commercial vlogs), then you don't need a permission form from the creator.

Getting Permission to Film People

In addition to obtaining permission to use creative works in your videos, you need to get permission to film an individual. In some cases, such as for your personal videoblog, a verbal agreement will be sufficient for permission. However, if you're making a video for a commercial entity, make sure you have permission in writing, usually by having the individual sign a model-release form or an on-camera release form.

The elevator permissions speech

The *elevator speech* is the common name for a very short sales pitch or persuasive speech. You might be familiar with it from job-hunting; career counselors suggest that you have an elevator speech prepared that highlights your strengths and ends with you putting your résumé in the hands of a potential employer. The term comes from the idea that you might be in an elevator with just the right person, and have the opportunity to talk for the duration of the elevator ride. And yes, punching the Emergency Stop button on an elevator is bad form — so you have to make your case quickly and effectively.

In an elevator speech, you must have a card or some sort of handout to give the person listening that will give them more information. In the case of an employment speech, the handout is your business card or résumé.

When you ask people for permission to videotape, try to give them the information quickly, so they don't reject you before they have some facts. As your handout, you can provide a business card or brochure with your videoblog's URL on it, or the permissions form itself. If you hand out the permissions form, make sure the part to be signed is detachable — or that you can make a copy for the individual to keep.

When you give an elevator speech to ask someone for permission to film, just hit the main points:

- ✔ **Who are you?** "Hi, my name is _____."
- ✔ **What are you doing?** "I'm shooting video for a Web site blog I run."
- ✔ **Where is your blog?** "At www.`myblog`.com."

    You may just want to let the person know that the address for your videoblog is on the handout you'll provide (and then offer it).

- ✔ **What is your blog about?** "It's a blog showcasing events in this city."
- ✔ **What do you want?** "I'd really like to film your participation at this event. May I do so, and post it to my videoblog on the Internet?"

As soon as the handout is in their hands, you will lose their attention for a moment while they look at it — so be sure to hand it to them at the end, not the beginning, of your speech.

The whole speech should take no more than 30 seconds, including simple responses. Practice it and time it. Then practice it by asking a few of your friends to act as the person being asked permission, so you can practice your answers to some common questions you might get, such as *How is the video going to be used?* or *Will people make fun of me?* or *How do I get a copy of the video?*

Sample permissions form

There are a couple of types of permissions forms you can use for videoblogging. One is a *model-release form* for people who appear in your vlog. Another type is the *location release*, which must be signed by the owner or manager of a privately owned site. Finally, there's the *media-release form,* in which you license video or music to appear in your videoblog post.

You can find several such permission forms on the Internet. Although you can't guarantee that they've been reviewed by a lawyer from your jurisdiction, they can provide a working model for you to customize. As with all things pertaining to the law, you may want to have a lawyer review your release form before you use it.

Here is a sample model-release permission form:

> I, _____, in exchange for consideration received, hereby consent to being the subject of or appearing in videos taken by [your name] and authorize [your name] to display and distribute said videos or derivative works, in any format they so choose.
>
> By this document I, _____, release [your name], their agents, employees or assigns, from any and all claims for damages, for libel, slander, invasion of privacy or any other claim based upon use of my likeness.
>
> Signature/Date: _____ _____
>
> Witness/Date: _____ _____

What to do when they say no

Sometimes your potential participant will say no to being filmed — or to having video of him or her posted on the Internet. Sometimes they will say yes initially, and then get cold feet later.

When a subject says no, you have a couple of choices. One is to do the human thing and turn the camera off or move on and film something or someone else. Another choice, particularly when filming small-venue events, is to ask the person to wear a sticker or something so you can edit his or her image out of the footage, if that's acceptable. If the subject is in front of you, facing away, in a crowd scene, you can film without permission, but if you go for a close-up, you're invading their privacy.

The third — often riskier — choice is to film anyway. In the U.S., this choice is only legitimate under a few limited circumstances. For instance, if the subject is a member of the government actively engaged in civil duty — say, a police officer on duty, or military personnel (though if they're doing something classified and tell you to go away, I suggest you comply). That usage is generally considered free use, because the government employee is doing government work, paid for by your taxes.

Then there's the public figure clause in the line between journalism and respecting a person's privacy. If the subject is a political candidate or politician, you can film that person in public — politicians deliberately put themselves in the public spotlight. (But stay away from their kids!) Celebrities get into more of an iffy territory; most celebrities like to be recognized, but also need to have as much of a normal life as they can. Also, movie and TV celebrities are usually members of the Screen Actors Guild, whose contract is so serious that SAG actors need to use that contract for *any* on-screen appearance, even non-deliberate ones; an actor appearing in your videoblog by accident can make a claim that you've harmed their ability to work for pay. Unless they're doing something to draw attention to themselves (beyond just going to a restaurant), leave them alone. The world doesn't need more paparazzi.

The gray area around high-profile criminals is a bit tougher. In general, you can film someone who has been charged with a serious crime, but you must make sure not to presume guilt before a trial in your blog. If you do, you run into slander and libel laws, which opens a whole big can of lawyers. Do your homework first.

Crediting Your Sources

Whenever you use other people's work or likenesses in your videoblog, be sure to credit them for their contribution(s). For other people's work, credits identify the source, so viewers can look for their work later. For your interview subjects or actors, credits give them the opportunity to promote themselves and/or their Web sites.

Introducing interview subjects

Whenever you interview people, introduce them to the camera, or ask them to introduce themselves. An interview is an opportunity to get to know a person, but without a name, viewers won't know who you're talking to or about.

If possible, use subtitles to identify the interview subject on-screen, as shown in Figure 15-1. In addition to remembering the person's name, your viewers are more likely to spell the name correctly if they see it written out.

Figure 15-1:
Use
subtitles to
identify your
interview
subjects.

When possible during the interview, use the subject's name as you ask questions. Again, repetition helps your viewers remember the name, and it is also a good way to build rapport with the interview subject.

Including end-reel credits

Some people prefer to give credit in the text of the blog post, but I prefer to put the credits at the end of the video itself. People watch videoblogs out of context all the time; making sure the credits are in the video file itself means your contributors and assistants are always given credit.

Ask your subjects, participants, and crew members how they want to be credited. Get them to write down their names with the correct spellings as they want them to appear in the credits.

Be sure to credit anyone who works on your vlog, but in particular don't leave out:

- ✔ **Actors and interview subjects:** Give your interview subjects a chance to get the publicity.

- ✔ **Musical performers:** Independent bands and musicians need the publicity, and it's usually a condition of their appearance.

✔ **Songwriters:** Songs aren't always written by the band performing them. Ask the band who wrote the song, and give credit there, too.

✔ **Visual artists:** Artists are often hesitant to appear in Internet video, so any gesture of goodwill will go a long way.

✔ **The location:** If you filmed on location and got permission, make sure to mention where you were.

✔ **Your crew:** If you had any help with carrying gear, holding lights or microphones, editing the video, or just setting stuff up, be sure to thank your crew, even if (especially if!) they're unpaid.

In the movie business, credits are what drive a performer or crew person's résumé. True, a name credit in a videoblog doesn't count for much in Hollywood, but it's your acknowledgment of people's contribution to your creative vision, and a crucial sign of respect.

Chapter 16

Monitoring Traffic

*T*alk to other vloggers about videoblogging, and the conversation will eventually turn to money. The cost that looms in most vloggers' minds is bandwidth. Vloggers love the exposure that comes from having a hundred visitors a day, but the cost of delivering a 15MB file a hundred times quickly (yikes) adds up. How do you deliver quality video without breaking your own bank? Invariably, discussion of sponsorships and advertising revenue comes up, which then requires the vlogger to know what kind of viewership he or she has, how many people visit, and whether they're actually watching the movies or not.

This chapter offers some pointers on how to keep up with your viewers, how to track their use of your videoblog, and how to control how much (and how fast) an individual can download your movies.

Gathering Traffic Data about Your Vlog

Every time a file on the Internet — be it a Web page, e-mail message, video, or picture — is downloaded, the server storing that file makes note that it was accessed and when, tucking that info into a plain-text file called a *server log*. The server also saves other useful data in the server log, such as where the visitor came from.

The server log enables you to find out who's watching your vlog, when, and how. You can read the server log directly as a plain-text file, or you can use server stat charts to get a visual representation of the server log's information. You also may find that a remote Web-tracking system is easier to use and interpret than the server logs.

Reading a server log

When interpreted correctly, server logs can tell you where in the world your visitors are from, what Web site they used to get to your vlog, what search engine terms they used to find your vlog, and whether they found what they were looking for. You can also use server logs to watch for suspicious activity and attempts by computer crackers and malicious programs (such as viruses) to break in.

The following is an example of a server's log entry:

```
68.142.249.129 - - [01/Jan/2006:00:33:15 -0800]
   "GET /personal/unforgettable.html HTTP/1.0" 200 780
   "-" "Mozilla/5.0 (compatible; Yahoo! Slurp;
   http://help.yahoo.com/help/us/ysearch/slurp)"
```

The first number is the IP address of the requesting computer. That's followed by the date and time (January 1, 2006 at 12:33 A.M.)

The next section is GET /personal/unforgettable.html HTTP/1.0 which is a communication line from the Web browser to the server asking the server to get a file called unforgettable.html from the personal directory under the main Web directory for this server. HTTP/1.0 is the protocol version — it basically tells the Web server to use version 1.0 of HTTP (HyperText Transfer Protocol) to get and send the file.

The next two numbers are the response from the server: The 200 code means it found the file; 780 refers to the size of the server's response.

Then the server logs information about the program being used to retrieve this file. Mozilla/5.0 (compatible; means the Web browser in this case is compatible with Mozilla, which is the most common Web browser architecture available. Internet Explorer, Netscape, Mozilla, and Firefox all appear with Mozilla as the compatible type. In this example, the request was actually made by the Yahoo! search-engine program as it indexed the content of the site. The folks at Yahoo! include the URL for their help page about their slurp program, in case curious webmasters need to know how it works.

The following code shows another example of a server log entry, this one from Google's search engine indexing bot:

```
66.249.64.26 - - [01/Jan/2006:01:25:09 -0800]
   "GET /robots.txt HTTP/1.0" 404 399 "-" "Google bot/2.1
   (+http://www.google.com/bot.html)"
```

In this case, Google's bot looked for the `robots.txt` file. 404 means the file wasn't found. Some search-engine crawlers first look to see if you have a `robots.txt` file specifying which directories they should ignore.

The next code sample shows a server log of Microsoft Internet Explorer accessing this Web server:

```
66.252.133.172 - - [27/Jan/2006:14:11:21 -0800]
   "GET /personal HTTP/1.0" 301 310 "-" "Mozilla/4.0
   (compatible; MSIE 6.0; Windows NT 5.1;)"
```

The 301 indicates that the requested URL redirects to another file — this is common when a Web browser requests a directory instead of a specific file (such as `index.html`).

As a Web user, you may see server logs like these when you go to a page that's missing, or hit a server that has problems. Some common server status codes (such as 200, and 301, and the infamous 404) are listed in Table 16-1.

Table 16-1	Server Status Codes
Code Number	*Meaning*
200	Success: The file was there and was returned. All of the 200 codes indicate some form of success.
301	Moved: The file has been moved and the Web browser was redirected.
400	Bad request: The server can't understand the request.
401	Unauthorized: The Web user must log in using an authorization scheme.
403	Forbidden: Usually for password-protected files and directories, the file may be there, but the Web browser cannot retrieve it.
404	Not found: The file isn't there (familiar to regular travelers in cyberspace).
500	Internal server error: This one crops up when the server is misconfigured, or a script isn't installed correctly.

Reading server stats charts

Most people don't read server logs directly. Between the number of hits a server can get in a day and how dense the log text gets, it's a little more than most people feel comfortable reading on-screen. Fortunately, however, taking raw text data and turning it into easily-read results and graphs is the sort of thing computers are very good at. Many Web-statistics programs have been written to help Web site owners interpret their Web traffic.

A typical server stats program will report the basics of your server activity, plus some information on who visits your site and when. For instance, at the most basic, you'll learn when visitors accessed your site, what files they downloaded, and what Web browser(s) they used.

Figure 16-1 shows an example of a server stats chart that shows how many hits per month a Web server gets.

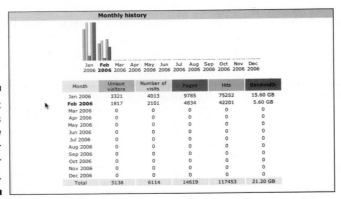

Figure 16-1: Server stats charts show you your hits per month.

Month	Unique visitors	Number of visits	Pages	Hits	Bandwidth
Jan 2006	3321	4013	9785	75252	15.60 GB
Feb 2006	1817	2101	4834	42201	5.60 GB
Mar 2006	0	0	0	0	0
Apr 2006	0	0	0	0	0
May 2006	0	0	0	0	0
Jun 2006	0	0	0	0	0
Jul 2006	0	0	0	0	0
Aug 2006	0	0	0	0	0
Sep 2006	0	0	0	0	0
Oct 2006	0	0	0	0	0
Nov 2006	0	0	0	0	0
Dec 2006	0	0	0	0	0
Total	5138	6114	14619	117453	21.20 GB

Since RSS readers aren't technically Web browsers, your stats may be skewed from reader and RSS aggregator hits. They can also be skewed by firewalls and local network caches.

Some server stats programs offer more detailed charts and graphs, showing which files were requested the most, and where they were requested from. Figure 16-2 shows a server chart with information on visitors' operating systems, browsers, and where they connected to the site from.

Operating Systems (Top 10) · Full list/Versions · Unknown		
Operating Systems	Hits	Percent
Windows	38511	91.2 %
Macintosh	1795	4.2 %
Unknown	1702	4 %
Linux	166	0.3 %
FreeBSD	25	0 %
Symbian OS	1	0 %
Irix	1	0 %

Browsers (Top 10) · Full list/Versions · Unknown			
Browsers	Grabber	Hits	Percent
MS Internet Explorer	No	35034	83 %
Firefox	No	3122	7.3 %
Safari	No	1157	2.7 %
Unknown	?	998	2.3 %
Mozilla	No	809	1.9 %
Netscape	No	322	0.7 %
Opera	No	270	0.6 %
WebCollage (PDA/Phone browser)	No	238	0.5 %
Apple iTunes (media player)	No	175	0.4 %
Camino	No	28	0 %
Others		48	0.1 %

Connect to site from				
Origin	Pages	Percent	Hits	Percent
Direct address / Bookmarks	972	37.7 %	2792	33 %
Links from a NewsGroup				
Links from an Internet Search Engine - Full list	1391	54 %	2472	29.2 %
- Yahoo	980 1883			
- AltaVista	281 281			
- MSN	74 206			

Figure 16-2: Server charts can also provide information on files requested and user demographics.

Installing a remote-stats system

A *remote-stats system* is a program that runs on an off-site Web server that tracks your Web traffic for you. Because the remote system doesn't actually have access to your Web server's logs, you usually have to add a file or JavaScript to your main Web page (or blog page).

If you use JavaScript, your Web stats can't include users who don't have JavaScript enabled.

An *image-based Web-stat service* is actually one of the simpler ways to track stats remotely. Image-based Web-stat services track visits from users who have their Web browser set up to download images — in other words, nearly all of the Web surfers out there. The service works by putting a simple (and sometimes invisible) graphic in your Web page or blog page template. The image is stored on the remote-stats server, so every time someone loads your main Web or blog page, the remote image gets loaded, and the stats server logs the hit to the image. The stats server has its own server logs to give it access information about any page on your Web site containing that graphic.

The advantage to this kind of program is that it's really easy to set up, and often free. The disadvantage is that you can't track stats generated by your RSS feeds at all, and you can't track how much bandwidth your video files consume.

I use a free Web-stats tracking program, webtracker, as an example to show how to install a stats program on your own site. Most Web-stats trackers are similar. When you sign up for a Web-stats program to use with your videoblog, check your blog site's limitations and make sure the Web-stats requirements will meet them. Table 16-2 describes common limitations blog services impose and how to work around them to use a remote stats service.

Table 16-2	Videoblog Remote Web-Stats Requirements
Blog Limitations	*Web-Stats Requirement*
Forbids JavaScript.	Must not use JavaScript. Uses an image that you add to your blog template.
Can't customize the main blog template to include a remote image.	You'll need a Web-stats service that tracks an image, and then include that image in every post you make. This will inflate your stats somewhat, but if it's the only blogging service you have available, it's a decent workaround.

In Chapter 4, the recipe for a vlog includes signing up for Blogger and FeedBurner. FeedBurner logs stats when people use your RSS feed to download your vlog posts, and has a paid option for tracking the stats on any individual vlog entry. Blogger lets you include JavaScript and customize your blog's template as you wish.

Setting up a simple Web tracker

To set up a simple Web-stats service, follow these steps:

1. **Visit www.sitemeter.com.**

   Alternatively, you can find a different Web-stats service by searching for *Web-tracking program* with your favorite search engine.

2. **Click the Sign Up button or link to create an account.**

   A form appears, where you give the information the stats service needs to track your vlog site, as shown in Figure 16-3.

3. **Click Next to continue.**

   For SiteMeter, you'll be prompted for demographic information about yourself, and to sign up for various newsletters and information. Click Next through these screens if you don't care to sign up.

Figure 16-3:
Fill in
your site's
information.

4. **When you're done, verify the information is correct and click Next to finish registering.**

5. **Click the <u>Manager</u> link at the top of the screen, and then select HTML Code from the options on the left side, as shown in Figure 16-4.**

6. **Click the <u>Using a Text Editor</u> link to get the plain HTML code.**

   A page appears with the HTML code in a text box, along with instructions on how to use the HTML code, as shown in Figure 16-5.

7. **Scroll down to the text box, select all the HTML text, and copy it to your clipboard.**

8. **In your Web site's pages, or in your blog template, paste the HTML code and then save the template or page.**

   After you save the HTML code into your Web pages or blog template, the Site Meter counter image appears, as shown in Figure 16-6.

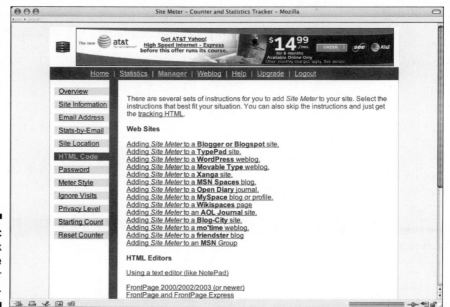

Figure 16-4:
Click
HTML Code
for your
options.

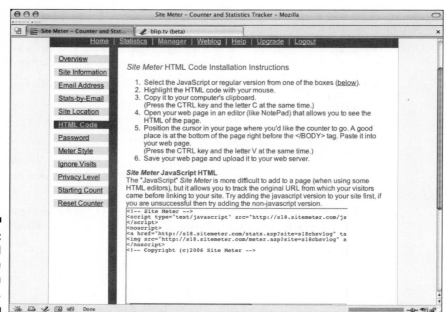

Figure 16-5:
Copy and
paste the
code from
the text box.

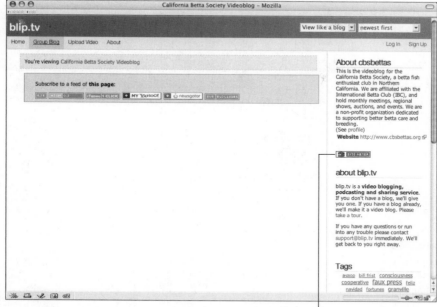

Figure 16-6:
The counter
will now
display on
your
videoblog's
main Web
page.

The Site Meter counter

Tracking stats with a third-party service

After you have installed your third-party Web-stats service, let it run for a few days (or even a few weeks) to accumulate data on your Web traffic. When you check your stats, you'll be able to get some of the more basic information on your visitors.

To view the tracking stats gathered by Site Meter, click the SiteMeter icon in your Web page. Figure 16-7 shows an example of a third-party Web-hits report (in this case, the number of visits and number of page views gathered by Site Meter).

Installing a stats system on your own server

You can also install a Web-stats analysis program on your own server if you store your video and/or blog files yourself. If you store these files with a third-party server — such as the Internet Archive (www.archive.org) — then you won't be able to install a stats system to track those files.

Figure 16-7:
A SiteMeter
tracking
report.

To install a stats script or program on your own Web server, you will need to have administrator's access to the server. If your Web server runs on Windows, you can use Windows' built-in Web-stats tracking to interpret your server logs.

The stats program I use in this example is called awstats, shown in Figure 16-8. It's an open-source Web-stats tracker for UNIX- and Linux-based servers.

Tracking RSS Subscriptions

RSS subscriptions and aggregators confuse the Web-stats programs by not always downloading graphic files, and not always accurately reporting the number of viewers of your vlog videos. Some aggregators store a copy of your posts to their own server and then deliver it to their subscribers on an as-needed basis. While you might not like losing out on those traffic stats, just remember that those viewers, while not necessarily being counted, are a part of your audience anyway.

Some RSS feed programs offer more complete stats analysis for your feed subscriptions. FeedBurner, for instance, provides basic stats and subscription information on any feed, and it offers a paid upgrade option if you want more thorough tracking. Figure 16-9 shows a typical RSS stat chart from FeedBurner.

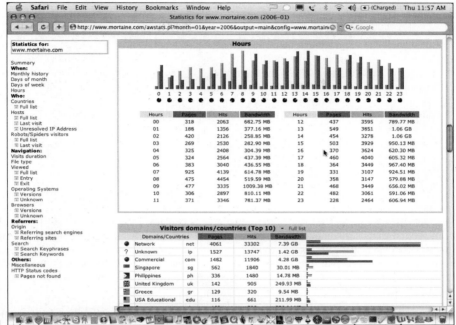

Figure 16-8:
Generate
server logs
with awstats
or similar
programs.

Figure 16-9:
A
FeedBurner
stats chart.

Tracking visitors to your vlog with cookies

You can use cookies to track visitors to your videoblog, provided the blog pages themselves are hosted on your own Web site. *Cookies* are small pieces of information that your visitors' Web browsers store for you. They're not programs, viruses, or files. They can be set up to track visitors' activities on the site, such as what pages they visit, and which links they choose to follow. You can also use cookies with JavaScript to set up user preferences.

Cookies are often used in conjunction with e-commerce sites, and users can choose not to accept them, as many perceive them as a privacy intrusion. Many Web sites resort to requiring cookies in order to function — but unless your videoblog is entirely commercial, and all of your content is on a paid-subscription basis, you probably won't want to risk turning away some visitors by forcing them to enable cookies before they can view your site.

If your videoblog is commercial in nature and you want to track users via cookies, be sure to post a privacy policy on your Web site to explain how and why you use cookies. Even the most Web-savvy users will accept the policy and motivations, even if they still do not accept the cookies themselves.

To use cookies to track your users, you'll need to know about cookies and how they work with your server logs. The most basic setup is to specify that your server put a cookie on the user's machine with some information, such as the user's login ID or session ID (some way to uniquely identify the user). The cookie information will appear in your server logs, and you can use server-side log-analysis tools that are specific to cookie-tracking to learn more about your visitors' experiences.

If the user's RSS reader is a standalone client, such as FireANT, which doesn't accept or store cookies, you won't be able to store and track the cookie data. However, if your visitors use Web-based RSS readers to view your vlog, the cookie can be saved, if their browsers are set up to do so.

There are several visitor-tracking packages available for various Web servers, including a module for Apache, the most common Web server, which tracks user stats for you. Many server-based cookie-tracking programs plug into the server logs system, to give you a more in-depth analysis of visitors to your site.

Giving detailed instructions to create cookies to track visitors to your vlog is well beyond the scope of this particular book, but you can learn more in *Building a Web Site For Dummies* by David A. Crowder or any other good Web design book.

Reading RSS stats

It's very easy to get hung up on your stats, especially when they fluctuate between 5 and 25 subscribers, seemingly overnight. The important thing to remember is that your RSS stats might only report the number of subscribers who have downloaded or attempted to download your vlog entries in the last day or so. Not everyone checks their videoblogs every day, of course — and with some setups, users can subscribe to be notified by e-mail when a new post goes up, so they won't bother checking when there's nothing new to watch.

If you decided to host everything on your own server — and you used the instructions in Chapter 13 to install your RSS feed on your server — then you'll have maximum control over your RSS feed stats. You'll be able to monitor how often your feed's URL is accessed — in other words, how often someone downloads your feed data. Note that you still won't be able to track when an aggregator re-indexes or republishes your feed content by storing it in its local cache.

Controlling subscription downloads

The vlogger's daydream is that, within a few months of publishing your videoblog, you will have hundreds of thousands of people subscribed to your vlog, and people on the street will wave at you and say "Hey! Aren't you on that popular vlog? Can I have your autograph?"

Okay, so maybe that's a little farfetched. Certainly, the dream of becoming a celebrity through your videoblog is about the same as becoming a celebrity through your blog. It's not impossible, but don't quit your day job yet.

While you're waiting for the *Enquirer* to catch wind of your vlog, though, you'll be building traffic and subscribers, slowly but surely. In six months of videoblogging, I racked up about 100 subscribers (though that number will hopefully increase after this book is published and you all decide to come visit me in my vlog). For each vlog post I made, I could calculate a sure-fire bandwidth hit to my server: however many megabytes my video file is, times one hundred. I could be fairly confident that any time I posted a vlog, I'd have to spend that much in bandwidth that month.

Now I store my videos on my own server; I like having control over where they are and how reliable the service will be. That server is connected to the Internet and has a set amount of bandwidth that it can spend each month. You will find that with most Web server plans, you have a limited amount of bandwidth. For most Web sites, the amount is large enough that you'll never run into a problem.

However, the cost of bandwidth isn't small, and it's something that you need to look at carefully when you create your own videoblog. For instance, a typical $30-per-month Web-server plan offers 20GB of bandwidth per month, with 2GB of storage and a fee of $2 per GB for each GB over the monthly bandwidth allowance. That sounds fine, but then I look at my video files — this month, I posted four vlogs, totaling almost 40MB. Multiply that by my 100 subscribers, and I'm sure to use almost 4GB of my bandwidth for the month. That doesn't include the people who come directly to my videoblog and don't subscribe to my feed. Nor does it include people who subscribe to my feed but then download my video more than once.

Using ads and sponsorships

There are many reasons to carefully track your visitors, but two of them come down to cold, hard cash. The first is something I discuss in this chapter: tracking usage to keep up with and control your bandwidth use, so you don't get hit with a bunch of unexpected costs.

The other reason to track your viewership is to sell advertising and sponsorships. Videoblogging is just starting to find ways to cover the costs of bandwidth and — perhaps — become a viable commercial enterprise. Advertising is billed on a per-hit basis, so your server logs are crucial to billing for advertising dollars. Additionally, many advertisers will want you to use their own site-tracking programs to ensure that your billing matches the number of ad hits they've received.

There are a number of advertising options out there for Web sites, if you want to simply put an ad into your Web site and not worry about its appearance in your videoblog's video files or RSS feed. You can also generate advertising revenue in your RSS feed through Google text ads — which, since they use embedded text, can be delivered along with your videoblog content to your subscribers.

Of course, if you really want to revolutionize advertising in videoblogging, put ads in your vlog video itself. Just remember that the vlog viewing audience is entirely voluntary — if they don't like your ads, or even the fact you put ads in, not only can they change the channel, they might just stop watching altogether. If you include ads with your video, make doubly sure you give a lot of value to your viewers.

Another popular revenue model is the sponsorship option. With a sponsorship, you ask for and get money from an organization. The organization pays you a flat amount, usually enough to cover the basic costs of putting on the videoblog. Sponsorships are a great option when your vlog is mainly educational or outreach-oriented, or if it promotes a particular technology in which sponsors might want to gain mindshare.

An example of a sponsored videoblog can be seen at the California Betta Society vlog, `http://cbsbettasvlog.blip.tv`. In this case, a nonprofit fish-enthusiast club sponsors a monthly videoblog to promote the club and better betta-keeping. As a nonprofit organization, the club is legally required to spend a certain portion of its funds on services that help its mission; a videoblog helps them do that by furthering their educational goals and at the same time encouraging new fish owners to consider joining.

There's more opportunity for sponsorships if you have a locally-oriented videoblog, because the sponsor can see how the market is targeted to a geographical area. When evaluating demographics for the return on their investment — whether it's for advertising or sponsorships — most for-profit organizations need to know something specific about the audience. The more information you can provide about your viewers, the more likely you are to hear yes when you ask a potential sponsor for money.

So, how do I control that? Well, for one thing, you can set up your RSS feed to not enclose your video files, but instead provide a link. Although that seems like a great way to throttle bandwidth costs, it adds an extra step to your viewers, and will result in fewer viewers overall.

You can also set up a third-party subscription service that caches your vlog's content for you. Even though you won't get the server logs from the file downloads, you will know that your files go to your subscribers without using your own bandwidth to deliver them. Alternatively, you can just make sure your Internet service plan for your server has a lot of bandwidth available, and then monitor your server's usage every day to keep abreast of new subscriptions and traffic spikes.

Improving performance

I've mentioned before that good videoblogs perform well. When a user comes to your vlog, or downloads your movies, they want the experience to be as seamless as possible.

The following list describes some of the ways you can ensure that visitors to your videoblog have a trouble-free experience viewing your vlog entries:

- **Avoid click-throughs.** Although there are cases where you'll want to use a poster file, unless it's necessary for download speed and time, avoid making your viewers click something extra to watch your movie.

- **Keep it small, fast, and cheap.** No, it's not the latest sports car — it's your vlog entries. Keep them small, fast, and therefore cheap (in terms of bandwidth) to download.

- **Guarantee fast downloads.** In addition to file size, also look at your server's speed and Internet connection. You just can't put a videoblog on a dial-up server in your garage and hope to handle a hundred downloads a day.

- **Use consistent and commonplace file types.** Use common file types, but also be consistent. If you decide to use Windows Media files for your vlog, then always use that file type. Your audience will expect Windows Media files from your vlog, so don't surprise them.

- **Use a common file and screen size.** I've seen videoblogs that take full advantage of the high-definition screen size and ratio. It took about an hour to download, and it was certainly gorgeous to watch. However, aside from a curiosity, it wasn't a sustainable format. Stick with common sizes and aspect ratios for screens (unless you want to make a specific artistic statement).

- **Play well with others.** Keep your ear to the ground as new videoblog viewers and devices become available, and test your vlog out in them if you can. Have a friend with an iPod video? Ask them to try subscribing to your feed in iTunes and see how it looks! Routine testing will help you diagnose problems early.

Above all — and this is true for all these practices — keep your audience and their needs in mind. Sometimes, you may need to revisit your audience profile, ask them how they watch your videoblog, and make sure they're not laboring under your file sizes, for example. But often, you will be impressed by how resilient your viewers are, how adaptable they are to your new ideas and new content you put into your vlog.

Part V
The Part of Tens

The 5th Wave   By Rich Tennant

"Ooo-wait! That's perfect for the clinic's videoblog. Just stretch it out a little further... little more..."

In this part . . .

Who doesn't love lists? This part is all about the lists. And they're useful lists, too (at least I think so). This part give you lists for ten vlogs you should definitely watch, ten ideas you might want to vlog about, and finally, ten ways to turn a videoblog into a business asset.

Chapter 17

Ten Core Vlogs to Watch

....

O ne of the best ways to learn about videoblogging is to watch other people's videoblogs. In this book, particularly in Chapters 1 and 2, I mention many videoblogs that you can visit and subscribe to. I hope you check out all the videoblogs I mention there because they are terrific ones to watch. Vloggers tend to be self-referential: One vlogger will post about another vlogger's movies, who will post about someone else's stuff. That's the only reason I could even narrow this list down to ten!

Anyway, I had to ask myself what videoblogs I'd want a new vlogger to watch first — so I dug around, and I think this is a good list of videoblogs that everyone should watch at least once.

Ask A Ninja

Want to lose an entire day laughing? Ask A Ninja is one of the funniest vlogs on the Internet, maybe because it's such a silly premise — a ninja assassin answers all types of questions, in a kind of advice-column parody — but also because its production quality lends itself to a kind of hyperactive camerawork style, with a lot of sudden cuts and a fast-talking black-masked ninja. It's almost reminiscent of old kung-fu movies.

A recent Radio Shack ad campaign involved a ninja making a decision about buying a cellphone. While there's no apparent connection between the Radio Shack ad and the Ask A Ninja vlog, the folks at Ask A Ninja were surely flattered.

Ask A Ninja is frequently updated every couple of days, and has feeds in most common video formats. The Web site is www.askaninja.com.

Chasing Windmills

I've mentioned Chasing Windmills before as an excellent fiction videoblog. It's the story of a young couple going through life together and apart. What's fascinating about this videoblog is that it's very well done, the lighting and camera work is never sloppy, it's all in black and white, and the storyline is just beautifully scripted.

Be aware that Chasing Windmills is definitely intended for a mature audience. There's nothing more in this videoblog than you might see on HBO, but you don't want to watch this one at work or with young children in the room. (At least, not before you prescreen it.)

Chasing Windmills is posted daily, in QuickTime movie format, here: `http://chasingmills.blogspot.com`.

Crash Test Kitchen

There's something about having a couple of Aussies demystify cooking that's really quite fun. It's particularly amusing when the hosts aren't afraid to show the mishaps and mistakes as they go along — like what happens to a Pyrex dish when it's exposed to direct flame.

Lenny and Waz don't post very long videos, but each one is a complete cooking show for a single dish. A typical vlog starts with the hosts talking about the dish, and then making it — often with a few mishaps and changes to the recipe along the way. At the end, they sit down to dinner over the dish and discuss whether or not it turned out well.

Crash Test Kitchen is posted frequently, in QuickTime movie format: `www.crashtestkitchen.com`.

Freevlog

If, after reading this book, you still want to find out more about how to videoblog, head over to Freevlog and watch some videos on how to videoblog. It's not the only resource for learning how to vlog, but it's a good one if you're starting out.

Freevlog is updated irregularly, in QuickTime format; you can get the how-to at `www.freevlog.org/tutorial`.

You should also check out the personal videoblogs of the creators of Freevlog, Ryanne Hodson, Michael Verdi, and Jay Dedman. Ryanne, Michael, and Jay are not only good friends and co-authors, they're also the founders of NODE101 (`http://node101.org`), a nonprofit organization dedicated to spreading the news and education about videoblogging. You'll find links to their personal vlogs and to NODE101 on Freevlog.

It's Jerry Time

This is a humorous, animated videoblog put together by two brothers — one does the animation, and the other serves as the talent by being the speaker and providing a piano music soundtrack. This is what you get when you let a guy with a lot of sardonic humor expose the foibles of his own life. It's so good, it was nominated for the 2006 Emmy award for new media programming, although it lost out to a nominee from the mainstream media.

It's Jerry Time is a monthly videoblog, with embedded QuickTime or Windows Media File in the Web page, or an RSS feed for QuickTime movies: www. itsjerrytime.com.

Izzy Video

I found out about Izzy Video through one of the many vlogs about vlogs (videoblogs that review other videoblogs), and I really like it. There are several videoblogs about making digital video, and this is one of the better ones.

I think Izzy's style is similar to Pouringdown (mentioned next), in the intimate quality to the videos — with voiceovers providing the bulk of the tutorials, illustrated with shots of the videoblogger's children. Again, production quality is high, but you expect that in a vlog about good digital video.

Izzy Video is produced weekly, in QuickTime format, at www.izzyvideo.com.

Pouringdown

It might be hard to explain what the appeal of Pouringdown is. Each vlog is a self-contained moment in the videoblogger's life, but it's the kind of moment that could happen to anyone, anywhere. Daniel's voiceover commentary, however, gives the vlogs more depth than just visual moments, and the audience is left with something more than a video moment. There's meaning to this vlog.

It helps that the production values are high — each vlog is well lit and superbly composed, with background audio that doesn't grate on the nerves.

Pouringdown is updated frequently, in QuickTime movie format, at `http://pouringdown.blogspot.com`.

Rocketboom

Rocketboom is the most popular videoblog on the Internet as of this writing, and for good reason. It's not just that it was featured on *CSI* in 2005. It's also a great show with a terrific format and an engaging hostess. Amanda Congden is the hostess of Rocketboom, and her timing and body language are reminiscent of Jon Stewart on Comedy Central's *Daily Show*.

People watching Rocketboom automatically think it's a humorous slant on the news, but aside from a few quips here and there, the show is actually more of a daily news show without being as dry as unbuttered toast.

This is a vlog that updates five days a week, with feeds in most major formats. The site: `www.rocketboom.com`.

Steve Garfield

Steve Garfield's was probably the first videoblog on the Internet, and he's credited with giving the technology its name. He's also a tireless evangelist for videoblogging, doing talks, seminars, workshops, and online community building nonstop.

Steve Garfield also has a videoblog on videoblogs, called Vlog Soup. He posted weekly episodes of The Carol and Steve Show in 2005, and you'll often find a 30-second vlog that was clearly taken during an educational session, and then posted to his videoblog.

Steve's vlog is updated often, sometimes more than once a day. The videos are available on his vlog's Web page in multiple formats, or through a feed using QuickTime movies. Here's where you find it: `www.stevegarfield.com`.

The Videoblogging For Dummies Book Vlog

After I finished writing this book, I made a videoblog for all you wonderful folks! I can't guarantee the production quality, though, since I'm inviting you to send in a vlog to post to it (see the Web site for instructions)! Here's the catch: Use a variation on the quest story from Chapter 8, and I'll post everyone's different interpretations on this theme.

I'll also be posting news and event appearances, and if you want to see some of the silly videos I made while writing this book, they'll be there.

The vlog is updated irregularly, with multiple formats available: `www.mortaine.com/vlogdummies`.

Chapter 18

Ten Ideas for Personal Vlogs

*P*ersonal videoblogs make up the majority of videoblogs out on the Internet, whether they're for your personal recordkeeping, sharing a hobby interest, giving your own opinion on the way the world works, or sharing something with a very particular someone in your life.

A personal videoblog can include many types of posts, or you can make an entire videoblog devoted to one particular type, such as the types discussed in this chapter. For example, I shoot videos on hiking and camping — a hobby — and post them to one particular videoblog.

I encourage all new videobloggers to create a personal vlog, even if your primary wish is to make a commercial or business videoblog. You're going to need to test out the technology — and that works best when you try it out by posting it to a personal site first, where the stakes are low.

Family Share Time

As with the sweetheart video (discussed later in this chapter), long-distance family videos can bring families closer together and bridge the generation gap. Through a videoblog, non-custodial parents can watch their kids growing up, or parents of grown children can get to know them better as adults.

Videoblogs are also a great way to send a note back home. When my young nephew came to visit for a week by himself, we posted a videoblog each evening so his mom and dad could see how he was doing. It was like a video postcard home.

A family video can include family history and documenting important moments. Family reunions are a great place to interview relatives, and any major milestone in your family's life is a good moment to document for posterity.

History and Documentary

I mentioned family history already, but of course you don't have to stick to documenting your own family. Are you a Civil War fan? Take the video camera out to a re-enactment group or a battle site to film your perspective on that historical moment. Sure, it's not the same as a documentary put on by PBS — it's better because it's your *own* words and perspective on that moment in history.

If you do have a particular tie to a time or place in history, make your historical or documentary vlog personal by connecting it to your world. After all, your personal vlog is the place to set aside any academic or professional detachment and really connect with your subject.

Humor

My favorite videoblogs are the ones that make me laugh. Don't get me wrong — I love to think, and I like to get to know people. But the vlogs that get me laughing are the ones I watch the most.

Humor is an inherently subjective thing. What makes me laugh might just annoy someone else. Don't be surprised if what you think is the funniest vlog entry ever doesn't get the reaction you'd hoped from your audience. And to keep things in perspective, remember the pro comedian's motto: "Dying is easy. Comedy is hard."

Humor comes in many different types, appealing to some very common elements all the way up to math jokes that you probably won't get if you don't have a Ph.D. Use whatever form of humor you like best in your vlog — for example:

- ✔ **Low:** This type of humor appeals to the most basic forms of human nature. Potty humor and sex jokes fall into this category. Another type of low humor you may want to use in a humorous vlog is physical comedy, also called slapstick.

- ✔ **High:** This type of humor uses some type of intellectual joke that the listeners can only get if they already know something else — kind of an in-joke for the intelligentsia.

  A popular form of high humor is the superiority humor. In this form, someone or something is shown to be stupid or inferior. There is a long-standing tradition of using humor to also poke fun at oneself with this type of humor, which could make for a very funny vlog.

This is also the genre of humor where potentially offensive or insulting jokes fall, such as jokes about race, gender, religion, politics, and so on. Some people believe that if you don't risk insulting some group of people, you can't be funny. Although I think it's entirely possible to be funny without insulting anyone, there is definitely an audience for this type of humor. Just be aware of the line between funny and offensive, even if you intentionally cross it in your vlog.

✔ **Language humor:** With this form of humor, a turn of phrase delivers the punch line. Puns are the most common forms of language humor. Imagine a vlog entry that uses language humor where a word's meaning is misunderstood, as in Abbott and Costello's famous "Who's on First?" gag.

✔ **Humor to lighten the mood:** You can also use humor to lighten up a serious situation, or to make fun of something very serious, such as illness or death. Although some people have a hard time with this kind of humor and find it distasteful, others just can't handle serious topics without cracking a joke and offering some levity.

Good taste is relative, yes, but there's also such a thing as knowing when to back off.

If you're not inherently a funny person, but you want to make a funny vlog, start by observing the things in your life that make you laugh, and then vlog them. Watch other funny videoblogs as well — timing is a major part of comedy, and you can pick up the cadences of other humorists and adapt the style to your own speech. It may take a while, but like any art form, comedy is improved through careful observation.

Interests and Hobbies

Hobbies are a great subject for videoblogging, because your enthusiasm for your interest will come through in your vlog. If you don't think you have any hobbies — or at least none that would interest others — think again. If you fix up your own house or car, you have a videoblogging subject ready to go. If you're a hard-core TV watcher, what would your commentary be on your favorite (or not-so-favorite) shows?

Hobbies fill in the spaces of people's lives between work, sleep, eating, driving, and changing diapers. What do you do in your off time? Read books? Watch movies? Knit? Fix old cars? Set up the Ultimate Stereo System? Play Dance Dance Revolution? Vlog it. All of it. Nothing says *you* like the things you do for pure fun.

Love Vlogs

Videoblogs don't have to be seen by a thousand people. Sometimes a videoblog can serve as a postcard between yourself and a loved one, whether far away or nearby. You can post your deepest secrets to your beloved in video form, and have them respond in kind.

If you're in a long-distance relationship, directed videoblogs can really help you connect and get that all-important face time with your beloved. Some videobloggers might even get a bit naughty with their vlogs, but how comfortable you are with that is really up to you.

If you set up a common blog to share videos between yourself and your significant other, I strongly encourage you to password-protect the blog and your video storage. Using a password that only you and your significant other know is the simplest and most effective way to keep your deepest, most intimate secrets from being posted all over the Internet through an RSS feed.

Personal Diaries

"Dear Diary . . . " A lot of people keep personal diaries on paper, on the Internet, as audio recordings, or in video form. The video diary has become a film form in its own right, although most people do not use a video diary as a commercial film environment.

There are many advantages to diary-keeping. Diaries help provide perspective on your life, and serve as a historical record if you ever need to know when something happened. A casual mention of a minor symptom in a diary has helped diagnose an illness later on — and diaries can serve as legal records for purposes of providing evidence in a court of law.

A video diary, at its most basic, can be just you talking into the camera. Sure, it means you're making another talking head video. But it's *your* head, and since it's *your* diary, it's okay to put your head on it.

For a personal vlog diary, you could also include footage of your day. For example, if you went somewhere or did something, include video of what you did or where you went. Or a photo you took, or even a scanned receipt (but make sure you blur out your credit-card numbers!).

You might be tempted in a video diary to only include things you're comfortable with. But a personal diary is little more than a minute log if you leave out the personal part. Don't shy away from the camera when you get emotional — that's a very important and human part of your daily life. And don't be afraid to capture moments where you are not at your best. If you can't laugh at yourself, then whom can you laugh at?

Another suggestion for a personal vlog diary is to post a "day in the life," where you take 5–10 second videos throughout the day, one every hour or so, and edit them together chronologically.

Finally, your personal video diary can explore the world in which you live, especially if that world is not typical. Videobloggers in war zones (from Baghdad to the South Side of Chicago) have an opportunity to make the world hear their voices and that of their community in times of upheaval and change. Anne Frank kept a personal diary through her years in hiding, a diary that has become a tremendous work to showcase an individual life in crisis. A personal diary vlog can do the same for you.

Rants

Is there anything quite so much fun as completely lambasting your pet peeves? Done right, ranting is as much an art form as rock'n'roll. Done with humor, it's high comedy.

A good rant should do a couple of things. Most importantly, it should release your own frustration with whatever you're ranting about. Yes, that might mean some strong language, but remember that you can always edit in a few bleeps if you need or want to.

Your rant should also be coherent enough to explain to your audience why you're so annoyed. If you're annoyed because something isn't logical, then look at your rant and make sure you can explain what's so illogical about it.

Good rant subjects are ones in which there's some inherent lack of consistency or oversight of logic on the part of the subject. For instance, I recently ranted about a company that makes tax and accounting software. In my rant, I went on an on about how ridiculous I found it that the tax software couldn't read the accounting software's files. This seemed to me to be a basic failing in consistency within the company.

Of course, there are always reasons why something is the way it is. People do not usually set out to annoy you, after all. If there's a stupid company policy preventing you from doing something spectacular, it's good to rant about it, and ignore the mitigating circumstances. Balanced opinions have no place in a really good rant. You can save them for the text of your blog post, if you want to make a disclaimer that you know why it is the way it is.

The one thing to be wary of when you rant is libel and slander. In the case of a vlog, it's slander — you're ranting audibly, not in print. In both libel and slander, a person may take umbrage at your harsh words against them. If your words are untrue, then they have legal cause to sue. Note that, since anyone can sue you for anything in the U.S., if you blast an individual or corporation, you should know that there's a risk there. However, the best defense against libel/slander suits is the truth. If your rant is 100 percent true, then it's not slander — but you had better be 100 percent *sure*.

Reviews of Cool Stuff

One of my favorite vlog formats are the vlogs of cool vlogs. In these, videobloggers show off the videoblogs they like or are watching, and why they think they're cool. This kind of videoblog is a review vlog, and the thing they're reviewing in this case is other videoblogs.

Of course, you don't have to review other vlogs — anything you have an opinion about can be reviewed. For example, you could do a review vlog of any of the following:

- Books, movies, or music
- Foods, recipes, or restaurants
- Sewing, knitting, or craft patterns
- Assembly instructions that come with products you have to put together

Can you imagine a whole videoblog about putting together kids' toys and which toys have the best instructions? Parents would flock to your vlog at Christmas!

If you do review music, you might wonder if you can legally play any of the music you're reviewing in your vlog. I'm not a lawyer, but the lawyers that I've asked about this say that you can play a short clip (less than 30 seconds) in a piece where you're reviewing or commenting on the work. It's like quoting from a book in an article. You still have to give credit to the artists, but it's a legitimate use.

When you do a review videoblog, it's customary to include the name of the item (and where someone can get it) as handy information. But be sure to tell your viewers what you like about the item, but also what you didn't like or what needs improvement. If it's a movie or book, avoid giving away the ending, also called *spoiling* the movie or book. If you do include a spoiler, start out your post with a spoiler warning so people can pause or stop the video before their enjoyment of the book or movie gets ruined.

Finally, if you have any financial interest in the item being reviewed, you must disclose it. If you're an investor, an employee, a contractor, or the spouse or child thereof, telling your audience about that relationship identifies you as a potentially biased source. Now, you might also be an inside source for the item, having an "in" with the company. But failure to reveal those relationships means when they come out (as they inevitably will), your audience will be suspicious of your motives.

Storytelling

Chapter 8 talks about storytelling and plots for videoblogging, using a classic heroic story structure to form a videoblog. But stories are everywhere. Stories can be about your regular day, about your family, or your life, or they can be completely made up, all fiction.

Most people believe that the difference between fiction and non-fiction is whether or not something is true. The word *fiction* comes from the Latin *fictus*, meaning to shape or fashion something. It means to put your finger on something, to get at something true and real and mold it. Fiction can be true-to-life, but what makes it fictional is that its truth is artistic — and *not* the same as fact. Facts attempt to provide data about what actually occurred. However, *truth* may describe not only things that actually happened, but also things that are universal to the human experience.

A fiction vlog can be very powerful. Consider Chasing Windmills (www.chasingmills.blogspot.com), a black-and-white videoblog that tells the story of a young couple's emerging relationship. Over the course of the videoblog, a story of love, commitment, arguments, and heartache unfolds through each vlog post.

Fiction can also be humorous, dramatic, suspenseful — in short, all the things that life is. However, there are some risks in a fictional videoblog, and the main one comes up when your audience does not know that your vlog is fictional.

The wrong way to add drama

In 2005, a videoblogger had been vlogging about his life for a while, complete with some minor drug use. One day, he posted a vlog about having had his kids taken away because of what his ex had seen in his vlog. The videoblogging community was shocked and saddened for his predicament, and many wanted to reach out and help. This was because they did not know that, although his videoblog reflected parts of his life, the drugs and the part where his kids were taken from him were fictional. Some of his viewers became disenchanted and stopped trusting him, or trusting anyone's so-called personal vlog. Members of the videoblogging community,

myself included, chalked up the experience to another case of emotional manipulation on the Internet.

It's not hard to lie with video. Even though video supposedly shows it as it really happened, editing and composition are easy to manipulate, and you can always get actors to participate in a fictional storyline.

If you want to make a fictional vlog, do it. But don't toy with your audience or lie to them. Be honest about the fictional nature of your vlog; your audience will respect you for it.

Travel Vlogs

Travelogues have been around since the days of Homer's *Odyssey*. They're a form of writing in which the author describes a place to their home-bound audience, in such a way as to really capture the essence of the place. Whenever people have traveled, whether for work or pleasure, documenting their travels has always been an important part of the journey. From the early travel diaries to the horrible slideshow of Aunt Mildred's trip to Egypt, people share their travels with others so they can feel they were really there, and to bring back a little taste of the experience to their loved ones.

Travel photography (and videography, as well) is an art unto itself. To capture the essence of a place, you really have to look beyond the tourist centers and find the images that make a place unique, and then compose your shots carefully to capture that unique quality on film.

Even though you can take a still or video camera out to all the standard tourist destinations, what happens when you approach your travel with a different perspective? What if you looked at your travel plans and deliberately went to a place during the off-season? You would get video of life there when it's not the height of the tourist season, when the majority of the people out and about are people who live and work there. Or if you prefer to travel during the on-season, what about escaping the tourist crowds by finding the real marketplaces and cafés, the spots where the local folks do their shopping or hang out?

A travel vlog can be a fascinating document of your time in a place, a walking tour, a montage of places you've been, or even just a really simple glimpse at a roadside attraction.

Chapter 19

Ten Ideas for Business Vlogs

One of the most common topics for discussion when videobloggers get together is how to use videoblogs in a business setting, either to make money or to improve a business's exposure and promotion.

As videoblogging matures as a medium and an industry, more business applications for it will evolve, so don't take this chapter as the final gospel on how to use videoblogs for your business. If you have the greatest idea for a business vlog, go for it. There is no limit to how these technologies can be used.

Activism

Some businesses are in political hotbeds and can't avoid becoming politically or socially aware, if not active. Some lines of business, of course, are less involved until lack of involvement affects their bottom lines. Some businesses engage in political or social activism, taking action to raise awareness about public issues.

For instance, a land developer needs to remain on top of land-use rights, and likely will try to lobby local and state governments for the right to develop land. A doctor must remain engaged in health-care law, to best serve her patients. A fast-food franchise must be aware of nutritional-education programs and decide how to support them in their town. In some cases — such as a not-for-profit homeless shelter — political and social activism isn't a sideline to a business, it's a way of life.

If there is a law or issue that threatens or benefits your business, you would do well to let your customers know. A videoblog can help raise awareness of issues that affect you and make your business successful. A new zoning rule, for instance, may seem like a great idea to your customers — until you point out to them that the new law opens up your community to competition from major chain stores that will almost certainly drive you out of business. A videoblog can help get that message to your customers and your community.

Advertising

The most blatant use of a videoblog — and the *least* successful — is to post an advertisement for your product or service to your videoblog. This particular method of videoblogging isn't known for its effectiveness, because when people download your videos, they want something valuable in exchange for their time; they see a blatant self-promotion as a waste of their time and bandwidth.. Since advertising is something that you as a business normally pay other people to show, asking people to download it of their own free will is counterintuitive.

However, there are two types of ads that do seem to work. First, if your ads are really clever and fresh, people will download them because they're interested in them. When I say *clever,* I mean the kind of fresh and surprising ads that you can expect during the Super Bowl (which many Americans watch only for the advertising, even if they don't say so).

The other kind of ad that works is a trailer for a movie (or, to a lesser degree, for a TV show). People love downloading and watching movie trailers online. If the online trailer contains content — scenes for example — that aren't in the theatrical trailer, all the better!

I should mention that there's a special kind of trailer — better called a *teaser* — used to advertise adult media and Web sites. Videoblogs for these teasers work for their audiences, and if you have such a site with teaser videos or the capability to make them, then you will have no trouble turning your teaser videoblog into a very successful moneymaker.

Announcements

Whenever your company has an announcement or event, in addition to your standard press release, you can post the announcement in video format to your videoblog. Delivering a keynote speech? Video the speech and post it, or excerpts of it, to your vlog.

You can do this for product launches as well, with a video showing the product and your announcement, though this runs perilously close to an advertisement if it's done with *too* slick a style.

In the vlog post, include a link to the related press release, and at least provide contact information for media outlets to license your announcement video. You can even put the licensing in the vlog post itself — if you do, more casual vloggers will feel comfortable re-vlogging your company's news.

Behind the Scenes

One advantage of a business vlog is that you can show parts of your business that no one else would normally have access to. You can show the world what your work process is like, or how you take an idea from its bare concept into full implementation.

If you're an artist, musician, or filmmaker, this behind-the-scenes look will fascinate your fans and help promote your work. If you're a businessperson with a product to sell, showing off the parts of your development cycle that are cool or effective gives your customers greater insight into your business and greater pride of ownership of your products.

Naturally, you'll want to keep in mind that some of your processes may be protected information, trade secrets, or otherwise not for public knowledge. (After all, your competition is part of the public.) If you own the company and want to disclose everything, that's your business. If you aren't the owner, though, you might want to run your vlog ideas past the corporate attorney, as well as the owner.

Disclaimers and Disclosures

Every year, publicly traded companies have to make an annual financial report to their shareholders and the SEC (Securities & Exchange Commission), as well as file quarterly reports. The number of legal disclaimers, disclosures, and related announcements a company has to produce can be staggering.

To make matters worse, the disclaimers and disclosures are usually several pages of legalese, and nobody actually wants to read those. So — instead — they wait for the media to pick up on the story, or hire an expert to interpret for them.

Although a lot of these documents have to be formatted a certain way when filed, what if you were able to present your annual report in a video format, where you could explain how the company is doing, and what's ahead? The market analysts would still analyze, but at least you would have the opportunity to get your side of the story out in the public.

Again, make sure you clear these types of vlogs with your legal department or attorney. Any kind of legal or financial statement on behalf of the company can be a fast track into hot water unless you know exactly what you're doing.

Educational

The easiest application for many businesses is to create educational videoblogs. These can be instructions or training for employees or potential employees, of course, but a more general application is to create a videoblog that helps customers understand and use your product or service better.

For example, if you run a vegetarian restaurant, you could produce a videoblog teaching people how to cook a healthy vegetarian meal, a vlog on the meat industry and its impact on society, or a vlog about organic local farms in your area. Another example is that a law firm can use videoblogs to explain how to behave in court, what particular acts are considered criminal, or to show interviews with experts on legal issues.

Now, you might wonder why you'd give away information for free. After all, people pay you to give them advice or your expert opinion, right? Sure, but you aren't going to lose business by giving away information for free. The people who won't buy what they can get for free would probably not have bought your service anyway.

Whatever your business, chances are there are things you want your customers to know. If they have already watched your vlogs, then you wouldn't have to answer the same questions when you first meet them, for instance. Or you believe that knowledge will naturally lead them to buy your product or service.

Finally, a little bit of education can be a real lure. Consider a magician who uses a videoblog to show how he does a simple trick. Now he has calls coming in all the time from people wanting him to perform — having seen one trick explained, customers now understand the kind of control it takes to pull off a magic trick, and how much talent and skill he has.

Games and Contests

Would you like to play a game? I know I would! Businesses have used contests for years to promote their products, and you can use your videoblog as a delivery mechanism. Contests like these work well when promoted in a business videoblog:

- **Sweepstakes:** These use a random drawing to pick a winner.
- **Trivia/knowledge contests:** These use trivia questions or knowledge questions to pick a winner, or to qualify entries for a sweepstakes.

✔ **Skill games:** These are often competitions of contestants' abilities, such as essay contests for kids, or film-festival contests.

✔ **Other games:** Puzzle-solving games and riddles can challenge contestants' minds and logic skills.

Games and contests don't necessarily have to have prizes, though simpler contests such as sweepstakes usually need a tangible reward. For skill contests, bragging rights work (though providing a prize is also nice). Prizes can be cash, products, services, trips to events, or even a simple certificate.

If you hold a contest in your videoblog, check your local gaming laws to make sure you aren't breaking any of them. All those "void where prohibited/ no purchase necessary" rules in the fine print of contest entries are basically there to protect the contest sponsors from legal liability. It goes without saying (or should) that for any contest of a significant size, disqualifying employees and their families is a smart way to avoid trouble.

Media Delivery

Some of the most commercial vlogs aren't even called videoblogs. They're called *video podcasts* or just *videos* in the iTunes Music Store. When Apple announced that iTunes would start carrying video in the store, the door opened for quick, inexpensive, video-on-demand downloads. It's now possible to miss an episode of *Lost* one day, and then buy and download it the next.

If you're a media producer looking for a new distribution method, a videoblog might be for you. Online Internet TV channels such as dtv.com (www.dtv.com) offer a way to deliver content and accept payment for it. But you can also use RSS to deliver content, even the sort you want users to pay for. With the password-protected RSS feeds now available, you can have paid subscribers downloading your vlogs automatically on a subscription basis.

If you make your commercial media downloadable, eventually it *will* escape into the Internet. Although there's a lot of argument about the rights of creators versus trends toward sharing, consider which is more valuable to you: the cost of a download subscription, or another viewer eagerly snapping up your video. The business impact of your videoblog is in your hands.

Other Promotions

Any promotional idea your marketing team can come up with can probably be videoblogged. Have a street team doing some guerilla marketing at a local event? Send a camera crew out to film it. Not only will you have a neat piece for your videoblog, but the very presence of the camera crew will get people interested in the street team and what they have to say.

Any publicity stunt you can think of can and should be recorded, at least for your own marketing analysis. If the film comes out well, or the stunt takes hold, grab that video and post it to your vlog.

Your vlog doesn't have to be planned, either. Accidental vlogs can be just as effective a viral campaign as if you'd planned one. In San Francisco recently, Sony filmed a commercial using several hundred thousand high-bouncing balls. San Francisco residents, surprised by the sight of thousands of rubber balls bouncing down the street, pulled out their camcorders and caught the action on film, which they then posted to the Internet. Sony's advertisement surprise may have been spoiled, but their bouncing-ball stunt put them on the map for a viral-video campaign.

Sneak Preview

Similar to a behind-the-scenes vlog, the sneak preview lets you show off a product before it's ready to launch. Car companies have done sneak previews at car shows for years, with the concept cars displaying all the new technology without ever making it to an assembly line.

Software companies provide sneak peeks to customers as well, through beta programs where customers can download and install a not-quite-finished version of the software before all the bugs are ironed out. Beta testers provide valuable public exposure to the product; they also help identify those bugs.

And of course, the idea of a sneak preview isn't new to film, either, with sneak previews showing up in theaters before a movie's release. You can use your videoblog to give a glance at an upcoming product or service to your potential customers — and gauge their reaction — as well as drum up a little buzz.

Index

• F •

• J •

• Q •

• R •

• S •

• W •

SPORTS, FITNESS, PARENTING, RELIGION & SPIRITUALITY

0-7645-5146-9

0-7645-5418-2

Also available:

Adoption For Dummies
0-7645-5488-3

Basketball For Dummies
0-7645-5248-1

The Bible For Dummies
0-7645-5296-1

Buddhism For Dummies
0-7645-5359-3

Catholicism For Dummies
0-7645-5391-7

Hockey For Dummies
0-7645-5228-7

Judaism For Dummies
0-7645-5299-6

Martial Arts For Dummies
0-7645-5358-5

Pilates For Dummies
0-7645-5397-6

Religion For Dummies
0-7645-5264-3

Teaching Kids to Read For Dummies
0-7645-4043-2

Weight Training For Dummies
0-7645-5168-X

Yoga For Dummies
0-7645-5117-5

TRAVEL

0-7645-5438-7

0-7645-5453-0

Also available:

Alaska For Dummies
0-7645-1761-9

Arizona For Dummies
0-7645-6938-4

Cancún and the Yucatán For Dummies
0-7645-2437-2

Cruise Vacations For Dummies
0-7645-6941-4

Europe For Dummies
0-7645-5456-5

Ireland For Dummies
0-7645-5455-7

Las Vegas For Dummies
0-7645-5448-4

London For Dummies
0-7645-4277-X

New York City For Dummies
0-7645-6945-7

Paris For Dummies
0-7645-5494-8

RV Vacations For Dummies
0-7645-5443-3

Walt Disney World & Orlando For Dummies
0-7645-6943-0

GRAPHICS, DESIGN & WEB DEVELOPMENT

0-7645-4345-8

0-7645-5589-8

Also available:

Adobe Acrobat 6 PDF For Dummies
0-7645-3760-1

Building a Web Site For Dummies
0-7645-7144-3

Dreamweaver MX 2004 For Dummies
0-7645-4342-3

FrontPage 2003 For Dummies
0-7645-3882-9

HTML 4 For Dummies
0-7645-1995-6

Illustrator CS For Dummies
0-7645-4084-X

Macromedia Flash MX 2004 For Dummies
0-7645-4358-X

Photoshop 7 All-in-One Desk Reference For Dummies
0-7645-1667-1

Photoshop CS Timesaving Techniques For Dummies
0-7645-6782-9

PHP 5 For Dummies
0-7645-4166-8

PowerPoint 2003 For Dummies
0-7645-3908-6

QuarkXPress 6 For Dummies
0-7645-2593-X

NETWORKING, SECURITY, PROGRAMMING & DATABASES

0-7645-6852-3

0-7645-5784-X

Also available:

A+ Certification For Dummies
0-7645-4187-0

Access 2003 All-in-One Desk Reference For Dummies
0-7645-3988-4

Beginning Programming For Dummies
0-7645-4997-9

C For Dummies
0-7645-7068-4

Firewalls For Dummies
0-7645-4048-3

Home Networking For Dummies
0-7645-42796

Network Security For Dummies
0-7645-1679-5

Networking For Dummies
0-7645-1677-9

TCP/IP For Dummies
0-7645-1760-0

VBA For Dummies
0-7645-3989-2

Wireless All In-One Desk Reference For Dummies
0-7645-7496-5

Wireless Home Networking For Dummies
0-7645-3910-8

ALTH & SELF-HELP

0-7645-6820-5 *†

0-7645-2566-2

Also available:

- Alzheimer's For Dummies
  0-7645-3899-3
- Asthma For Dummies
  0-7645-4233-8
- Controlling Cholesterol For Dummies
  0-7645-5440-9
- Depression For Dummies
  0-7645-3900-0
- Dieting For Dummies
  0-7645-4149-8
- Fertility For Dummies
  0-7645-2549-2

- Fibromyalgia For Dummies
  0-7645-5441-7
- Improving Your Memory For Dummies
  0-7645-5435-2
- Pregnancy For Dummies †
  0-7645-4483-7
- Quitting Smoking For Dummies
  0-7645-2629-4
- Relationships For Dummies
  0-7645-5384-4
- Thyroid For Dummies
  0-7645-5385-2

JCATION, HISTORY, REFERENCE & TEST PREPARATION

0-7645-5194-9

0-7645-4186-2

Also available:

- Algebra For Dummies
  0-7645-5325-9
- British History For Dummies
  0-7645-7021-8
- Calculus For Dummies
  0-7645-2498-4
- English Grammar For Dummies
  0-7645-5322-4
- Forensics For Dummies
  0-7645-5580-4
- The GMAT For Dummies
  0-7645-5251-1
- Inglés Para Dummies
  0-7645-5427-1

- Italian For Dummies
  0-7645-5196-5
- Latin For Dummies
  0-7645-5431-X
- Lewis & Clark For Dummies
  0-7645-2545-X
- Research Papers For Dummies
  0-7645-5426-3
- The SAT I For Dummies
  0-7645-7193-1
- Science Fair Projects For Dummies
  0-7645-5460-3
- U.S. History For Dummies
  0-7645-5249-X

Get smart @ dummies.com®

- **Find a full list of Dummies titles**
- **Look into loads of FREE on-site articles**
- **Sign up for FREE eTips e-mailed to you weekly**
- **See what other products carry the Dummies name**
- **Shop directly from the Dummies bookstore**
- **Enter to win new prizes every month!**

arate Canadian edition also available
arate U.K. edition also available

ble wherever books are sold. For more information or to order direct: U.S. customers visit www.dummies.com or call 1-877-762-2974.
ustomers visit www.wileyeurope.com or call 0800 243407. Canadian customers visit www.wiley.ca or call 1-800-567-4797.